Old House Woodwork Restoration

Ed Johnson, in addition to being a teacher, is the proprietor of Johnson's Restoration Service in Oak Park, Illinois. An expert restorer, he has refinished the woodwork in many old homes in the Chicago area, most notably the furniture and woodwork in the Frank Lloyd Wright Home and Studio. He holds an Ed.D. degree and teaches business education in the City Colleges of Chicago.

A SPECTRUM BOOK

PRENTICE-HALL, INC., Englewood Cliffs, New Jersey 07632

Ed Johnson

How to Restore
Doors, Windows, Walls,
Stairs, and Decorative Trim
to Their Original Beauty

Old House
Woodwork
Restoration

Library of Congress Cataloging in Publication Data

Johnson, Edwin.
  Old house woodwork restoration.

  "A Spectrum Book"—Verso t.p.
  Includes index.
  1. Dwellings—Remodeling.   2. Wood finishing.
  I. Title.
  TH4816.J625   694'.6.0288   82-7484
  ISBN 0-13-634022-9   AACR2
  ISBN 0-13-634014-8 (pbk.)

Front cover photograph courtesy of
The Preservation Society of Newport County, Newport, RI
All photographs of the Frank Lloyd Wright Home by permission
and courtesy of the Frank Lloyd Wright Home and Studio Foundation
Chapter opening page and interior drawings by Pamela J. Johnson

A SPECTRUM BOOK

This book is available at a special discount when ordered in
bulk quantities. Contact Prentice-Hall, Inc., General Publishing Division,
Special Sales, Englewood Cliffs, N.J. 07632.

10 9 8 7 6 5 4 3 2 1

Printed in the United States of America

Editorial/production supervision: Marlys Lehmann
Manufacturing buyers: Cathie Lenard and Barbara A. Frick
Cover design: Hal Siegel
Page layout: Mary Alice Lento

ISBN 0-13-634022-9

ISBN 0-13-634014-8 {PBK.}

Prentice-Hall International, Inc., *London*
Prentice-Hall of Australia Pty. Limited, *Sydney*
Prentice-Hall Canada Inc., *Toronto*
Prentice-Hall of India Private Limited, *New Delhi*
Prentice-Hall of Japan, Inc., *Tokyo*
Prentice-Hall of Southeast Asia Pte. Ltd., *Singapore*
Whitehall Books Limited, *Wellington, New Zealand*
Editora Prentice-Hall do Brasil Ltda., *Rio de Janeiro*

To Jean—my wife, my friend, my support

Contents

Preface

This is my story about one aspect of house restoration, a very important one: woodwork, trim, and siding. Up to now little more than cursory attention has been paid to this subject while many owners of old houses were struggling with the task, working without a definitive coverage of the topic.

Now it will be possible for one to go about the task of woodwork restoration in an organized, orderly, and knowledgeable manner. Though success is not guaranteed (no phase of old house restoration can be), it is assured.

The material between these covers has been assembled through nearly a decade of experience. Work has taken me into homes built from a century ago to ten years ago. Some have been landmarks and historic sites designed by famous architects, although most were just ordinary houses. A few were very difficult jobs started by the owners themselves, who gave up, but most were commissioned by those who either didn't know how or where to start or else didn't even want to try.

It was at City House, Chicago's home improvement show, in 1979, where I demonstrated woodwork restoration along with several other craftsmen, that I realized the great number of homeowners who wanted to do their own work. And they were very interested in what I had to say.

So this book is my response to you. I trust it will tell you what you want to know.

Acknowledgments

I want to thank all of those who assisted me in generating and gathering the material in this book. Specifically, I thank the many customers whose homes served as my learning labs, the very first of whom were Mary and Charlie Strizak.

Several people were kind enough to grant me interviews. They are Cindy and Gregg Maholic, Jim Shimon, Don Palmgren, and Ferd Johnson. The principal organizations for whom I worked and who allowed me to take work-in-progress photographs are the Frank Lloyd Wright Home and Studio Foundation, Carla Lind, home and studio director, and John Thorpe, president; and the Chicago Architectural Foundation, Dick Combs, director.

Finally, I want to thank my antique furniture associates, the old-time authorities and dealers such as Sue and Jim Bohenstengel, who got me started in all this. Thanks to all of you.

Old House
Woodwork
Restoration

Chapter One

Why Restore Your
Woodwork and House Trim?

So you're thinking about restoring the trim or the woodwork in your house—the door and window frames, doors, staircase, or perhaps the fireplace mantel. Congratulations. You may join the thousands who have turned this into one of the most popular indoor pastimes in America.

The "strippers," as I call them, come home from their nine-to-five job, gulping a hamburger on the way, change into their grubbiest of jeans, and begin another five-hour stint at woodwork stripping. All over the country otherwise normal people are being deprived of their usual good books, theater, or concerts because they want attractive veranda posts or staircase balusters. Don't apologize. I'm with you!

Caution: Unless you know what you're about to undertake, this project may well be the undoing of your marriage, your friendships, or your sanity. Fortunately, you now have my book. With it, your task will be a lot easier and the outcome more rewarding.

You see, woodwork and trim restoration can be a very soul-trying experience. It is far from being a simple decorating task; it is not a problem that can be solved with a paint roller. On the contrary, it can be much hard, smelly, messy, dirty, grubby work. And that's just the stripping part.

After stripping off the old finish, hard questions have to be answered. What should the new finish be? How can I match colors? How does one refinish, anyway? Finally, how should I care for the new finish into which I have poured my very soul for weeks, months (I hope not) years? Without some assistance you'll be asking yourself, "Why did I start this in the first place? Help!"

Help is what you'll get from me, the "woodwork doctor," because I've been stripping and refinishing woodwork and antique furniture for nearly ten years. Included are some historical places: five rooms in the Frank Lloyd Wright Home and Studio, Oak Park, Illinois, 1889; Frank Lloyd Wright's Chauncey Williams House, River Forest, Illinois, 1895; and Henry Hobson Richardson's James J. Glessner House, Chicago, 1886. The furniture restoration part of my business has included Frank Lloyd Wright's family dining room suite in his former home and studio and Wright-designed furniture in Unity Temple, Oak Park. After all this historically important work and much, much more for just ordinary people in ordinary old homes, I have decided to make my experience and know-how available to potential strippers like you.

Now, I'm going to be discussing both interior and exterior trim in this book. In the beginning it will be sort of general, because their restoration has much in common. Later on, the material will be specific. To keep the two architectural elements separate in your mind, I will use the term *woodwork* for interior trim such as door and window jambs, sills, sashes, muntins, mullions, staircase risers, treads, balusters, newels, and, baseboard and cove molding. Exterior wood around windows and doorways, eaves, fasciae, porch posts, and pediments is labeled *trim*. As woodwork restoration is more complex because of the need for very careful refinishing, it will get more attention.

Here it is a beautiful summer day in the woods of Door County, Wisconsin, on the Lake Michigan shore. All this beauty puts me in a reflective mood.

3

Far left: *The author finishing the doorway of James J. Glessner House, Chicago. H. H. Richardson, 1886. The oak trim has been stripped, sanded, stained, and sealed. This is the finish coat.* Photo by Jim Kuba

Near left, top: *Frank Lloyd Wright Home and Studio, 1889–1909, Oak Park, IL.* Photo by Dina Johnson

Near left, bottom: *James J. Glessner House, Chicago. H. H. Richardson, 1886.* Photo by Jim Kuba

As I sit here at my typewriter, I wonder what a nice person or couple like you wants with trim and woodwork restoration, anyway.

Good question. Maybe you want to get involved because the woodwork in your home or condominium is a pretty important part of the place. Every day when you return home you're greeted by that paint-peeled door and trim, or the shutters are shedding. At holiday time you'll have all the relatives over for dinner and you'll be sitting around the lovely antique round oak table under ceiling beams painted "office green." Maybe you don't know the answer to my question. But if each day of the year you are living with ugly woodwork or molting trim, boy, am I motivated to assist you!

WHAT IS RESTORATION?

Woodwork restoration is the process of removing old finish from doors, windows, staircases, built-ins, and all sorts of interior trim and refinishing them much as they were originally finished. It is taking what you presently have and making it both functionally and aesthetically more livable.

Restoration differs considerably from remodeling, as the latter changes the form of things, sometimes for the better and sometimes for the worse. When remodeling, old paneled doors are discarded because they are damaged or too heavily painted. They are replaced with new flush doors. Restoration, on the other hand, entails making repairs, removing the old finish, and refinishing the original paneled doors.

In remodeling one may remove an old back staircase and turn the resulting space into a storage closet (heaven forbid!). An open porch on a Queen Anne style house may be enclosed and may eventually become a winter storage place for kids' summer toys. A fireplace may be covered over in remodeling and then become part of the wall, perhaps because it took up valuable wall space or maybe old bird nests have blocked the flue. Restoration, however, calls for fixing the fireplace, perhaps sandblasting the brick to clean it, and using it once again to provide warmth, a glow, and romance.

Don't get me wrong. Remodeling is not necessarily bad. I concede that some old homes were poorly designed, with too many small rooms, large useless areas, high, heat-wasting ceilings. The dangers of remodeling lie in its irreversible nature, its often disunifying effect, and its destruction of authenticity. Restoration, however, is (or at least should be) reversible. It should continue the unity of the original design and preserve the authenticity of the structure.

4

Unrestored staircase, 72 Anson Street, Charleston, SC. Photo by Louis Schwartz, Charleston, S.C. *(Courtesy of Historic Charleston Foundation)*

Restored staircase, 72 Anson Street, Charleston. Photo by Louis Schwartz, Charleston, S.C. *(Courtesy of Historic Charleston Foundation)*

WHY RESTORE?

The emphasis of my book is on restoration, and for many good reasons besides those already mentioned. There is a great interest in historic preservation, and you desire to preserve your entire house, including the woodwork. You may be concerned about the monetary as well as the aesthetic value of your property. Current house replacement costs are high. You may also want to preserve your neighborhood, and, finally, you may want to reduce house care.

Now, you may be mumbling to yourself that most of these reasons do not apply to your situation. True, but you may want to read about them in the following pages anyway, as they are designed to motivate you not only to start your job, which is presumably in the planning stage, but to follow through with it in relatively quick order. Besides, this material will give you something else to think about during the coming weekends and evenings when you do rather monotonous woodwork stripping.

The National Interest in Restoration

A really big interest in house restoration exists in the United States today. I have personally observed fervent activity in the restoration districts of such cities as Richmond, Virginia; Charleston, South Carolina; Newburyport, Massachusetts; Seattle; Vancouver; Atlanta; and Chicago.

A good illustration of this interest is in Savannah, Georgia, where preservation has been taken seriously since about 1955. There, an alliance between preservationists and the city government

Unrestored second-floor drawing room, left, and in restored condition, 72 Anson Street, Charleston. Photos by Louis Schwartz, Charleston, S.C. *(Courtesy of Historic Charleston Foundation)*

called Savannah Landmark is restoring that city's Victorian neighborhood. Another illustration is the city of Baltimore, which is helping preservation-oriented persons by operating the Salvage Depot, a place where many architectural items can be found.

Preservation groups across the land supported the National Historic Preservation Act Amendments of 1980. Passed by Congress, it:

• Identifies remaining natural, historic, and cultural heritage resources.
• Protects the finest examples of our heritage.
• Cuts costs for developers by providing easily accessible information on each state's significant resources.
• Reduces expensive development conflicts by identifying natural and cultural sites early in the planning process.
• Promotes citizen participation in all stages of heritage resource identification and protection.

Heading the long list of preservation is the National Trust for Historic Preservation. It is the only nonprofit organization chartered by Congress to encourage public participation in the preservation of sites, buildings, and objects in our history and culture. Two publications come from the Trust: *Preservation News* and *Historic Preservation.* Privately owned historical property protection is the province of the Historic House Association of America. There are also state organizations, such as the Landmarks Preservation Council of Illinois and the Maryland Association of Historic District Commissions. City organizations abound, such as Historic Nashville, Inc., Historic Kansas City Foundation, and Historic Fredricksburg Foundation, Inc.

Old house restoration has even been on television. A twenty-six-week series, first aired in the summer of 1980 by Boston's WGBH Educational TV, featured the Bigelow House in Newton, Massachusetts. Designed by Henry Hobson Richardson, the late Victorian building had befallen evil times. The only way it could survive was to convert it into a five-unit condominium, a project the TV cameras followed during the series.

Seminars and trade shows featuring restoration are also very current. For example, City House, "a home improvement fair for older houses" sponsored by the Commission on Chicago Historical and Architectural Landmarks, held its fourth show in 1982. The Landmarks Preservation Council of Illinois and the Restoration College Association sponsored five workshops in the summer of 1981 detailing the preservation of buildings and their interiors. A final illustration is the Second Annual Illinois Preservation Conference sponsored by the Landmarks Preservation Council of Illinois and held in April 1982 in Woodstock, Illinois.

A leading publication in the restoration of old houses is *The Old-House Journal.* On its mast is written, "Restoration and Maintenance Techniques for the Antique House." I get a lot out of reading it; perhaps you would, too.

Well, you can see that everywhere there is a revival of old houses and old neighborhoods. Call it rehab or call it restoration. I call it good for our nation!

Why the interest? you ask. Well, I think that more people want the real and the authentic rather than the new or the remodeled. What I mean is you want real oak floors, real plaster walls, real marble sinks, and real stained-glass windows. That's the big reason why you bought your old home, isn't it?

Maybe the desire for the authentic stems from a feeling that there is just too much plastic in

OAK PARK RESTORATION COURSE

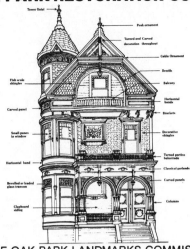

THE OAK PARK LANDMARKS COMMISSION
ANNOUNCES
A COURSE IN HOUSE RESTORATION
ON SIX MONDAY EVENINGS
MARCH 2 TO APRIL 6

☐ Session 1 – March 2 – Identification of Styles
☐ Session 2 – March 9 – Historical Sensitivity
☐ Session 3 – March 16 – Wood Restoration
☐ Session 4 – March 23 – Plaster and Stucco
☐ Session 5 – March 30 – Energy Conservation
☐ Session 6 – April 6 – Color and Landscape

Greater Chicago Celebrates
Historic Preservation Week
May 11-18, 1980

continued on page 8

Some examples of public interest in historic preservation.

WOODSTOCK OPERA HOUSE

WOODSTOCK ILLINOIS

organizations, corporations and foundations which provided nearly two-thirds of the necessary funds.

Before the restoration began, the City of Woodstock had moved its offices to an attractively restored and adapted 1906 brick schoolhouse also located in the downtown area.

The Woodstock Opera House Community Center now provides service as a cultural, recreational and meeting center.

ARCHITECTURAL NOTES

The Opera House was designed and constructed by Smith Hoag. Its architectural style has been colorfully described as "steamboat gothic," reflecting the cathedral shape of its exterior and the similarities of the auditorium's interior to a riverboat salon. John Vincent Anderson is the restoration architect. The Opera House restoration has been honored by an award from the Northern Illinois Chapter of the American Institute of Architects.

The architectural treasure of the Opera House is its stenciled auditorium ceiling, which has been meticulously reproduced in pattern and in color. Design consultant, Robert Furhoff, provided the necessary research to insure its accuracy. The same attention to exacting detail and period has been shown in the restoration or reproduction of woodwork, lighting fixtures, hardware, flooring and wall surfaces, stained glass windows, and furnishings.

HISTORY HIGHLIGHTS

The Woodstock Opera House was built in 1889 to house City Hall, the public library, fire department and second-floor auditorium.

The Patti Rosa Company provided the inaugural performance on September 2, 1890. The main floor and balcony were filled to capacity for the company's production of MARGERY DAW.

The Opera House became McHenry County's center for entertainment and hospitality. Touring vaudeville, minstrel, and dramatic companies provided diversion after a week's labor. Farmers' wives chatted among themselves in the "parlour" while their husbands attended market.

this world, so to make the present more livable many people want to restore the great homes and rooms of the past. Certainly higher gasoline prices have made close-in neighborhoods with their old houses much more desirable than in the recent past.

Because we have wasted so much in this country, there is a motivation to conserve; because we now have a significant past, there is the desire to preserve. Preservation districts exist everywhere. In Oak Park, Illinois, the location of our city home, there is the Frank Lloyd Wright Historic District. This mid-northwest part of the village is the location of Wright's old home and studio as well as the site of many homes he designed and Unity Temple, his first church design.

Without doubt economic motives as well as aesthetic and historical are operative. In the Oak Park historic district Victorian homes in good condition are so in demand that they rarely reach the real estate market. They are snatched up by new owners when the former owners first decide to sell. Most Frank Lloyd Wright homes have a waiting list of buyers despite their premium prices. Clearly, preservation is in.

Impossible Woodwork and Trim Finishes

Over the years your house has probably served various families who have applied numerous coats of varnish or paint or both on woodwork and paint on trim. Figure on the average of ten years per coat. So if your house is ninety years old, there is an excellent chance that trim and woodwork are

Staircase, the Hunter House, Newport, RI. Note the thick blistered finish on the staircase risers. Restoration would refinish these. Rail and balusters are made of solid mahogany. (Permission and courtesy of The Preservation Society of Newport County, Newport, RI)

holding nine layers. If paint was used inside and even though it is the original, intended, and correctly traditional covering, nine coats is probably too many for the wood to hold gracefully. No wonder your paneled doors look lumpy and your windowsills look bumpy!

There may have also been incorrect, non-authentic paints applied, such as calcimine. Since calcimine was a favorite plaster ceiling covering for years, it is possible that your painted ceiling beams and cove molding have a few coats of it.

Of course, many old homes are located in neighborhoods that have been allowed by property owners to deteriorate. Take, for example, Oakdale Avenue west of Halsted Street in Chicago. A late Victorian neighborhood of once prosperous citizens, it had become practically a slum by the 1950s. Some of the buildings had been cut up into apartments or, worse, converted into rooming houses. This gave a lot of people an opportunity to decorate—with varying degrees of success. If this sounds like your house, your assignment: mission impossible.

Even in the homes of the well-to-do, house

painters were called in with great regularity to put another coat of varnish on the woodwork and another coat of paint on the trim. As this was usually done right over accumulated dirt, each successive coat left the surface just a little darker in the case of woodwork and just a little thicker in the case of trim. Couple this process with the inferior varnish and paint of the past and the results are, well, what some of you got.

At times this thick varnish found on woodwork became blistered, crazed, checked, and discolored, mostly the result of too many coats of old varnish exposed to too much heat, humidity, and dirt for too many years. Many homes in northern cities have been heated too much in past winters creating low-humidity conditions; and just the opposite are homes in the Southwest, which have been exposed to extreme dryness in the summer. Low humidity causes wood to dry out; glued joints come loose, and hairline cracks, even splits, appear. Too much humidity, as one often finds in Seattle and Houston, causes old finishes to come loose and separate from wood.

Much old woodwork, especially in finer homes, was selected for its beauty and intrinsic color. Successive coats of stain, varnish, varnish stain, and dirt have caused this beauty to disappear. Restoration of such woodwork will prove that the attractive grain and color are still there. The results will amaze you!

House trim has been even more subject to the elements: the sandstorms of the Southwest, the sea dust of ocean coastal areas, the humidity of Florida, and the baking dryness of cities built in former deserts. It appears that little thought was given to how trim looked so long as it got covered at the lowest cost.

REPAIRS. Repairing is often the forgotten part of trim and woodwork restoration. Nearly everyone rushes right in and strips off old finish and applies the new before even considering the repair of such things as loose staircase balusters and loose and missing veneer on doors. If you follow my book's recommendations, and I trust you will, such repairs as these will be made before you do anything else. Remember the old saying about a "stitch in time." It will not only "save nine" but be a lot easier to make in the beginning.

The laundry list of woodwork structural problems is long. It includes windows that won't stay open because of broken sash cords or won't

This exterior sill of the west bedroom, Frank Lloyd Wright Home and Studio, Oak Park, IL, 1889, is badly in need of repair. Restoration a few weeks later corrected the rotting. Photo by Edwin Johnson (Permission and courtesy of Frank Lloyd Wright Home and Studio Foundation)

An excellent example of house preservation: the hallway of the Hunter House, ca. 1750, Newport. The wainscot is William and Mary design, hall interior design is Queen Anne, and the furniture is Chippendale. Restoration took place 1952–53. (Permission and courtesy of The Preservation Society of Newport County, Newport, RI)

open at all because they are painted shut; missing pieces such as doors that have been removed and lost; doorways walled in and the doorway trim removed and discarded; and windows moved and removed.

Such a butchering process was carried on endlessly in some old houses. Even Frank Lloyd Wright's original home and studio in Oak Park was cut up into four apartments after he left it and his wife and family, and started all over in Spring Green, Wisconsin. It was a virtual rooming house when the National Trust for Historic Preservation bought it and turned it over to the Frank Lloyd Wright Home and Studio Foundation for management and restoration.

House Preservation

Maybe you never thought of it this way, but your old house is an antique, especially if it is over a hundred years old. So you could look at it this way: interior architectural pieces like the built-in sideboard in your dining room and even your doors are just as authentically antique as the Eastlake furniture that perhaps graces the same Victorian rooms. Consequently, these and other woodwork items

deserve the same care and concern as your furniture. The question is, Are they getting it?

There is such a thing, too, as preventative maintenance. Properly refinished woodwork and trim will stop checking and rotting; refinished doors will not have to be replaced with new and expensive ones; and unstuck windows will once again open to bring in cool breezes. Results such as these can be yours.

Aesthetic Values in Restoration

There is certainly an aesthetic value to many architectural pieces in old homes. Take, for example, built-in sideboards, fireplace mantels, and staircases. Their intrinsic beauty is the result of their grain, the careful selection of the wood, the choice of the particular species, and the mode of construction employed at that time. Thus, you may have quarter-sawed oak, mahogany veneer doors, and Early American pine. Restoration can bring back the beauty of former years.

In my humble opinion woodwork sets the decorating tone of a room. One can take both the style and the color of wallpaper and, more important, window treatment from the woodwork style, configuration, and color. Similarly, interior architectural pieces are a room's focal point. An exposed, curved staircase with graceful balusters as in some Federal homes in Charleston, is the first thing anyone sees inside your home. Fireplace mantels are clearly the focus of each room possessing them; ceiling beams and windows all draw one's visual attention.

If these woodwork items in your home look sick today, they can be cured tomorrow. Read my book, provide the necessary labor and material input, and that architectural piece will once again be an attractive center of attention.

This 1980 advertisement illustrates the kind of money "restored" houses are getting in Chicago. There may well be more remodeling inside than restoration, though! (From the Reader, *Dec. 19, 1980, p. 15. Advertisement courtesy 2051 North Bissell Partnership)*

Monetary Values

Money is always a favorite subject of mine, so let's discuss it. Naturally, restoration is going to cost you some money. Paint and varnish remover at 1982 prices are fifteen dollars a gallon, as are stain and polyurethane. How much you will use depends on your room size, the amount and complexity of the woodwork, its condition, and your skill. For example, I can restore the woodwork in a fairly large and complicated room using seven gallons of chemical stripper, three quarts of stain, and two gallons of polyurethane. At the other extreme is one stripper I heard of who used nearly forty gallons of paint and varnish remover for one room! Even the cost of all that material is a lot less than the $500 to $2,500 a professional refinisher would likely charge.

The other side of the coin is that, while all home improvements enhance the value of your place, the most profitable ones are the visual. Ranking high on this list of visuals are woodwork and floor refinishing. The capital/return ratio for these improvements may run as high as 3:1 when the job is done by a woodwork specialist. When *you* do it, using the figures in the preceding paragraph, the return could run as high as 15:1. Now I ask you, Where can you find a better investment than that?

While most folks who have been along the woodwork restoration route claim they never want to sell their house—in fact, they get upset at the very mention of it—it's nice to know that in so doing you have increased the value of your house. And even though well-maintained structures have always sold better and for more than the poorly

Restoration has maintained and improved the value of this old house for sale in 1980 in Kentucky. (Courtesy of The Old House Journal, *69A Seventh Avenue, Brooklyn, NY 11217)*

maintained, the new wrinkle is the old, the authentic, and the natural. As naturally grained old woodwork is part of that scene, this project, assuming you don't goof, is one on which you can hardly lose.

In addition to restoration being something on which you can hardly lose, maybe you'll be able to make big bucks on it as some people have. For example, a couple in the East claimed they made a million dollars in ten years recycling old houses. They even wrote a book on the subject; from what I know about publishing, I'm certain they made a lot more on restoration than on writing. Anyway, one house they bought for $26,500 in 1972, put $10,000 into it, and sold it five years later for $55,000. Though these are not suitable figures for the eighties, I think you get the idea. There's money to be made in restoration!

House Replacement Costs and Values

Now we come to another economic matter. It is the replacement value of your house and its architectural members. Consider the cost, if you will, of replacing your old 2,500-square-foot house at today's building costs. Consider also its location, more than likely a close-in neighborhood. Then compare the replacement cost with your purchase cost, unless you bought it very recently. Do you realize that most of you living in older, larger homes could not afford to buy that much housing if it were newly constructed?

That's the building. Now take the individual architectural members inside and outside your house. Just for fun, get your local lumber company to quote a price on duplicating your present front door; same design, wood, configuration, and dimensions. Now that you've recovered from the shock of that price, consider another example. An ordinary 4 × 4-inch 4½-foot-long oak newel, completely plain, cost $230 in 1980. I made one for less than $10 in materials. Price your built-in sideboard, bookshelves, window seat, and shutters. Finally, get a quote on new kitchen cabinets to convince yourself that proper restoration really pays.

Neighborhood Preservation

The offices of the National Trust for Historic Preservation are not the only quarters where preservation is held sacred. Old house preservation is clearly the savior of many old neighborhoods across the nation.

Oak Park, Illinois, is a classic example. Interest in the Frank Lloyd Wright Home and Studio and the preservation of the many architectural designs of his in the village have helped preserve the entire community from urban decay. Tour buses constantly bring students, architects, and tourists from all over the world to go through the place where this creative genius got his start, and to walk Forest Avenue and see Heurtley House, Beachey House, Moore House, Thomas House, and end up at Unity Temple a few blocks away.

Other Prairie School architects—John S. Van Bergen, Walter Burley Griffin, Barry Byrne, Tallmadge and Watson, and Purcell and Elmslie—

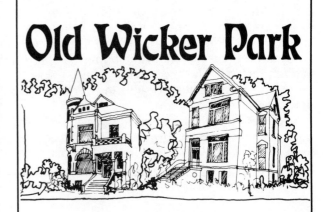

Old Wicker Park

second annual greening festival

august 19th & 20th

refreshments
entertainment
arts and crafts
garage and yard sales
plant sales
and
neighborhood walking tours

A restoration-conscious Chicago neighborhood.

have their works on display in Oak Park. The presence of such outstanding architecture coupled with the strong desire to preserve it has, in effect, stopped and possibly reversed West Side Chicago's spread of urban decay.

Valuable from an antique standpoint, and viable from a living standpoint, old homes have become landfill in the past. Today, preservation of homes has saved the Chicago metropolitan neighborhoods of Hyde Park, Beverly Hills, Lakeview, Wicker Park, and Old Town Triangle. If given half a chance, it can save yours, too.

Restoration Can Reduce House Care

Restored woodwork should reduce house care. Painted-over doors are harder to keep clean, as they show fingerprints. Windowsills that are painted mark, scratch, and easily chip. Painted staircase handrails and newels take a beating from everyday traffic. Painted baseboard shows every vacuum-cleaner nick, and stair risers display every kick. Removal of this paint and replacement with stained and sealed surfaces should considerably reduce cleaning care and costs.

With all that I've written so far, you may be thinking that I'm against painted woodwork. Not at all, not at all. Actually, I am in favor of it *if* it is authentic, that is, if it was meant to be. For traditionally painted surfaces restoration consists of removing excess paint buildup so that the surface can be repainted. Paint used as a cover-up

of bad finish or bad surfaces should be removed, never again to be seen!

Besides reducing maintenance by ridding your home of the painted-over woodwork finishes, you should cut future decorating costs. While it is true that "varnished" or clear surfaces require another finish coat from time to time depending on local conditions and care, they will require much less attention than painted woodwork, especially if the painted surfaces match wall treatment.

Restoration out of Sheer Necessity

After numerous coats of paint, woodwork finish begins to check and chip off. As mentioned earlier, numerous coats of varnish soon begin to mask the natural color and grain of the wood. Putting another coat over such surfaces is a futile act. The old finish must be removed; there is no other alternative.

Many woodwork repairs are made out of sheer necessity. For example, rotting window sashes and sills must be replaced, loose door veneer must be reglued, split panels must be glued and pulled together, missing balusters must be replaced, ceiling beams showing roof water damage must be refinished, and base kitchen cabinet doors with dog claw and teeth marks should be restored. With these tasks you are more concerned with functional than aesthetic variables. No matter. Though the motives are different, they will result in the same process and the same end.

GETTING READY TO RESTORE

One night not so long ago Jean (my wife) and I were sitting in a German restaurant drinking beer with our friends Kathy and Tom. They were recounting their early experiences refinishing woodwork.

"Remember, Tom," Kathy said, "you'd drop me off at Burling Street and then you'd go to your law office. Here I was practically nine months pregnant and I'd strip the bedroom woodwork all day. At about four in the afternoon you'd come

back and would be ready and raring to start work, and I was ready to quit. We'd be there until eleven and then go back to our State Street apartment. *Every* night—it seemed forever. Several mornings, after you left, I sat at the top of the stairs and cried and cried."

"Yeah, I remember," replied Tom, "although I'd rather forget. But then I finished the room when you went to the hospital to have Andrew. In fact, I worked day and night to surprise you when you got out."

"I'll say so," Kathy retorted. "You hardly ever visited me. In fact, the nurses asked me if I was married!"

From that point on, the verbal exchange went downhill, a testimony to the difficulties they had encountered. It was after that grim experience in 1975 that this couple called me in to restore their entry hall, staircase, and upstairs hall woodwork and wainscot. Then in 1977 I did their back bedroom, in 1978 their kitchen was restored, and in 1979 I refinished the entire third floor of this eleven-room house in Chicago's Lakeview neighborhood. They have often kiddingly said that I not only helped restore their ninety-year-old house but in 1975 helped save their two-year-old marriage. Maybe they weren't kidding!

What bothered Kathy and Tom, and what's probably bugging you, is that there is no authority to turn to for woodwork restoration assistance. At least this couple was smart enough to apply George Grotz's (*The Furniture Doctor*) principles of furniture restoration to their woodwork. But the long hours, the lack of know-how, and the uncertain outcome were almost too much for them.

Preparation Checklist

I think that you really have to get ready for restoration. This means having the correct attitude, knowing what to expect, possessing knowledge and techniques, having the correct materials, and, finally, getting organized.

It might be helpful in the beginning of this task to psych yourself up with positive thoughts of a successful outcome of your labors. Try to acquire a feeling of confidence that you *have* the power to do a great job. Since nothing succeeds like success, I suggest that you undertake a small furniture restoration project or two as openers. Similar skills and techniques are employed with woodwork. That's how I got started way back when.

Know what to expect. Look at the successful outcomes of friends and neighbors. Realize that part of your house will be torn up for a while. Be aware of the smells, the mess, and the dirt that you will have to live with for the next few weeks or months.

As to knowledge, you should get most of what you'll need from my book. You may wish, however, to consult books on furniture restoration, including my own, *Restoring Antique Furniture* (New York: Sterling Publishing, Inc., 1981). Other ways to acquire knowledge (and by the way, confidence too) are to work on a local restoration project as a volunteer, talk to others who have restored their own woodwork, and go to house rehab shows where seminars and experts are often available. Get an experienced woodwork restoration friend to give you a Saturday to help you get started.

Top-quality materials and a dependable, helpful supplier are essential. For example, buy and use the best brushes available, the strongest paint and varnish remover, and high-quality finishing materials. This is no time to scrimp and save. Woodwork and trim restoration is what they call in management circles "labor intensive." High-grade materials and tools generally make the job better and the work easier, so be kind to yourself and good to your job and spend a little more.

And finally, unless you have a five-year plan, you must be organized. A family once asked me to come over to their home and advise them on their woodwork restoration. It was a very large seventy-year-old house. I found the entire first floor, except for the kitchen and a study, torn up, with the extensive oak woodwork in various stages of restoration. Their project extended up the wide staircase and into the upstairs hall. Various family members were working on various parts and in various stages when they felt like it. It was a Saturday afternoon. A game was on television, and opened cans of beer and soft drinks were lying about. Very laid back.

This place was a shambles. Yet a family wedding was scheduled in three weeks with plans for home entertaining. No way could that task have been finished, let alone the wall and ceiling decoration that was to follow. Does this sound like your project? I certainly hope not!

A sane approach to the restoration job is to divide it up in workable units. Never do more than a room or an exterior wall at one time. Start it and finish it. Period. In working on that one unit divide it still further into workable units, like a window, a door, or the cove. Tie up only one entry at a time.

Try to start and complete stripping one item within your allotted work period, say, six hours, and set aside the best time periods in which to do it. If you're a morning person as I am, plan your trim or woodwork project for that time of day.

I suggest that you keep sane hours. Working way into the night not only will disturb your rest but may also disturb your neighbors. Restoration is not a crash program. After all, your house may have taken a hundred years to get where it's at today. So try not to work beyond your individual capacity. Put in a good day's work and know when to quit.

As so much trim and woodwork restoration is setting up and later cleaning up, it is better to work fewer longer blocks of time than many smaller blocks. To assist you in securing a bigger chunk of time, why not hire a baby-sitter for your stripping hours, unplug your telephone, avoid friendly neighbors, cancel your Saturday golf game, and stay away from TV. Such sacrifices we have to make!

Rehabilitation Guidelines

I assume that your old house is like most old houses. It is not a historically important home, it wasn't designed by a famous architect, nobody famous ever lived there, nothing important ever happened there, and it is not a particularly exquisite example of any particular architectural style. It is, in short, an ordinary old house. Therefore, my references in this chapter and hereafter to being faithful to the original design intent in your restoration are to be taken as relative. After all, "form [should] follows function" (or is it fiasco?), as Frank Lloyd Wright used to say.

It might be helpful at this point to look at some commonsense rehabilitation guidelines as published in the January 1977 issue of *Old-House Journal* (a must publication for old house owners involved in restoration). I have paraphrased these guidelines for the sake of brevity.

1. When bringing an old house up to modern functional standards, do not destroy its architectural character in the process.
2. Provide for compatible structure usage, thus minimizing building and environmental alterations.
3. Preserve the distinguishing qualities or character of the property and minimize removal or alteration of historic material or architectural features.
4. Repair rather than replace deteriorated features. However, any necessary replacements should duplicate the former.
5. Respect former structural alterations, as they may have developed a significance in their own right.
6. As all buildings should be recognized as products of their own time, attempts to create earlier or later appearances should be discouraged.
7. Additions and alterations should not impair the essential form and integrity of the original building.

CONCLUDING THOUGHTS

Dusk has come to our lakeshore. It has been a long day at the typewriter and there is so much more I want to tell you. Since my editors have informed me that this is supposed to be only the introductory chapter, the rest will have to wait for the chapters that follow.

Please bear with me for two more things that should be said here. One is that this book tells *my* story—*my* techniques and *my* experiences. It is not a compendium of woodwork restoration. That volume would require a lifetime of experience or more and a volume much larger than this one.

I have another confession. Even if you carefully follow what I have written, I cannot guarantee success. There are a lot of variables in this inexact trade. What I *will* guarantee is that a great deal of success is assured if you follow my directions and my good wishes.

Why not experiment a little? Test colors on your woodwork before you begin serious staining, try the heat gun if you can't seem to operate the electric paint remover, and try different brands of paint and varnish remover. In this process you will come to realize that there are many opinions on techniques, tools, and finishes. Ask those offering their opinions if you can inspect their work, because "the proof is in the pudding." You can check mine out, too, if you'd like. Just visit the Frank Lloyd Wright Home and Studio in Oak Park, Illinois.

SOME WOODWORK RESTORATION SUCCESS STORIES

Maybe a few success stories from my files would be helpful at this juncture. They may encourage you to go and do likewise; then again, you may want to quit now.

Chauncey Williams House

PROBLEM: Strip three or four coats of paint off woodwork and beams in living room measuring twenty-five by forty feet. There are twelve wide beams, ornate fireplace in alcove, six doorways (no doors to do), three small windows set in deep panels. Refinish either stain or natural on all-pine woodwork. Particular problems include damaged base, two doorways remodeled from former windows, and two-part picture molding separated by plaster. Frank Lloyd Wright design—1895.

SOLUTION: Accessibility to beams provided by three ladders and two long planks set up between the beams so two beams could be handled from one position. Paint removed with electric paint remover throughout, followed by chemical stripper. Paint also removed from fireplace tiles and hearth. Newly remodeled doorway trim matched to color of the old, which was refinished natural (no stain). Split picture molding plaster gap painted to match natural molding. Time: 150 hours.

Ashley C. Smith House

PROBLEM: Strip and refinish mahogany ceiling beams in thirty by fifty living room in the Tallmadge and Watson-designed house built in 1908. They are the only painted woodwork. As living room is all paneled mahogany, protection from ceiling work is a must. Also, beams must match color and light reflection of remainder of paneling and woodwork in living room.

SOLUTION: Paint removed with electric paint remover, and remainder of old finish dug, scraped, and wire-brushed out of intricate beam configurations. Plastic drop cloths taped up around entire room to protect finished paneling. Match to old woodwork made with careful stain selection. Satin-finish polyurethane had correct light reflection. Time: 45 hours.

The Ashley C. Smith House, Oak Park, IL, Tallmadge and Watson design built in 1908. While the living room mahogany paneling and woodwork had been well cared for, the mahogany ceiling beams had been painted white by a former owner. Present owners wanted the beams restored; the refinishing task was to match the refinished color of the beams to the original floor-to-ceiling mahogany paneling in the room.

Here the author is stripping paint from the white-painted wide, flat ceiling beams at the Ashley C. Smith House. He is standing on a twelve-foot plank between two stepladders. Photos by Nadine Johnson

Lakefront Condominium

PROBLEM: Remove paint from mahogany French doors, extensive trim, panel molding, and curved glass windows in converted condominium (ca. 1911) on Chicago's lakefront. As curved glass was fragile and costly to replace, no heat could be used on them to remove paint. Old wiring prevented sufficient current to operate electric paint remover efficiently. Four kinds of wood had been used: mahogany, birch, poplar, and oak. Woodwork painted over raw wood (unsealed); four to six coats had to be stripped.

SOLUTION: The removable French doors (four of six) were sent out to a *good* and dependable commercial stripper. Long soaking of woodwork required to get paint off, even after electric paint remover. Two different stain colors used: brown for the red mahogany and oak, and red brown for the lighter birch and poplar. Result, perfect match. Time: 125 hours.

H. P. Young House

PROBLEM: Strip and refinish the pine fireplace mantel in the master bedroom of this house designed by Frank Lloyd Wright about 1895. The mantel had been refinished once before and then painted white. Subsequent owners had put on several more coats of paint making a thick layer of six coats. The big problems were removing paint

H. P. Young House, Oak Park, IL. Frank Lloyd Wright, 1895. Author was commissioned to restore the fireplace mantel in the master bedroom. Photo by Jim Kuba

The fireplace mantel before restoration began. Note plastic drop cloth protecting the floor finish.

Using the electric paint remover to strip the bulk of the six coats of paint.

Author stripping off paint with electric paint remover. Note thick paint strip coming off.

Mantel before stripping off the "impossible" as well as nonauthentic painted finish.

Author brushing stripper on bead molding of fireplace mantel. A two-inch brush is the right size for this job. The paint and varnish remover is allowed to soak about an hour before removal begins. *continued on page 18*

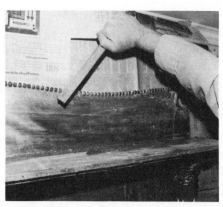

Removing paint from beaded molding carefully with a wire brush. Note newspaper held with masking tape to protect wallpaper.

Residue, a combination of paint, old varnish, and stripper is removed with a three-inch flexible putty knife. It is then flicked on newspaper on the floor.

Fireplace mantel with stain and sealer.

Pine fireplace mantel with finish coat. Note prominent wood grain.

Detail of master bedroom fireplace mantel. All photos of H. P. Young House by Jim Kuba

from the flutes in the columns and from the beaded trim.

SOLUTION: Paint was stripped from flat surfaces using electric paint remover. To avoid singeing the wood, however, paint was soaked from depressed flutes and beads with chemical paint remover. Then a screwdriver blade was machined to fit the flute configuration so that necessary scraping could be done. Paint was wire-brushed from the bead molding, carefully because it was fragile. The mantel was stained fruitwood, sealed with thinned polyurethane, and finished with full-strength polyurethane. Time: 19 hours.

Chapter Two

How Trim
and Woodwork Were
Made: Materials

How trim and woodwork were made—the kinds of wood that were used, some construction details, and the original finishes—can be useful information in the restoration process. With it you could really get an assist in being faithful to the original as much as is humanly and economically possible. And even if nothing I am going to tell you helps your project, at least you'll be able to impress your tennis pals when you know the difference between a baluster and a bracket.

There isn't a whole lot of information on this subject in any one place despite the great need for it. To completely fulfill that need in this book would be impossible; but, based on my wood restoration experience, I've tried to select what I think will be helpful to you. So although this chapter is not an encyclopedia, it should be a handy guide.

COMMON WOODS USED IN OLD HOUSE TRIM AND WOODWORK

Knowing what kind of wood was used for your house trim and woodwork is clearly necessary if you are going to replace damaged or missing elements. Thus, if all your doors are identified as mahogany after the five coats of paint have been removed, the replacement door you need for the missing closet door should also be mahogany (if you can afford it).

Learning about the various wood species is also good, because different woods strip differently, require different refinishing techniques, and have different finish characteristics. All this can be quickly learned.

Taking a sort of general overview of wood species, one finds that pine was a commonly used material and that different species were found not only on different floors of the same house but also in different adjoining rooms. Nearly all window sashes, trim, and mullions were made of pine, although there are several varieties of pine around. Perhaps the next most common trim wood was western and native cedar.

Inside homes, economics were clearly the governing factor as to what species of wood was used and where it was used. Decor or aesthetic beauty came in second in the average home. Therefore, finer, more beautiful, and consequently more expensive woods were used in rooms open to persons outside the family, such as the hall, parlor, living room, and dining room. Show was a prime mover then as now. Kitchens and upstairs bedrooms got cheaper grades of lumber for woodwork, and maids' quarters, if any, got the leavings.

Model kitchen cupboards, ca. 1910. (Carr, Ryder & Adams Co.)

Model oak sideboard, ca. 1910. (Carr, Ryder & Adams Co.)

To achieve decorating effects in the finer houses, decorators and designers often used different woods in different, often adjoining rooms, sometimes in unusual ways. Thus, oak was installed in the dining room for window and door trim, the built-in sideboard, and exposed ceiling beams. The adjoining music room may have mahogany trim, and the sliding doors separating the two rooms may have oak veneer on one side and mahogany on the other! In one home where I restored the woodwork, the hall and living room has oak woodwork, the dining room has rosewood door and window frames and rosewood wainscot paneling and doors, and the kitchen was painted pine. It was built around 1905 by a lumber company owner. That figures!

Well, what are the common woods found in woodwork and trim? Let's take a quick look, verbally and photographically. Besides pine there are ash, oak, birch, mahogany, cherry, walnut, rosewood, poplar, maple, cedar, and basswood. Some have two names. Rosewood is also called purplewood, poplar is also called whitewood.

ASH. Ash has a grain, texture, and finished color similar to oak, thereby causing some confusion. Its natural color is light brown with yellowish veins, similar to oak. What distinguishes ash from oak is its roey grain compared to oak's typically tight straight grain. Further, ash has a medium

density. In parts of this country where ash was more accessible and therefore cheaper, it was used in place of the more expensive hardwood. And hardly anyone knew the difference.

BASSWOOD. This is a light straight-grained softwood chiefly used where cost was to be kept to a minimum. However, because of both its softness and its uninteresting grain, I doubt if it was used very often for woodwork in older homes when pine was available. Basswood did find its way into furniture making as early as the eighteenth century. And it is to be found as painted woodwork in contemporary budget-conscious house construction.

BIRCH. Birch is a very strong, heavy, close-grained wood which varies from soft to hard. It possesses an even, fine texture and a cream to light brown color tinged with red. Its grain is typically plain, though it is often curly, wavy, or undulating. Sometimes it has a soft narrow band of more circular swirling grain. I can often identify birch by its smell after the old finish has been removed. Birch is confusingly similar to maple.

Because birch takes a color stain very well, it has been used in the past to imitate maple, mahogany, and walnut depending on the applied color. And because of its relative abundance and cheapness, it has also been painted. It's a fooler!

Walnut, plain sliced

Eastern red cedar

Mahogany

American black walnut (solid panels)

White oak

Oak

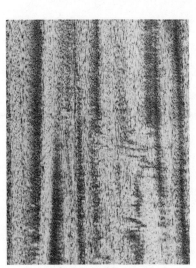

Mahogany, ribbon striped

Yellow poplar

What one must deal with in stripping birch woodwork is its tendency toward softness, causing it to scratch and mark easily and causing a porosity, or material absorption, quite difficult to remove completely. For example, the late nineteenth- and early twentieth-century red water stain commonly used on birch to imitate mahogany is impossible to remove completely. Similarly, birch that has been painted when raw, a practice common in midwestern kitchen woodwork, has less than satisfactory refinishing potential.

CEDAR. The five types of cedar all belong to the cypress family. There are southern white, Alaskan or yellow, Port Oxford, western red, and northern white cedar. Of these the cedar most likely on your home is either southern white or western red. Some northern white (also called native) is used in local construction in the Great Lakes states and in New England.

Cedar is known for its lightness; yet it is very durable in resisting the elements. It is straight-grained, even-textured, and pale yellow in color. Cedar is more likely to be stained than painted, even for exterior surfaces. Many contemporary homes have cedar exteriors, and the rough-sawn cut is very popular.

CHERRY. Cherrywood found in all woodwork and most furniture is black cherry. Black cherry trees grow tall and straight, producing a wood not too different from varieties of pine in grain appearance, but darker and harder. Although it was used extensively by furniture makers in the eighteenth and nineteenth centuries, it was also so plentiful in some places that railroad ties were made from it!

Sometimes confused with mahogany, cherry is reddish brown in color and has about the same hardness factor. It differs in that pores are less visible than in mahogany and that the grain is more swirly or roey.

Although I have not encountered cherrywood woodwork, I imagine some exists in places like West Virginia, eastern Pennsylvania, and other states through which the Appalachians run, the principal habitat of black cherry trees. Cherrywood panels in early American walls and doors, as well as in veneer in contemporary paneling, are noted for their intrinsic beauty. Today, authorities rate cherry highest in beauty, with mahogany second.

MAHOGANY. The mahogany found in antique and older homes came from Africa and Honduras; today, what mahogany is found in ranches and split-levels is from the Philippines. While I doubt if any mahogany found its way into house woodwork prior to 1800, the great use of it made by Duncan Phyfe, who brought American cabinetmaking from the Federal to the early Victorian period, undoubtedly introduced it to early Victorian rooms. And Talbert, writing in 1867, depicts a parlor suite complete with built-in bookcase and chimney piece constructed of mahogany in Gothic style.

Varying from a deep reddish brown to red with brown undertones, mahogany typically has a tight straight grain and visible pores. Crotch-cut mahogany, however, has a sort of arched grain and a very dark pattern flowing through the arches. Some African mahogany has a definite swirl pattern.

Many homes and fine apartments built at the beginning of this century have mahogany-veneered doors. Yet the woodwork around these doors was birch or poplar dyed mahogany. The differences in wood species are not noticeable until the old finish is removed. Then, surprise! Less expensive construction took the budget route and cheated on the doors as well as on the woodwork, substituting poplar or another cheap wood for mahogany. No doubt about it, mahogany was a popular woodwork material either to use or to imitate.

Mahogany is relatively soft and therefore easily damaged. Loose mahogany veneer on doors, for example, is easily broken off. Care must be exercised in stripping and sanding mahogany to avoid scratching or removing too much material. When stripped of all finish, mahogany typically has too much red. So refinish as the original decorator did; apply a dark greenish-brown stain, such as Fuller O'Brien's English Oak.

Much of the Philippine mahogany in houses built since 1946 has been finished in the "limed" manner. Paint, usually gray or a yellowish brown, was brushed on and wiped off, leaving different quantities of pigment in the wood grain. This coat was generally sealed and covered with varnish. If you want to eliminate the painted look and go natural, you will have to work quite hard to strip all of the old pigment out of rather soft mahogany pores. A handy tool is a wire brush worked very carefully with (parallel to) the grain. Subsequent stain will not be absorbed if any old finish remains.

MAPLE. Maple is a native hardwood that may have been used as woodwork in your home, particularly if you live where it grows, or grew. Although it is usually straight-grained, maple can also be bird's eye, curly, fiddleback, blistered, and even quilted. Characteristically, maple is heavy, hard, strong, close-grained; it can therefore be easily worked and is not likely to warp. Naturally whitish, its color when finished varies from a light brownish yellow to rich amber.

Over the years maple has been considered a cheap wood. This economic characteristic, besides its resistance to wear and its staining aptitude permitting it to resemble more expensive species, means that it must have been used in some homes at some past times. Your problem, however, will be to identify it positively.

OAK. Next to pine, oak has to be the most common material from which woodwork was made. It was chosen for its hardness, its relative abundance, particularly in eastern and southern states, and its beauty. Cut in normal fashion, oak has a tight, often straight grain, referred to by wood authorities as "pronounced long rays and a plain-striped figure." That is the rift cut; plain slicing produces a pattern of plain striped and leafy grain. And quarter-sawed production, common in the late nineteenth and early twentieth centuries, provides oak with the tiger pattern. Oak is clearly a very flexible material for decorating; no wonder it's been so popular in woodwork and furniture over the years!

Oak, however, has had a sort of spotty history. Summer beams and rafters in early American houses were hand-hewn from oak trees. Early Puritan and Stuart furniture was also made from oak, often combined with pine. Floors in Queen Anne, Georgian, and Federal homes were frequently made from oak, but window and floor trim was other species. It wasn't until the late Victorian period that oak trim appeared around doors and windows or that doors were commonly made of oak. This late appearance was probably as much a matter of taste as it was of millwork capability. Taste, because oak became the principal furniture wood in Golden Oak, Eastlake, and Mission Oak styles, popular from about 1875 to 1915. And since oak is very hard to work, carpenters probably had trouble with it fabricating woodwork as they did in on-the-job sites, while mills incurred higher costs producing oak woodwork. Later, oak was to become the principal interior wood of the Prairie School of Architecture and of the Craftsman period.

Three factors make the refinishing of oak woodwork gratifying. One, it was rarely painted by the original decorator, but stained, sealed, and varnished. This simplifies your stripping task. Two, because of its hardness and consequently its lack of porosity, old finishes were not readily absorbed, also making stripping easier. Finally, old oak has a very attractive grain and color, often making possible a natural finish.

PINE. Perhaps the first thing one should know about pine is that in olden days it was available in at least three species: southern hard, northern yellow, and white. Today, the lumber companies have added Idaho white, northern white, sugar white, and southern yellow. To simplify matters, though, the most common species found in old woodwork and trim are white and northern yellow.

Pine is probably the most common woodwork and trim material around, because it is plentiful, cheap, and easy for carpenters to work. It is relatively soft, porous, and light. White pine is straight-grained and was once available in very wide, knot-free boards. Yellow pine has a more pronounced, roey grain. These characteristics made it necessary for early decorators, handymen, and owners to paint the doors and woodwork, or paint and false-grain them or stain them. The earliest homes in each section of the country probably had unfinished pine woodwork, although I'm told that this was a sign of poverty and neglect even then.

Trim that was not cedar, which means most of it, was milled and cut from pine. In all but the most primitive houses it was whitewashed, painted, or stained. This is still the case today.

ROSEWOOD. Sometimes labeled purplewood, a name derived from its color, rosewood, although a dark purple to ebony in nature, becomes red purplish when finished. Both exotic and valuable, it is a very hard, firm, close-texture wood that stands up exceptionally well under all conditions. Its pattern is small to medium pores in wavy lines. Rosewood's appearance in woodwork is probably limited to either solid or veneer panels and inlays. The only home I have ever seen having rosewood is one built in 1905 by a lumber company owner. Does that tell you anything?

WALNUT. The popularity of American walnut over the years has been due to its exceptional beauty, its density and strength, and its availability. Yes, it seems strange today that walnut was once so plentiful that it was used not only for woodwork, like doors and newels, but for hand-hewn beams in colonial homes. In both nineteenth- and twentieth-century homes it was a decorative wood used in wainscot paneling, bookshelves, and staircases. No longer is that true, so if you're fortunate to have some walnut woodwork, you own a treasure.

The grain pattern of walnut varies. When plain-sliced, it can be narrow heart, wide heart, figured, or character-marked. It can also be quarter-sliced to give a pin-striped pattern and butt-plain-sliced to give a crotch-grain look to it. Walnut's color ranges from light gray brown to dark purplish brown.

As with rosewood, the beauty of walnut has been highly regarded. Hence, it is unlikely that interior woodwork made of walnut has been painted by former owners of your house. If perchance it has, the (dastardly) job was done over a sealed surface making its removal normal.

WHITEWOOD. Called poplar south and west of New York, whitewood is also labeled yellow poplar and tulip tree by some. Poplar is canary color, sometimes with a slightly greenish cast. Because it is a softwood, readily available, and cheap, it was used extensively in low-cost housing woodwork and doors. In my opinion its use was a twentieth-century phenomenon, when there was an attempt to copy finer woods like mahogany and walnut, although it has a less pronounced grain.

The poplar woodwork I've encountered was originally stained and sealed. Because of its softness, however, it retains much of its original stain color when stripped while giving up its sealers and varnishes. Thus, if it was stained or dyed mahogany in 1910 or so, it will still look like mahogany when stripped. Finishing it should be as if one were finishing mahogany.

ORIGINAL WOODWORK AND TRIM FINISHES

Woodwork and trim over the years have been finished with whitewash, paint, shellac, various oils, polishes, waxes, stain only, varnish, false grain, fuming, and nothing at all. One house I have visited, Larkin House in Monterey, California, had its woodwork since 1842 wiped regularly with ox blood to give it a rich, deep red look! That practice stopped when protesters recently picketed the landmark; today, all its woodwork has been painted white. Another loss to faithful restoration, I'm afraid.

Although it may be only of passing importance, the original finish on your trim and woodwork may well influence how you finish it after restoration. It may also affect the stripping process. Now, don't get me wrong. Faithfulness to the original does not extend to such materials as ox blood, whitewash, or even shellac; one has to utilize technology when it proves superior to older materials. Nonetheless, a look at the past can be of assistance in telling us where we should go.

No Finish

The original colonial houses in America were very crude and medieval by our standards today. Many did not have windows at all at first; trim and molding were not available or when present were simply flush with the exterior wall. Hand surfacing was seen everywhere and interiors were never painted. Thus, it is not strange to find primitive houses that have never had *any* woodwork finish and only a limited amount on the trim. Such was the case for a restorer who bought a Pennsylvania farmhouse built about 1775. To this day the woodwork is still bare, a tribute to faithfulness!

If you should be one of those fortunate but rare individuals restoring a primitive house, whether in Maine or Wisconsin, and you discover the original woodwork was bare, try to get it back to that state by cleaning it or stripping off the finishes that have been applied over time. Then seal it with a clear sealer and apply a clear finish

Model stairway, one of the popular colonial stairs, ca. 1925. Balusters are white enamel and rail is stained mahogany. (Carr, Ryder, & Adams Co.)

Paint

Paint is the material that has covered trim and woodwork for centuries. In some instances it is the traditional or original cover; in others it is merely the cover over the original. There is quite a history to paint.

Much paint today is probably a variety of a latex compound, but carbonate white lead in oil was the standard ingredient in paint in the early eighteenth century until around 1920. Then came the ready-mixed paints containing white lead and zinc oxide followed by titanium dioxide pigments in 1925, which permitted brighter colors. Pure titanium dioxide appeared in 1932. Over the years better hiding qualities and non-yellowing were achieved by adding various substances. Fast drying, hardness, color retention, and resistance to various agents were also qualities given to paint through research.

In stripping paint from surfaces, chemical solutions cause latex paint to flake and separate from the paint underneath. This prevents the stripper from soaking through, so about all you can do is scrape off the loosened latex and brush stripper on the oil-based paint underneath. Keep brushing it on until it soaks through and bubbles, the signal that removal can begin. *All* paints are subject to the powers of paint and varnish remover, even milk paint, given time and patience.

If your house is of historical interest because it was designed by a famous architect or because somebody famous lived there or something important happened there, or if it is a particularly good

coat such as satin polyurethane. This technique makes the woodwork "natural" but protects it and makes it easy to maintain. If you're a purist, though, apply beeswax to the wood and rub it in just as some did in olden times. This affords protection, though it *does* require maintenance.

Some house exteriors in the beginning were never treated at all, although many houses were treated with a form of whitewash. Today, all houses are painted if made of wood, or at least stained. After all, who would live in an unpainted or an unstained house? The answer is, some!

Take, for example, the man who bought a "catslide" (saltbox) in North Carolina. After he decided it had originally been unpainted, he sandblasted the paint that had been applied in more modern times, returning it to its original bare condition. To protect the old wood, however, he brushed exterior tung oil on it and painted the window and door trim. I only question the sandblasting because of the damage it can cause.

Model mantel and bookcase combination, colonial style, ca. 1923. Painted finish. (Carr, Ryder & Adams Co.)

example of a certain architectural style, you may want to preserve the various finishes applied to the woodwork or trim. Try to keep intact each coat of paint in an unobtrusive spot.

Besides the record aspect of restoration, you may want to have the paint analyzed. There are experts who can take a paint chip and inform you what kind of paint it is and the date of its application. Check the National Trust for Historic Preservation for names.

Painted woodwork has a long history, about as long as that of paint, as a matter of fact. In the early 1700s paint was used by those who could afford it, because it offered a better protection than the shellac then available and at the same time lightened and enlarged typically small rooms that also had small windows. An example of popular early paint colors were the so-called Connecticut colors of blue green and rusty red.

For finer, high-style rooms, painted wainscot, panels, and ceiling beams were popular decorating devices despite the fact that fine woods often possessing their own intrinsic beauty were covered up. The painted Queen Anne, Georgian, and Federal interiors were styled to copy classical Greek themes, and paint gave woodwork a sculptured appearance that shellac did not. So a tradition was established: early American window and door frames, doors and sashes, and mantels were all painted.

Another reason for painting was purely decorative. With considerable skill, a pine door could be made to look mahogany by painting it mahogany color and graining it as mahogany wood

is grained. Such graining was commonly done on furniture made from pine and native hardwoods like maple, which possess uninteresting grains.

Your old house could also have such "false-grained" woodwork under coats of paint or varnish. I have seen this finish method in New England houses built in the late eighteenth century, a mid-nineteenth-century Victorian house in Poynette, Wisconsin, and a Frank Lloyd Wright house built in Lake Delavan, Wisconsin, in the early twentieth century. Later I will tell you how to achieve this look.

Painted exteriors were the tradition during the first half of the nineteenth century, continuing the style established by the middle of the previous hundred years. Their color was white and they had trim painted dark green. Under Andrew Jackson Downing's influence exterior colors changed in the middle of the century to fawns, grays, and drab greens. Colors became deep and intense during the last quarter of that century. A warm red brown appears to have been the most popular, with deep greens, umbers, and golden ochres close behind. Even maroon, burnt orange, and stone gray were used on occasion.

Interestingly, owners of many Queen Anne (revival) houses rarely settled on two colors. As many as five colors, all contrasting and harmonious, were brushed on, which tells us something about the cost of labor in 1885!

Paint as the original woodwork finish practically disappeared during the Victorian period, as the emphasis then was on dark shades. The era began with dark mahogany furnishings, peaked

Model kitchen cabinets and breakfast nook, ca. 1925. Painted finish. (Carr, Ryder & Adams Co.)

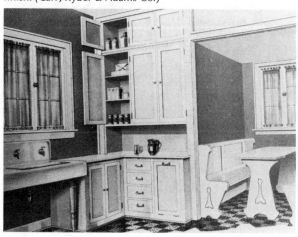

Model colonnade with leaded-glass bookcases, ca. 1925. Painted finish. (Carr, Ryder & Adams Co.)

with dark walnut furniture shades, and though the tone became lighter as the era drew to an end, dark woodwork continued. A typical Queen Anne (revival) hall, for example, was lined with dark oak wainscoting and woodwork.

The twentieth century brought in the Mission Oak furniture style, which was also dark, and the Prairie style and Craftsman style architecture, which stressed stained and varnished woodwork.

By then, however, inside baths were becoming common, with a resulting emphasis on cleanliness. Light painted surfaces lent themselves to this attitude. Home economics was developing as a science; among other things it stressed better working conditions in kitchens, which included lighting, cleanliness, and overall efficiency. Painted counters, cupboards, and cabinets appeared; woodwork was also painted to match. In general, other rooms were still unpainted.

The Art Deco movement in furniture design (1925–39), which featured some painted pieces, the rise in popularity of the California life style, and a renewed interest in the colonial (like the Dutch colonial house) all brought with them a demand for painted woodwork and interior doors. Then in the late 1930s, after the housing industry had recovered from a roughly ten-year hiatus brought on by the Great Depression, the Cape Cod and the Georgian styles came back and with them painted woodwork. Again, when housing resumed following the World War II hiatus, "limed" finishes became popular. Essentially a painted and wiped finish, it had an antique, though not authentic, quality to it.

Today, woodwork, when wood, is often painted because it is a poor-quality wood. It is also the style in modern houses and fits the budget of cost-conscious builders and prospective owners.

So much for original finishes. Now, you ask, Why did previous owners paint over the original wax, shellac, or varnish finish? No one really knows. I've got some theories, though. One is that there have been several colonial revivals in our history. The first came around the centennial in 1876, when Early American briefly interrupted the late Victorian era then in full swing. Interior decoration became colonial, in obviously Victorian houses. That it didn't fit at all seemed to make no difference. Some dark woodwork painting took place then.

The other big revival was in the mid to late 1920s. This was carried to the extent of removing beautiful old verandas from large Victorian homes

There is a slight Art Deco influence in this interior door design, ca. 1925. Door is stained mahogany, woodwork is painted. (Carr, Ryder & Adams Co.)

to make them colonial. Some onion domes and turrets were removed from late Victorian Queen Annes, and probably gingerbread from some lovely Gothics was taken off to simplify the lines and make then "Early American." Some trim probably also fell off due to neglect!

Inside, everything that could be painted was brushed over with white. By this time, too, we must keep in mind, many old house interiors had suffered from years of neglect, on the one hand, or too much attention, on the other. In either case the result was a dark material buildup of varnish, varnish stains, polishes, waxes, and dirt. As modern refinish methods were unavailable, woodwork and built-ins were painted to "brighten them up a little." Finally, some old dark homes, many surrounded by large dark trees, were depressing places in which to live. Coupled with the depressive psychosis of some older people living in these places, it is easy to understand why many grabbed a paintbrush and covered their gloomy interiors.

Was it a mistake to paint the interior woodwork? If you're not planning to repaint, the answer is a clear yes! But that is not necessarily the right answer. Painted woodwork belongs in a restored or remodeled Georgian or Greek revival as much as it did in the original. So paint *is* a traditional finish. As noted, paint lightens a room in homes not blessed with good natural light. For example, though Frank Lloyd Wright is an architect of great renown, some of his room designs featured small high windows and cavernous interiors that sunlight barely reached. In such a room dark woodwork helped create a very dark interior.

Finally, I think paint provides a change in decor and provides creative decorating possibilities. For example, I restored the living room woodwork in Wright's Chauncey Williams House to the original 1895 patina. Adjacent to that room was a large added and enclosed porch, called in the modern vernacular the family room. It is a decorator-designed room interior. The painted woodwork is a work of art, executed in multicolored stripes, making the room contrast nicely with the original rooms in this landmark house.

Painted woodwork can be a problem, though. Material buildups occur much more rapidly with paint than with other materials. This causes subsequent chipping, peeling, crazing, and cracking. It also means that at some time in the future paint must be removed so that more paint can be brushed on. Then, too, paint does not seal wood as well as other finishes. For example, door panels shrink, check, and split more readily when painted than when sealed with shellac or varnish. Finally, paint seems harder to maintain. It scratches and marks easily, chips, and shows fingerprints. Painted windowsills are the housewife's bane.

It would appear, then, that those who painted their woodwork for reasons other than being faithful to the original finish were shortsighted. Many are discovering this today and doing something about it by removing the paint and replacing it with a more practical finish.

Shellac

H. Hudson Holly, writing *Modern Dwellings in Town and Country* in 1876, mentions both shellac and varnish as the finish of a built-in sideboard. And we know from a historic study of furniture that shellac was almost the exclusive clear finish prior to lacquer introduced in the twentieth century. For example, Bruce J. Talbert, also writing in 1876, notes a "polish" for oak furniture. It is "One-half gallon of methylated spirit [alcohol]; one-half

Model stairway with seat arrangement, ca. 1910. The oak woodwork was stained, shellacked, and varnished. (Carr, Ryder & Adams Co.)

pound of shellac, bleached, 1 oz. of gum benzoin and ¼ oz. of gum mastic." This is to be "bruised well and allowed to stand till it is dissolved." So Talbert recommended a thinned version of shellac.

The extent to which shellac was used as the sole finish on woodwork, however, is pure speculation. So I will proceed to speculate that shellac was used as a clear finish until varnish was commercially available. And that date I would guess is about 1865, a time when American manufacturing was really coming into its own. Of course, varnish was known from the mid-eighteenth century when the Martin brothers in Paris began mixing and using it.

Shellac is made from the residue of the lac bug of Ceylon and India. Shipped worldwide in lac flakes, it is mixed with denatured alcohol by the manufacturers. The "cut" of shellac refers to the pounds of lac to one gallon of alcohol; thus, a three-pound cut is a mixture of three pounds of lac flakes to one gallon of alcohol.

It is a clear wood sealer that can be applied to a given surface many times and, if skillfully done, does not acquire the material buildup of paint. Shellac dries fast and does not cause the bleeding through of stain, because it has a different solvent from most stains.

Craftsmen found that shellacked boxes and even furniture withstood the elements satisfactorily, though it was often too delicate a material for floors and doors. It neither wore so well nor withstood moisture without turning dark. So people sealed the wood with shellac and then applied wax over the shellac to protect it. I suspect that this procedure lasted until varnish became readily available; I am certain that shellac continued to be used as a sealer under the varnish for another hundred years.

It is highly unlikely that your woodwork has only shellac on it, but you can determine the substance by testing it. To test for shellac—you're probably way ahead of me—put some denatured alcohol on a rag and wipe it on the woodwork, preferably in an out-of-the-way corner. If the finish dissolves, sure enough, it's shellac. Among other things, this means that if you're going to strip that old finish, you can use denatured alcohol as the solvent. This is good because it's cheaper and easier to use than paint and varnish remover; just be sure you have a lot of ventilation unless you want to get a new high working with it!

Model sideboard kalitan colonnade and wainscoting, ca. 1910. (Carr, Ryder & Adams Co.)

and Japanese products, so much so that it was considered a lacquer product. And so it was that varnish technology preceded that of paint.

The principal varnish oils were linseed and tung with some perilla. Predominant among the varnish resins were the hard fossil gums of congo and kauri. Faster-drying varnishes and those that did not turn white in water were developed by combining tung oil and ester gum. Viscosity was reduced next, followed by still faster-drying varnish made with phenol-modified rosin esters. By now there was a varnish that could withstand exterior elements as well as interior.

Varnish utilizes a mineral spirit solvent such as benzine, oleum, or turpentine in contrast to the alcohol solvent of shellac. The most important difference between varnish and shellac is that varnish resists everything, making it clearly superior to its time-honored predecessor.

The disadvantages of varnish are that it dries much more slowly than shellac or lacquer and its protective coat is, by today's standards, soft. Heavy traffic causes wear, too much sun can cause it to dry and flake, heat can cause crazing, and too many coats cause a buildup that can darken wood and cover grain.

Model living room, fireplace, and bookcases, ca. 1910. A good illustration of Mission-style interior. (Carr, Ryder & Adams Co.)

Varnish

If your woodwork has a clear finish on it, more than likely it is varnish. Historically, varnish is first mentioned in connection with "French Varnish," developed by the four Martin brothers, who were in business in Paris from about 1725 to 1765. Labeled Martin's Varnish, it is said to have had a fine luster, which compared favorably with Chinese

Stain

Stain as we know it today is also a product of technology. The penetrating oil stains, alcohol stains, and water stains are a far cry from the

Burgoyne-style colonnade. Model for ca. 1910 Mission-style home. (Carr, Ryder & Adams Co.)

materials used in olden times. Ox blood, as noted, was one of these substances. Red filler was a stain made from Spanish brown pigment, linseed oil, and turpentine. An acid wash applied to walnut furniture in the Victorian era turned it "black," the current fashionable color.

Various dyes were also applied to woodwork to achieve the desired color before and after commercial stains were available. Much "mahogany" is birch with a mahogany dye; it's impossible to completely remove by stripping and must be sanded out of the wood after stripping.

Stain is a pigmented solution in penetrating oil having a mineral spirit solvent designed to give wood a desired color that it does not possess naturally. Stain can also enhance a wood's natural color, cover imperfections, and enable different wood species to be color matched. For example, I had the task of matching mahogany French doors to birch woodwork in a 1911 vintage room. After some experimentation and a little mixing I stained the doors mostly a dark greenish brown and the frames around them mostly a walnut shade. The match was perfect; everything now has a rich mahogany appearance.

Other advantages of stain are that it will stabilize the color of the wood, an asset for wood not possessing a good intrinsic color like pine, and can entirely change the character of wood. Thus, birch can become walnut and poplar can become mahogany when stained. On the other hand, stain is not always necessary if the wood possesses the

natural color that you desire. It is also more work, requires drying time, has a tendency to bleed if you're not careful, and hides wood grain.

Graining

Graining, or as I call it, false graining, is a finishing technique in which a semitransparent paint is brushed on the woodwork and then smeared and streaked with fingers, palms, feathers, erasers, or even rather sophisticated graining tools to create an interesting design. At times wood grains were authentically reproduced by graining. Not only is this process decorative but it can hide a multitude of sins in damaged woodwork, poor surface conditions, and woodwork not worth stripping and refinishing.

Basically, a graining glaze is applied on an enamel base coat. This is where the skill comes in as one is attempting to copy a natural wood grain. Then the pattern is protected by applying a varnish over it. (A detailed, step-by-step procedure is outlined in the December 1979 issue of *The Old-House Journal*.)

Fuming

Some Mission Oak furniture and some oak woodwork in Prairie School and Craftsman houses received their dark brown color from fuming.

Model kitchen cabinets in yellow pine, ca. 1919. (Carr, Ryder & Adams Co.)

Unrestored room at 72 Anson Street, Charleston, SC.

Restored room at 72 Anson Street, Charleston. Woodwork is painted in keeping with authentic restoration. Photos by Louis Schwartz *(Photos courtesy of Historic Charleston Foundation.)*

Woodwork was fumed by setting a number of dishes of 26 percent aqua ammonia in the room after it was made airtight and leaving them there until the desired color was achieved. The Craftsman Workshop of Gustav Stickley lays claim to discovering the fact that ammonia reacts with the large amount of tannic acid in white oak, turning the wood a pleasant dark brown.

In any event, one can duplicate that process today without the smoking. One can apply a solution called 880 ammonia with a brush, and the fumes will do the trick, or you can brush on a dark English oak to Flemish black shade of penetrating oil stain. This latter technique, I feel, provides an authentic color without all the mess.

Other even more esoteric finishes were also used around 1910, such as sulfuric acid and an iron oxide solution. A diluted solution of sulfuric acid created a warm brown gray on cypress when brushed on. Pieces of iron allowed to sit in vinegar a few days makes a clear silver gray color on maple woodwork when brushed on. These finishes and fumed woodwork were protected either with wax or sealed with shellac. At times the shellac had a black aniline dye added to it to darken the wood. Finally, the woodwork sealed with shellac was, at times, covered with varnish, although another coat of shellac was more common.

Well, that's how they made and finished woodwork. How you will finish yours is the topic of a later chapter. But first let's continue our background research by learning a little about old architecture.

Chapter Three

Woodwork and Trim Designs of the Past

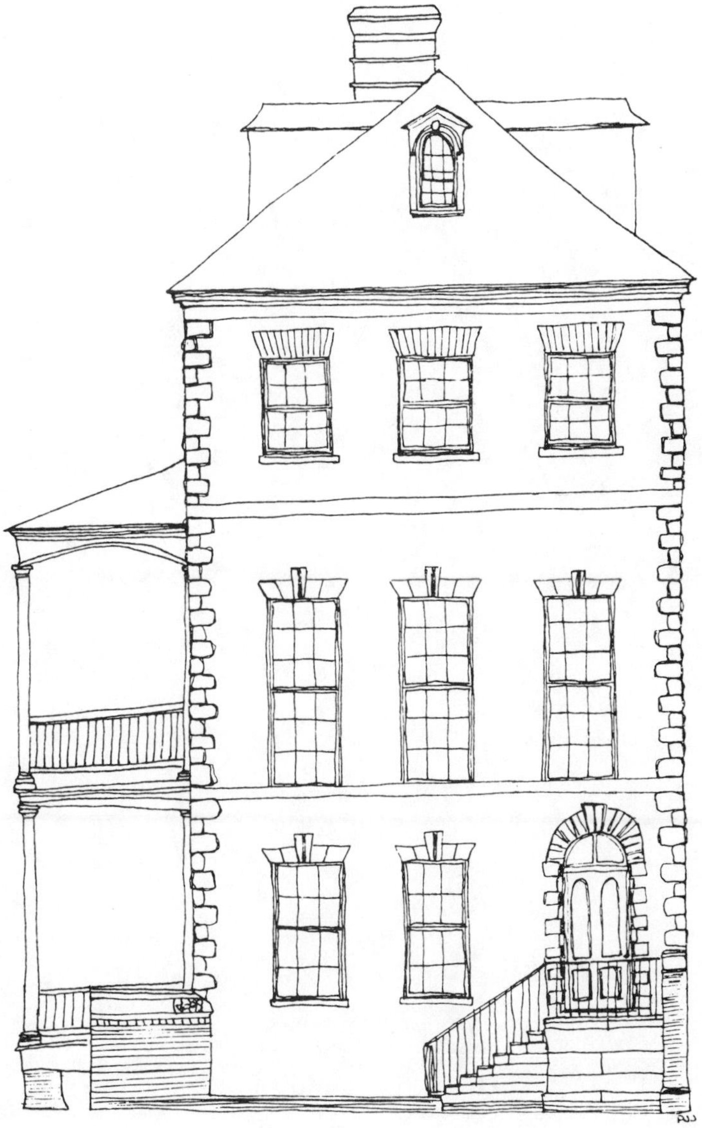

A few houses have survived the rigors of time from the very beginning of America. In addition, entire rooms have been taken from buildings to be demolished, from those that had deteriorated beyond repair and even from those that are still standing in good shape today. All of this is very helpful to the restorer who wants to be faithful to his or her home's style and construction period.

Of course, it's not required that one remain faithful to the original trim and woodwork. Zealous concern is left primarily to historical sites and the foundations and committees managing them. Being faithful, further, is rather hypocritical, since most houses are a collection of several styles (and sometimes no style), assuming that former owners and their handymen have not tampered with them since their erection. Since few owners could resist remodeling, removing, and renovating in a sort of restless quest, many of us have really inherited quite a collection to restore. Nonetheless, I'm sure you'll agree that it's good to have some knowledge of architectural styles, with an emphasis on trim and woodwork and their respective restoration.

I'm kind of proud of this chapter because it contains a brief history of architecture in America, a description of woodwork and trim styles, and some facts on materials, finishes, and configurations. All of this is the result of a great deal of research, for while exteriors are very topical, interiors, especially the nitty-gritty details, are, strangely missing. So I put together my experience working in old houses, my travels to practically every old city in our land in which I studied old landmarks, and material from over a dozen books.

In the organizing process of all the material

Model "period" buffet in quarter white oak, ca. 1919. The furniture is William and Mary revival, a popular 1920s style. Wainscoting and woodwork are from that historic period. (Carr, Ryder & Adams Co.)

for this chapter I began to discover that my attempt to fit houses into styles and styles into time periods was a little frustrating because they often defied classification. For example, the Gothic revival architectural style reportedly began about 1835, earning it a place in "early Victorian" styles. Yet landmark Gothics like General Mariano Vallejo's Lachrymae Montis in Sonoma, California, was built in 1851–52, and Rest Cottage in Evanston, Illinois, was built in 1865, placing them in the mid-Victorian

Model oak built-in buffet for dining room, ca. 1925. (Carr, Ryder & Adams Co.)

period. Another illustration is the Georgian style noted in a Connecticut house built in 1710, although Georgian's official "debut" was 1750.

Evidently style periods are approximations. Some designers and carpenters were ahead of their time and others lagged. So, considering the approximations regarding dating and the eclectic nature of many houses, even landmarks, some of the material that follows *may* be debated.

Perhaps you will wonder why, in the following pages, I make so much reference to furniture styles. It is because furniture design and building design are related. At first, historically, furniture styles provided the leadership. Architects were conspicuously absent and buildings were designed by carpenters and by such dilettantes as Thomas Jefferson. So our initial look into trim and woodwork origins will be heavily furniture-oriented.

After about 1800 architects occupied the building design driver's seat. In fact, as the nineteeth century progressed to its conclusion, some architects, notably Henry Hobson Richardson, Frank Lloyd Wright, and Charles S. Greene, designed the furniture to be used in their own creations. Let's see how all this came about.

THE SEVENTEENTH CENTURY

The earliest homes in America were not much more substantial than the wigwams of the Wampanoag Indians, the first permanent settlers found in 1620. A visit to Plymouth Plantation in Plymouth, Massachusetts, shows us small, dark, clapboard abodes with a few tiny casement windows and doors set close to the wall surface.

Gradually these were replaced by such places as the Stockwell House. Typical of the 1650s, it was dark, low-ceilinged, massively constructed, and medieval in character. Inside, the framing members—ceiling beams, corner posts, and intermediate posts—are visible. Hand finishing was obvious, because interiors were rarely painted or finished in any way. Wainscot of wide pine boards rose from floor to ceiling, and the furniture of the period, which was labeled Puritan, Stuart by others, and Wainscot by still others, derived its name from the paneling.

Windows were leaded-glass sashes, some fixed and some casements. Trim was unpainted, as were the doors. Exterior plaster walls, however, were whitewashed.

So the hardy settlers lived their lives in small, two-room cabins. The kitchen doubled as the sitting room after the evening meal, and the bedroom contained the average family's most prized possession, the bedstead. Their interior lives were centered in front of the huge fireplace, as yet without a mantel.

THE EIGHTEENTH CENTURY

Things began to happen in the eighteenth century. Several definite architectural styles emerged bearing the names of the leading furniture styles: William and Mary, Queen Anne, Chippendale-Georgian, and Federal. The latter combined Hepplewhite and Sheraton.

William and Mary (1700–25)

In the first quarter of the century design formed a fork in the road. One way led to the higher style of emerging urban centers, and the other led to the country. The great monument to high-style William and Mary is Williamsburg, Virginia, made capital of that colony in 1699. The best example in Williamsburg is the Governor's Palace. Destroyed by fire in 1781, the edifice was authentically rebuilt. Its façade, with two windows on each side of the main doorway, five second-floor windows above each of the first-floor openings, and five roof dormers, is a portrait of symmetry.

The new wealth was also reflected in the Morattico Hall flock room, one of many moved, restored, and reconstructed rooms open to public view. Built in 1719 and now located in the H. F. du Pont Winterthur Museum, it has wainscot paneling above chair height on three walls, and on the end wall is a large fireplace framed by bolection molding. Windows of twenty-four lights (panes of glass) are set deep in floor-to-ceiling panels. Floors, in medieval tradition, are wide board, either pine or oak, stained dark.

Just as such a room departs considerably from the distinctly medieval rooms of the past century, so did its furnishings. William and Mary introduced walnut and maple as the basic materials of a much lighter piece than the wainscot style. Turned legs had bulbous ball-, bun-, or turnip-shaped feet and put furniture a good twenty inches from the floor.

Organized interior unity made its first appearance in this period. As in the exterior, symmetry and balance are emphasized in carved room decorations, the articulation of wall paneling, and the spacing and organization of architectural elements. Summer beams and rafters are now covered with plaster or sheathing; ax and saw marks are less in evidence, and planes and rulers are being used more frequently by carpenters. Most important, sash windows made their first appearance in the Colonies.

While homes for the great and the wealthy were being built in Virginia, Philadelphia, and Boston, New England architecture evolved into the so-called Yankee House. A gentle roof rise replaced the pointed façades of the previous decades; sash windows replaced casements and came into better proportion with each other. This house had no porches, bays, recessed windows, or eaves, making

Old Ogden House, Fairfield, CT, ca. 1700. Colonial-style saltbox. Drawing by Pamela J. Johnson

it plain and declarative. Labeled saltbox, stone-ender, Garrison, and other names, many are still standing in such Massachusetts towns as Worthington, Newburyport, Barnstable, and Stockbridge.

The interior of this everyman's house can be seen in the Concord Antiquarian Society's "pine-ceilinged room." Nearly everything in it is made of wood. The floor-to-ceiling wainscot and the ceiling panels were made of soft pine, as was the flooring. Paneling, doors, and trim were left natural. Wall sheathing was feather-edged at the double-hung windows, making framing unnecessary. Such a room was frugal, orderly, and untainted by modern machines.

Queen Anne (1725–50)

Though a robust style, Queen Anne seems to have made a complete break with the past. Both the medieval tradition of William and Mary furniture as seen in its bulk and the principle of adding elements to achieve the complete piece were replaced by more delicate, simple, and self-contained style. Important features of the new style are the cabriole leg and pad foot, the carved shell motif, the fan, and the sunburst "logo," all of which created a distinctive style and a focal point to each piece.

In similar fashion Queen Anne exteriors and interiors also featured greater unity and emphasis, marking the beginning of the Classical period. Rooms were conceived as subtle variations on a single theme. Chair curves were picked up and echoed in the lines of desks, beds, and curtains. They were reinforced in doorjambs, mantels, and paneling in moderate and bold relief.

Rooms were often paneled floor to ceiling and painted light colors. Floorboards became narrower and in fine homes came from oak trees. Take, for example, the Rose House in North Bramford, Connecticut. The summer beams, corner posts, and girts are encased, and the floor is constructed of narrow oak boards laid in unbroken lengths. All other woodwork, including the wainscot paneling, is made of white pine. Although the floor has never been painted, the walls have had many coats over the original greenish blue. Sashes were painted white, the corner cupboard top interior, vermilion.

Another Queen Anne room interior is found in a Connecticut parlor now in the Metropolitan Museum of Art in New York. The fireplace is enclosed in an arched wainscot paneling and flanked by fluted pilasters. No other wall is paneled, however, giving the impression of simple wood treatment and emphasizing one wall, that of the fireplace. Framing around doorways and window openings is achieved by nailing a small molding to the surface of flat boards. The color that survives was probably achieved by mixing a buttermilk or egg base to a rusty red paint. Today, one sees a natural wood color with a trace of red.

The exterior façade of the Queen Anne featured main doorways framed in pilasters and entablatures which interrupt the first-story belt course (a row, course, of stone flush with the wall used on a house exterior either to mark the floor line or bring about an apparent reduction in height), giving a visual focus lacking in William and Mary. Unfortunately, visual proportion took precedence over interior structure, so inside not everything came off that great. Design was concentrated in a few robust patches like entrance porticoes, dentils under outside eaves, and pediments on roof dormers. It all added up to a unified whole and repeated interior designs, only on a larger scale.

Chippendale-Georgian (1750–75)

In Chippendale furniture the last vestiges of medieval verticality disappeared. Chair backs became almost square, and the proportionate height of their legs lowered. These differences seem greater than they really were, for the new designs of Thomas Chippendale of London were mostly an extension of Queen Anne.

Similarly, house façades were practically the same as before except that they became more symmetrical and were dressed up a little more. Now every window to the right of the door had its mate to the left. Rough clapboarding was smooth. Deep hallways are more likely to feature gracious staircases. Cove moldings grace the tops of walls, and all doors are paneled.

The consumer-oriented market had its beginning in the Queen Anne period. New England carpenters, formerly suiting themselves as to what they built, began to listen to their customers' wishes. Often the customers' demands were ideas published in the volumes then available on home design and ornamentation. Trim like pilasters, cornices, pediments, arches, and mantels were depicted in these books. Prospective homeowners could pick and choose.

Plain windows were out of style; now they had to be capped with attractive cornices and had to be larger than before. Cove molding, chair rails, and banisters were not only a must but artistically designed as well. Wood paneling also disappeared, and the only wood paneling used in rooms covered the chimney breast and the dado. The old stile and bolection molded wood paneling was replaced with molding applied to plaster surfaces to simulate wainscot.

In finer Chippendale-Georgians, doors were paneled and made of mahogany. Fireplaces received their first mantels and were often flanked with pilasters and crowned with an overmantel elaborately trimmed with a broken pediment and cartouche. The simple woodwork of Queen Anne gave way to doorways and window frames topped with architraves and broken pediments and framed with pilasters. All woodwork was painted, giving the room a sculptured look. As all this was reminiscent of Greek temples, the style has received a sort of sublabel of Greek Revival.

Chippendale furniture set in a room paneled from floor to ceiling further identifies the Hunter House as Chippendale-Georgian and Queen Anne. Windows are large, twenty-four-light, reminiscent of William and Mary.

Built in about 1750, the Hunter House was extensively remodeled in 1850. Restoration took place in 1952–53. The house, labeled late colonial, combines the paneled interior of Queen Anne and the exterior of Chippendale-Georgian. As windows appear William and Mary, this house well illustrates the eclectic nature of most homes.

Here, as in other fine Chippendale-Georgian homes, the fireplace has a mantel. The throwback to Queen Anne lies in the floor-to-ceiling paneling, grained ("false-grained" or "grained-painted") to imitate walnut. The painting is The Hunter Dogs, by Gilbert Stuart.

The paneling was originally painted a red tone, pilasters and baseboards were later "marbleized" a black paint veined with gold, to imitate marble. Flanking cupboard interiors were painted dark blue, and wainscoting a solid greenish putty color. Paint research determined the original colors. (Hunter House photographs by permission of The Preservation Society of Newport County, Newport, RI)

Peirce-Nichols House, Salem, MA. Samuel McIntire, 1782. Late Georgian style. Drawing by Pamela J. Johnson

Gadsden House, Charleston, SC, ca. 1800. Federal style. Drawing by Pamela J. Johnson

Plenty of examples of Georgian architecture have survived, particularly in New England. Quickly identifiable by its column- or pilaster-flanked front entry, its Palladian window above the entry, and its symmetry, Georgian was undoubtedly a very popular style. It still is!

Federal (1785–1825)

One does not have to look any farther than the White House, home of American Presidents, or to portions of Mt. Vernon, the home of *one* President, for examples of the Federal style. Many other examples abound, from High Street, Newburyport, Massachusetts, to Beacon Hill in Boston, to Anson Street in Charleston.

Federal embodies all the classical qualities of the preceding three periods often to a self-conscious excess. Labeled classical decadence by some, Federal was what successful shippers in Salem wanted from Samuel McIntire, as well as what wealthy merchants in New York and rich rice planters in Charleston wanted from their builders and designers.

While New England designs continued to be relatively simple, the scale became imposing under the first American architect of note, Charles Bulfinch. Pilasters became columns and porticoes, two stories became three, with a smaller Palladian-style window often above the typical second-story one. Because of renewed interest in columns and other trappings of the Greek temple, some also call this period Greek Revival, and others labeled it Adamesque-Federal, as in the case of the Nathaniel Russell House in Charleston, built in 1803.

Carvers made extensive use of pilasters in the finer homes for ceilings, cornices, moldings, and case work. Their renderings were often so realistic it is hard to tell whether a given piece is carved in wood or molded in plaster. McIntire, the renowned builder of many houses in Salem, is said to have had forty-six planes in his possession for the shaping of white pine. Though most woodwork was painted white, other colors were used. The Oak Hill living room now reposing in the Museum of Fine Arts in Boston has ecru-painted woodwork.

Portico of Nathaniel Russell House, Charleston, SC. Federal style, 1809. Considered an unusual example of Adam architecture.

The famous "flying" stairs in the Nathaniel Russell House which spiral unsupported from floor to floor. (Photos courtesy of Historic Charleston Foundation)

The high-style furniture of the period was Hepplewhite and Sheraton, produced mostly by British cabinetmakers. However, there was one famous American, Duncan Phyfe, who lived and worked in New York from about 1795 to 1847. The first American cabinetmaker of note, he leaned toward heaviness, though lightness in materials, mass, colors, and shapes is characteristic of pieces of that period. Satinwood, holly, tulipwood, curly maple, and pine cut in thin strips and used as veneer and inlay were introduced by cabinet-

makers. Phyfe used mahogany and really introduced the early Victorian styles.

Frequently, Federal furniture was painted white, gold, or pastel shades. Another innovation was the dark marblelike quality of Chippendale mahogany set off by strawberry- and orange-colored inlays. The center of gravity of rooms was lowered as chair legs became shorter, sideboards, desks, and chests lost their upper sections, and windows were brought down to floor level. It was a style the new republic could be proud of.

THE NINETEENTH CENTURY—VICTORIANA

Victoria Regina became Queen of England in 1837. She did not announce at that time that she was initiating a new era, but she may as well have, for the next seventy years or so bear her name.

To continue our relationship of furniture to architecture, we should note the furniture styles of this period: American Empire, early Victorian, Gothic, Spool Turned, Cottage, Renaissance, Louis

XV, Eastlake, Golden Oak and Mission Oak, and Art Nouveau. Compared to the previous century, there was a great deal more innovation, and a characteristic heaviness and mass that sort of went back to the beginning of the eighteenth century. Ornamentation, too, differed. It ranged from the sometimes plain Gothic and early Eastlake pieces to the baroque Belter, rococo Renaissance, gaudy Gothic, and elegant Eastlake.

In addition to design and ornamentation, the various Victorian substyles can be delineated by wood species. Thus, there is the mahogany of the Empire and early Victorian, the walnut of much Gothic and Louis XV, the pine of Cottage and Spool Turned, and the oak of Eastlake, Golden Oak, and Mission Oak.

Architecturally, the era began with Andrew Jackson Downing and ended with Adler and Sullivan. It was the spawning ground of Frank Lloyd Wright's Prairie School, Gustav Stickley's Arts and Crafts Movement, and Greene and Greene's bungalows. Victoriana can be rather roughly divided into three fuzzy periods: early Victorian (1820–50), high Victorian (1850–80), and late Victorian (1880–1910).

Early Victorian (1820–50)

The nineteenth century witnessed a rather sudden shift in furniture design from the functional delicacy of Federal pieces to ponderous Empire pedantry. To many the first few decades of that century exhibited a strange collapse of taste. The Empire style with its columns, caryatids, lyres, and scrolls leaned heavily on archaeology whether one is discussing chairs, doorway frames, or newels.

Dozens of furniture factories, those of Duncan Phyfe and Lambert Hitchcock being the most famous, turned out handmade reproductions of designs of others like Thomas Sheraton, George Hepplewhite, and Ithiel Town, the American architect. Their furniture was characteristically bulky and lacking in grace. It had heavy table pedestals, thick columns on chests of drawers, heavy cyma-curved legs and feet for settees, and cupboards sitting squarely on the floor. Although most of this was veneer, country cabinetmakers still used solid wood. They were producing early Ohio and early Pennsylvania pieces still more bulky and

cumbersome and made of native hardwoods cut in one-inch-thick boards.

One illustration of high-style Empire is a parlor copied from an Albany, New York, house, circa 1830, to be found in the Winterthur Museum in Williamsburg. One notes wide, flat pilasters painted white and flanking windows and doorways, which, in turn, are capped with entablatures. The window sash and muntins are painted white, extend nearly from floor to ceiling, and have twelve lights in the bottom sash and nine in the top. The paneled door is either mahogany or stained a dark shade. The focal point of the room is a marble fireplace with Egyptian figures as supporting columns (connoting permanence).

Another illustration of Empire interiors is now in the Brooklyn Museum, although it once was the parlor in an Irvington, New Jersey, early Victorian house. As with many homes of that period one wall is curved, the entrance wall. Thus, the doorway, its alcove, entablature, flanking pilasters, and base and cove all had to follow the curved line. Walls are pale-tinted foil, and there is no trace of wainscoting. This results in a lightening of the architectural mass. Windows are narrower, typically six-light mutined sashes. Woodwork has a carved geometric motif and is painted white, as in the Winterthur Museum room.

The new architect, more of an intellectual than his predecessors, possessed an eclectic mind. Borrowing from the past, he revived classical designs, including Roman suggesting civic virtue, Greek for liberty, Egyptian for permanence, and Gothic for Christian ideals.

The Italianate period in this era illustrates the Roman Revival and lasted in New York from about 1845 to 1860. It sired the famous New York brownstone in the city and the Hudson River bracket house in the country. Another popular style was the Gothic Revival, begun as early as 1835 and lasting as long as the Italianate. Finally, the Greek Revival, begun about 1830 and also ending with the Civil War, was chiefly the development of Ithiel Town.

The hallmark of Greek Revival is the low triangular pediment in rooflines and over doors and windows. Particularly good examples are the row houses numbers 22, 24, and 26 Willow Street in Brooklyn Heights, Brooklyn, New York. They have a higher basement housing the kitchen and the family room, the first floor comprising two parlors,

Italianate (Tuscan). Drawing by Pamela J. Johnson

Gothic Revival. Drawing by Pamela J. Johnson

Frederick Stahl House, Galena, IL, 1844. Greek Revival. **Drawing** by Pamela J. Johnson

and two more floors of bedrooms. Ceilings are high, and the twin parlors are separated by wide sliding doors flanked by a screen or pilasters.

Not all brownstones were Greek Revival, however. In addition to Italianate, they were also Gothic. Roosevelt House, built in the 1840s, is sort of a Gothic eclectic style. Inside there is the heavy stuffed furniture of the forties, the marble mantels with realistic foliage, and heavy plaster moldings. The door trim is wide, flat, and has a crossette at each upper corner; cove appears to be a combination of decorative plaster and wood molding. The door is paneled and its frame rests on plinths almost as high as the rather high base. Of note are the two French doors in this room.

In the country the Gothic Revival took the form of the "cottage residence," a design attributed to Andrew Jackson Downing and Alexander Davis. Hardly cottages, they were made entirely of wood and featured pointed roofs. Because they contained much gingerbread exterior trim, they earned another label, that of Carpenter Gothic. In contrast to many of the styles depicted so far, the Gothic was not limited to any one region. For example, Rest Cottage in Evanston, Illinois; Lachrymae Montis, Sonoma, California; and Surgeon's Quarters, Fort Dallas, Oregon, illustrate the geographical diversity of this style.

It became possible to achieve total Gothic in one's rooms as Gothic furniture, clocks, lamps, stoves, and even tableware were designed and manufactured. Most of the rooms were Tudor in feeling, though. Ceilings were flat and ornamented with ribs; pointed arches appear on windows, door cases, and mantels. Those homes that did not follow the Gothic theme throughout had at least one Gothic room, the library. Here dark woods, narrow windows, and rich wood-grained surfaces created a feeling of scholarly isolation.

It was, however, the Italianate style that led most directly from early Victorian to high Victorian. It compromised the columns, gables, and pediments of classical Italy with the towers, arches, and asymmetrical plans of the early Christian and Romanesque era.

Italianate exteriors were elegant yet informal, simple in line yet lavish in decoration, classical in derivation and picturesque in execution. Interiors completed the picture. Though there was no Italianate furniture style, the baroque Belter line was considered high style. This was furniture made by John Henry Belter in rosewood laminates, pierced with designs, all very classy. Room details and proportions are reminiscent of the Empire style: marble fittings in fireplaces, marble-topped tables, decorated columns, and ornate plaster cove molding and even ceilings.

Captain's Cottage No. 2, Sailors' Snug Harbor, Staten Island, NY, 1885. Late Second Empire style. Drawing by Pamela J. Johnson

High Victorian (1850–80)

Victorian styles reached their zenith about the middle of the Italianate period, 1860, and the thirty or so years constituting that time span have been labeled high Victorian. In furniture the Gothic continued its popularity, while Spool Turned, Cottage, Louis XV and XVI, and Renaissance were all introduced. Spool Turned and Cottage represented the lower end of the styles as they were mass-produced by an industry quickly becoming mechanized. Made from native hardwoods and pine, these pieces were often stained to imitate more expensive woods like mahogany, or else painted, as in the case of most Cottage, to cover very cheap wood. One can see such pieces in the Gothic Cottage and the Carpenter Gothic house of the day, and one can speculate that at least some of the woodwork in these homes was originally painted to match the furniture.

In many respects, Louis XV and XVI were a continuation of previous styles: the cabriole legs of the Queen Anne found in Louis XV and the slender, tapered chair legs of Sheraton found in Louis XVI. However, the best known piece in these styles is the medallion sofa and settee of the Louis XV style.

Renaissance is more a genuine Victorian creation. The furniture of Lincoln's time, it combines the large mass of the Empire style, the ornateness of early Victorian, and the height of Gothic. Finer pieces were walnut, treated to achieve a dark tone.

While Gothic and Italianate architectural styles continued to be built, the Queen Anne (revival) style came into being in this period and continued into later Victorian years. Thousands of Queen Annes once lined the streets from Stanford to San Francisco. Although it was "introduced" in the Philadelphia exposition in 1876, this is the style of Harry Truman's home in Independence, Missouri, built in 1865.

Queen Anne was everyman's dream house till almost 1910, perhaps because it combines all the popular elements of the Elizabethan, Jacobian, Gothic, and Italianate styles. As you can see in the drawing, it was indeed a bric-a-brac design. Although the exterior focal point is the tower, its interior focal point is the entry hall. It was typically a squarish room lined with a dark oak wainscoting and woodwork. At times a large fireplace occupied

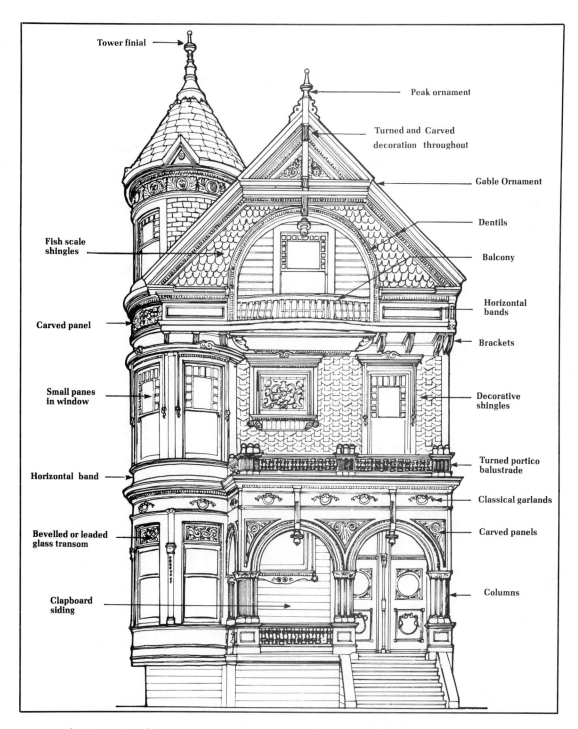

Tower finial

Peak ornament

Turned and Carved decoration throughout

Gable Ornament

Dentils

Fish scale shingles

Balcony

Horizontal bands

Carved panel

Brackets

Small panes in window

Decorative shingles

Horizontal band

Turned portico balustrade

Classical garlands

Bevelled or leaded glass transom

Carved panels

Clapboard siding

Columns

This Queen Anne house contains many features found in this picturesque style—a variety of textures with three different types of shingles plus clapboarding, many different kinds of windows, and different kinds of wood decoration. The drawing is adapted from an excellent book about Victorian architecture in San Francisco, A Gift to the Street. *(Reprinted with permission of* The Old-House Journal, *69A Seventh Avenue, Brooklyn, NY 11217)*

the wall at the end of the hall and a built-in bench sat beneath the staircase. Clearly, it was designed to impress the visitor.

Above the wainscot paneling was either wallpaper with exotic patterns or damask or velour fabric. Boxed-in beams, outside light filtering through stained glass, or windows bordered with stained glass gave the hall a medieval atmosphere.

Main rooms led off the central hall; portieres replaced the doors of prior periods. Upstairs were the bedrooms and the *only* bath, as indoor plumbing was still a luxury.

Late Victorian (1880–1910)

From about 1880 to 1910 the Victorian era was drawing to a close. It was hardly as a spring running down or an engine running out of steam. Without exaggeration this important century ended on a very high note. These decades were the time span of Charles Eastlake, Henry Hobson Richardson, John Root, and Louis Henri Sullivan; they were the infant years of Frank Lloyd Wright, Gustav Stickley, and Charles and Henry Greene.

The furniture of the period was Eastlake, Golden Oak, Mission Oak, and Art Nouveau. And it can be said that design, construction, and manufacture were a distinctive departure from what had preceded them.

Eastlake furniture had a straight line and a rectilinear shape. It was somewhat reminiscent of Gothic, but its mass was lighter and its designs more geometric, accenting the line of the individual piece. Oak was the material of the finer pieces, as was burl veneer; ash was used on cheaper pieces. The color was immeasurably lighter than in past decades, a sort of light yellowish brown or light fruitwood.

Golden Oak continued the lighter shades of Eastlake as well as the material. It differed,

DESIGNS FOR SCROLLS AND BRACKETS.

DESIGNS FOR CORNICES.

FRONT STAIRCASE

CHIMNEY TOPS.

Victorian homes, interior woodwork and exterior trim details. (Reprinted with permission of The Old-House Journal, 69A Seventh Avenue, Brooklyn, NY 11217)

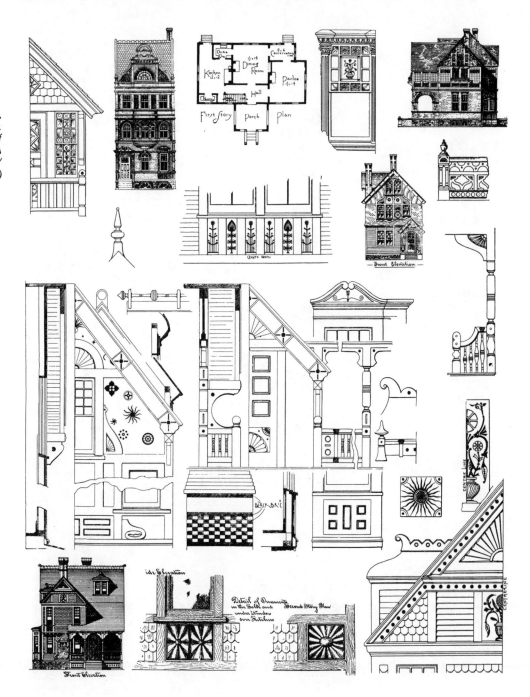

Victorian Romanesque designs, woodwork and trim details. (Reprinted with permission of The Old-House Journal, 69A Seventh Avenue, Brooklyn, NY 11217)

however, in being more curvilinear—a sort of Empire Revival in some designs—and bulkier, too. Typically it was less ornate than Eastlake. The signal was clear that oak was in.

Mission Oak took up where Golden Oak left off. Using the same material, it reflected earthy lines of the Prairie School architecture and the Craftsman bungalow by taking on a dark, earthen color. Line-wise, this style also reflected the straight line, especially that of the Prairie School. The verticality of most Mission Oak pieces, however, contrasted greatly with the horizontal line of the homes that housed them. So Mission Oak was a kind of functional Gothic, as it were.

Art Nouveau furniture is an entity unto itself, having little precedence. It is often asymmetrically curvilinear; edges are also often rounded. Though it did reflect the "natural" orientation of many designers by having no paint, and little stain on it, it was a product of a growing machine age with its use of metal as an accent. Both Art Nouveau furniture and architecture are western European creations, and little is found in this country.

Late Victorian architects have been loosely divided into two groups, the Beaux-Arts and the Progressives (or Pioneers or Rebels). The Beaux-Arts were represented by Henry Hobson Richardson and the firm that followed him, Shepley, Rutan,

Victorian Italianate home designs, woodwork and trim details. (Reprinted with permission of The Old-House Journal, 69A Seventh Avenue, Brooklyn, NY 11217)

Late Victorian Gothic style.
Drawing by Pamela J. Johnson

and Coolidge, and by Richard Morris Hunt, among others. These designers were interested in revival architecture like Tudor, Gothic, and Roman. Their work exuded a certain romanticism.

Two houses should illustrate their thinking. One is Richardson's Romanesque James J. Glessner House in Chicago (1886). It consists of heavy stonework and ponderous forms. The north wall is 150 feet of unbroken granite! Another is illustrated by the Watts Sherman House in Newport, Rhode Island, also by Richardson, designed in 1875. Featured is a hall of exposed ceiling beams, panels, posts, and balusters, all representing a revival of a seventeenth-century New England folk building combined with Romanesque eclecticism.

Richardson's design of furniture, mostly Golden Oak, reversed the eighteenth-century situation in which furniture designers influenced architecture! The old unity between architecture and furniture design had been restored; later the ball passed to Wright, who scored more points than Richardson.

There was a symbolism to building design. Richard Morris Hunt's architectural masterpiece, The Breakers, designed for the Vanderbilts and built in 1892 in Newport, seems to represent the imperial power of that family. Bigness was the theme of many other homes (though they were hardly the size of The Breakers) and commercial buildings in this period. In Chicago it is illustrated

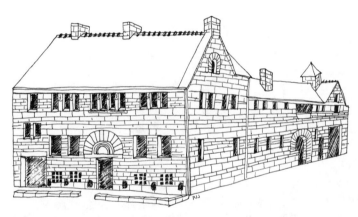

James J. Glessner House, Chicago, IL. H. H. Richardson, 1886. Drawing by Pamela J. Johnson

President John F. Kennedy's birthplace, Brookline, MA, ca. 1908. Vernacular Victorian. Drawing by Pamela J. Johnson

Frank Lloyd Wright Home and Studio, Oak Park, IL, 1889–1909. Begun as a modified Queen Anne, which reflected the Craftsman period, it evolved in twenty years to this eclectic residence and drafting studio. This façade will be changed via restoration to Wright's 1909 design. (Photo by permission and courtesy of Frank Lloyd Wright Home and Studio Foundation)

in the Auditorium Theater and the Monadnock Building, both Adler and Sullivan designs.

Favored materials were heavy oak and walnut, polished marble, gilt fittings, velvet draperies, and tile flooring. Material innovations consisted of glass in walls, ceilings, and roofs, and concrete. These were used as much for their construction qualities as their aesthetics.

The Progressive School, represented by Sullivan, Root, Wright, and others, reacted against high Victorian styles and *any* revivals. Honesty characterized these architects: honesty as to the real nature of structure (form follows function), as to making use of the true character of materials, and honesty of expression. Both Sullivan and Wright are well known for their arrogance, believed today to be a result of their honest convictions.

Sullivan demonstrated this when he said that one does not learn how to create beauty; one becomes the kind of person who can create it. Wright proved to be prophetic when he made the now famous statement "Not only do I intend to be the greatest architect who has yet lived, but the greatest who will ever live!" How about that!

Besides changes in architectural design, social, and technological changes were occurring that would influence the entire housing industry. Suburbs were being developed and large cities expanded their boundaries. The housing industry was being formed to meet the increasing demands of the public.

Technological advances in design like balloon construction and lumber cut in standardized dimensions by circular and gang saws revolutionized construction. This pine framing lumber came from Michigan and Wisconsin; pine cut in six-inch tongue-and-groove boards was the principal floor material, later replaced by three-inch-wide pine, which was oiled, shellacked, and waxed after laying. Toward the end of the late Victorian period hardwood flooring cut narrow, with tongue and groove from maple, beech, or oak, replaced pine. For example, Wright's Chauncey Williams House in River Forest, Illinois, was originally constructed with pine flooring in 1895. Doorways and windows were framed in oak, native cherry, or walnut; they were refinished by sanding, staining, and sealing with shellac and finished either with varnish or with wax.

Although I have worked in a number of Victorian houses, I naturally never saw one as it was originally decorated. I was therefore fascinated by some of the interiors depicted in *Photographs of New York Interiors at the Turn of the Century,* by Joseph Byron (Dover Publications, Inc., 1976).

What I first notice is the dark, heavy, cluttered appearance of most of the rooms. Tapestry, drapery, and upholstery are rich, full, and everywhere imaginable. The woodwork seems quite glossy and looks like dark walnut or mahogany and is typically flat. There is considerable clutter in each room. For example, a sitting room in an ordinary house in 1896 has two windows, each with two pairs of drapes, one inside the other and hanging below a piece of fretwork. There is a shade in each window plus a café curtain hanging so as to block the view from the street above the porch rail outside.

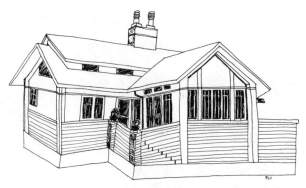

T. S. Estabrook House, Oak Park, IL. Tallmadge and Watson, ca. 1909. Though labeled Prairie School, there appears a heavy bungalow orientation. Drawing by Pamela J. Johnson

Many rooms have chandeliers hanging from the center of the ceiling. Pictures cover whole walls (thank God for picture molding). Fireplaces, found in most of the rooms pictured, often have mantels covered with fabric, either completely or partially. Drapery hangs from poles in doorways. Fabric hangs in long sheets from walls, almost like tapestry. And bric-a-brac is unbelievable.

Rugs are laid *on* rugs, including, of course, animal skins. Although the old four-poster bed is gone, canopies still cover beds using innovative means for support.

As Byron's photos move out of the late nineteenth century and into the twentieth, the scene changes a little. Rooms are much less cluttered, lightly painted woodwork begins to appear, and the heavy draperies disappear. Ornate, heavy furniture, however, remains.

THE TWENTIETH CENTURY

The present century took furniture and architecture out of Victoriana. As noted with furniture, this was not just a facelift, not just a little gathering and removal of loose skin. It represented a distinct change in line, shape, and function.

A radical change in line took place in which the vertical was replaced by the horizontal, the earth hugging of the Prairie School and the bungalow. Gone were the square of the Georgian, the vertical rectangle of the Queen Anne. In their places was the rectangle lying on its side. As to function the new architecture was, in most respects, much more functional than its predecessors. Heat-wasting high ceilings were replaced with low ones, large kitchens with small, and porches and verandas either reduced in size or completely eliminated. Such was the way this century began, and except for a few brief interruptions with various revivals, this appears to be the way it is ending architecturally.

Important designs in this century are the Prairie School, pioneered by Frank Lloyd Wright, the bungalow, a brainchild of the Arts and Crafts Movement of Gustav Stickley and developed by Greene and Greene, Art Nouveau, Art Deco, the split-level of Walter Burley Griffin, and the ranch. Let's examine each of these.

The Prairie School

As the label states, the Prairie School is a collective effort rather than the work of a single individual. Its acknowledged leader is, of course, Frank Lloyd Wright. Others of note are Barry Byrne, Walter Burley Griffin, Guenzel and Drummond (Louis Guenzel and William E. Drummond), George W. Maher, Purcell and Elmslie (George Grant Elmslie and William Gray Purcell), Spencer and Powers (Robert C. Spencer, Jr., and Horace C. Powers), Eben E. Roberts, William L. Steele, Louis H. Sullivan, Tallmadge and Watson (Thomas E. Tallmadge and Vernon S. Watson), and John S. Van Bergen.

You may have an original Prairie School house, but it is much more likely that you have a copy, because there are many, many around. Oak Park, Illinois, Wright's hometown, for example, is full of them. Whole blocks using a modified Prairie

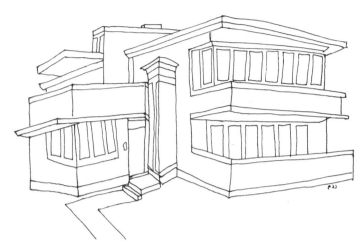

Mrs. Thomas Gale House, Oak Park, IL. Frank Lloyd Wright, 1909. Prairie School. Drawing by Pamela J. Johnson

School plan can be seen. This being the case, let's take a closer look at this style.

Prairie School architecture emphasizes the visual, and many of its creations are considered works of art. Most of the designs of this group, which started in 1897 and lasted about twenty years, accent the horizontal and hug the ground. Frank Lloyd Wright initiated the Prairie School with his Winslow House design of 1893 in River Forest, Illinois, and ended his interest some twenty-five years later with his Avery Coonley House in Riverside, Illinois, in a blaze of glory.

Prairie School house exteriors made extensive use of wood trim to outline eaves, gables, chimneys,

Model French doors and sun porch, ca. 1910. (Carr, Ryder & Adams Co.)

and belt courses. Some were a Tudor Revival style, like Wright's Nathan Moore House and H. P. Young House in Oak Park, and the combination wood and stucco looked like it came straight out of jolly old England. Sets of windows with their heads at the level of door heads were entirely framed to form a separate entity. While these designers avoided columns, colonnades, and cornices to cut costs and maintenance, they certainly stressed wide framing, corner beads, and exceptionally wide fasciae. So maintenance of trim is still a problem!

Interiors were lower than in previous periods; first-story ceilings were nine and a half feet, and second-story ceilings were a whole foot lower. An illusion of height, however, was often given in main first-story rooms with a cathedral ceiling, or a higher center of the room ceiling in front of the fireplace, as in the Wright-designed house in Lake Delavan, Wisconsin. Corner bead woodwork was present everywhere, adding further to an illusion of height. Room sizes were also enhanced by cove molding and picture molding running a foot to two feet apart all around the room. Ceilings had decorative beams running across their narrowest width, although Tallmadge and Watson sometimes ran beams the length of the room or made a ceiling border with them. Their Ashley C. Smith House in Oak Park has a double beam border with interesting interlocking corners. All such beams were decorative following the visual orientation of this school of architecture.

Model colonnade with writing desk pedestal arrangement. Mission-style furniture (Stickley) found in Prairie School homes and Greene and Greene bungalows, ca. 1910. (Carr, Ryder & Adams Co.)

Interior woodwork detail as well as exterior trim bordered on being fussy. Perhaps in no other design have these elements played such an important role, with the possible exception of Queen Anne houses. Trim and woodwork were typically thin and flat; where it was thick, the depth thereby created was modified with molding. Staircase balusters and newels, however, were square. Oak was the material of most woodwork and pine and cedar that of trim. Trim was generally stained, although oil and wax were also used. The colors were autumnal: delicate browns, light greens, and golden yellows. Woodwork was both stained and painted. I will generalize that one tends to find more painted Prairie School woodwork in summer and other country houses. Clearly dark-stained, varnish-stained, and fumed woodwork predominated in this style, corresponding to the Mission Oak furniture of the period. Frank Lloyd Wright's own home in Oak Park, however, has woodwork that was originally a light reddish brown color. Then, when he had established his Prairie School design he had all his woodwork covered with a dark brown alcohol stain and shellacked. That finish remained until 1976–82 when the author restored it to the original Victorian patina.

I cannot leave this section without commenting on the livability of some Prairie School houses. Their high strip casement windows, their overhanging eaves, and their dark woodwork and furniture woods created rather gloomy interiors. But Wright, and perhaps his colleagues as well, was a romanticist. His designs often have disproportionately large living rooms and master bedrooms, whereas his kitchens are pitifully small and his bathrooms dreary. So while he always stated that form follows function, it would appear that he either didn't follow his own philosophy or else spent little time in the kitchen and bath.

As a possible Prairie School design owner, these adverse characteristics may affect your restoration. For example, Wright's Peter A. Beachy House in Oak Park has ceiling beams and woodwork that have been painted by former owners because the dark interiors were too depressing for them. Proper restoration, following the "being faithful" principle, would call for a dark stain replacing the cream-colored paint. Here is an instance where I would counsel a lighter wood stain, like pecan. In any event, the paint should go!

Model colonnade of plain red oak, ca. 1919. (Carr, Ryder & Adams Co.)

The Bungalow Style

The most important and most popular house design in America for the first thirty years of this century was the bungalow. Though there was considerable variation as to size and details, this style is loosely defined as a one-story, two-, or three-bedroom dwelling with a porch across the front, wide eaves, and most or all living quarters located on one floor. Wags once described it as "a house that looks like it had been built for less money than it actually cost." In truth, the larger roof area and additional land requirements made the bungalow more costly than a two-story dwelling.

The Arts and Crafts Movement expounded by Gustav Stickley in his monthly magazine, *The Craftsman*, published the first decade and a half of this century, stressed structural honesty and an honest use of materials. His designs for cottages and bungalows called for the decorative use of structural elements and those materials to be simple and rustic and not highly finished.

Though Stickley was an easterner, both his Mission Oak furniture and his architectural designs influenced two West Coast architects who took the bungalow plan and carried it to its ultimate. The two are brothers, Charles and Henry Greene, who operated the successful architectural firm of Greene and Greene in Pasadena for well over three decades. Like Wright, they developed in the late Victorian period, designing Queen Annes at first,

then Beaux-Arts revivals, finally developing the bungalow to its ultimate in 1909. Unlike Wright, however, they were not experimenters, did not achieve worldwide acclaim as Wright did, and did not evolve and continue their work nearly as long as he did. Nevertheless, there are many more bungalows in this country than Wright-oriented dwellings. In most cities and suburbs there are literally solid blocks upon solid blocks of bungalows, a tribute to the influence of Greene and Greene. These, however, are mostly uncraftsman-like, built of often cheap materials to meet the demands of the mass market, and do not stress rough, natural materials.

The true Craftsman house features a liberal use of wood in beamed ceilings, wainscoting, fireside nooks, window seats, and often built-in furnishings. The furniture built to fit in these rooms heavily emphasized wood, too. Mission Oak was straight, plain, and very functional. Furniture, lamp, and glass designers were also influenced by Art Nouveau patterns. This contrasted starkly with Mission pieces in that it was curvilinear, ornate, flowing, and, some say, overtly erotic. Tiffany lamps are an excellent example of Art Nouveau.

It may be of passing interest to take a close look at a masterpiece Greene and Greene built in Pasadena in 1907 for about $100,000. The Robert R. Blacker House is a twin-gabled, two-story stucco with an exposed basement in the rear, totaling twelve thousand square feet. Though hardly a city bungalow, it certainly expresses the extent to which the Arts and Crafts Movement went.

Interior paneling and woodwork in the dining room are in teak and mahogany; peg detailing (sometimes square in shape) is ebony and mahogany. Light fixtures are Tiffany glass and wood; doors are concealed in the paneling. Paneling in the billiard room is redwood brushed to bring out the grain and toned with a faint stain.

Structurally, the Blacker House appears Oriental with the heavy timberwork, the joinery, and porch railings. The large entry hall features a wide staircase with heavy timber balusters on one side and paneling on the other. Very heavy beams, obviously structural in function, support a wooden tongue-and-groove board ceiling and floor above.

Greene and Greene also designed their own furniture, following the tradition established by Richardson and continued by Wright and Stickley. At first it was very Mission Oak in design, if not in materials. Later one notes the Art Nouveau design

Front hall closet mirror door and nest of drawers in closet, ca. 1910. (Carr, Ryder & Adams Co.)

Art Nouveau

Begun about 1885 by a group of avant-garde European architects as a reaction to the eclectics of the period, Art Nouveau was in full swing in Europe by 1900. Although it has had little influence on American architecture, it shows up every now and then in such elements as carved and scroll-cut panels, stained glass, and light fixtures. Greene and Greene were clearly influenced by this style.

Art Nouveau is an attempt to be new and novel. Most of it was decorative and floral. In line it was a willowy curve, a direct feminine contrast to the masculine line of Mission Oak and Prairie School. Derived from nature, Art Nouveau's subject matter was vines, flowers, trees, and leaves. Some see erotic images in its subject matter and line.

The lamps of Louis Comfort Tiffany, his Favrile glass and furniture, are about the extent of Art Nouveau, although I must quickly add Louis Henri Sullivan's Carson Pirie Scott building wrought iron in Chicago as a classic example. Despite its limited influence for its own sake, I feel that Art Nouveau paved a path for Art Deco, a more architecturally significant style to come in the late 1920s and 30s.

and even a Chippendale influence in some chair backs. There was also a rough look to some of their pieces, sort of a predecessor to the Ranch Oak of today. Woods used were birch, white cedar, redwood, and ash. Their ash pieces, for example, were finished with soft stains washed into the wood which practically disappeared when oiled, leaving a subtle tone to the coloration of the wood. Ebony pegs, both round and square, were the sole furniture fastener at first; later they became decorative filling for countersunk screw holes.

Perhaps a clue as to how the woodwork was finished is given in a description of how their furniture was finished. In 1907 furniture made for the Greene brothers by Peter Hall was finished "natural" according to the dictates of Charles Greene. This consisted of repeated hand rubbing of boiled linseed oil and Japan drier on soft stains until the friction produced the heat necessary for the final finish.

Transition Period

A period of rapid change took place between 1920 and 1945, perhaps understating the meaning of the word "transition." A world war and a worldwide economic depression occupied most of the two and a half decades. One would think that a war and a slump would have hampered all architectural activity. True, the quantity of new construction was down, but not the quality of creativity. And that quality was best expressed in the Art Deco movement. The remainder of the design lacked direction; it was, like so many other transition periods, an eclectic mix.

Part of this mix was the upper middle class suburban residence called the period house. Its allusions to specific historical styles were, however, more generalized and simplified than in the past. Nonetheless, houses were recognizable as Tudor, Spanish, Normandy, and colonial. The bungalow of the Craftsman period was adapted to the narrow

Colonial-style stairway and hall with painted balusters and mahogany-stained rail and volute, ca. 1925. (Carr, Ryder & Adams Co.)

Model study showing interior door and wainscoting, ca. 1919. Reminiscent of colonial William and Mary style. (Carr, Ryder & Adams Co.)

city lot, simplified, taken out of the Mission period, relabeled city bungalow, and built by the thousands across America for the lower middle and upper lower class family.

The interiors of all these houses were simplified and stylized. Woodwork and trim were no more than what relatively good taste would consider. There was the simple framing of doorways and windows, and windows were more likely than not to have no muntins. Spanish colonial interiors, a very popular design, often called for little woodwork, and some windows and doors were not framed at all. There was a functionalism to it all, probably borrowed or continued from Mission houses. Built-ins became rare, except in kitchens, where cabinets were standard equipment replacing the pantry.

Art Deco

The forward thrust in architecture during this time slot was clearly Art Deco, and among those on its cutting edge is our old friend Frank Lloyd Wright. As to line it was a curvilinear approach to design based on geometric figures in contrast to the rectangles and squares of prior designs and the willowy curves of Art Nouveau. As such it was more architecturally sound than the latter.

In addition to differences in line, Art Deco used new materials and a lot of color in new ways. The new materials were chrome, stainless steel, and lighter woods. Color can be depicted as often brilliant blues, yellows, reds, greens, you name it.

A sort of neo-neoclassical symbol, like a 1927 design of winged gods and goddesses, appeared on public and business buildings. The simplicity of the prior Mission style was often carried to excess, and a flat, stark functionalism often prevailed. This functionalism was evident not only in the visual aspects of Art Deco but also in its utility. Thus, there was a return to built-in construction: bars, beds, and baths, among other elements, shared in the overall design theme of a room.

The only things in a room not painted were constructed of polished chrome and stainless steel, or used light, natural veneers. Glass block in metal-trimmed windows made wood framing unnecessary; staircases often lacked balusters, and when they were present they were made of metal. So to restore an Art Deco house you may also have to be a welder.

But there aren't many such houses around. Started in the late twenties, Art Deco was just catching on when the Depression hit. Because of the avant-garde nature of Art Deco, there was little public demand for it, and architects, hard pressed for work, even if they believed in Art Deco, would not dare to suggest it to the typically conservative customer. By the time housing got started again, World War II stopped it, and by the time the war ended, Art Deco was mostly of historical interest, where it remains today.

The Jet Age

America entered the Jet Age about 1950. Accompanying this, modern architecture became almost synonymous with American architecture. What had once been the revolutionary concepts of Wright, Gropius, and others in terms of flat roofs, horizontal window strips, wide plain expanses of wall, exposed steel and concrete and glass, and a general lack of ornament were becoming more commonplace. It was an international architecture, with buildings in Tokyo and Buenos Aires looking much like those in Houston or Los Angeles.

Huge housing projects came into being in this period spurred on by heavy population growth and urban decay. The ranch house, a design that can certainly trace its inception to the California bungalow, became popular. It was horizontal, low (lower than the bungalow), often with appendages like a carport, a garage, a breezeway, picture windows (reminiscent of the Chicago window of Adler and Sullivan), and was placed on a lot parallel to the street rather than at a right angle to it.

Simplicity of design predominated. Flush doors often replaced the paneled doors of the transition period; door and window trim became the narrowest in history, and nearly nonexistent in some homes. Hardwood floors became rarer as carpeting and rising costs necessitated plywood;

hardwood also began to disappear from woodwork as painted pine, basswood, linden, and even metal took over.

The other favorite house in tract development, particularly in the early years, was the colonial, especially the Cape Cod. Barely recognizable from the original, and historically inaccurate, probably millions of these were built. Another revival was the two-story Georgian (now labeled crackerbox), characterized by a similar lack of interest in historical accuracy. Both were built to meet the demands of a rapidly expanding population, and meet it they did.

A rather innovative design, however, was the split-level, pioneered by Walter Burley Griffin fifty years earlier. It provided economy of space that the ranch home did not and an improved aesthetic line, particularly in tract developments. Here again, though, compared to past interiors, aesthetics were lacking, space was economized, material costs held in line, and often cell-like rooms were the result.

Restoration and Revitalization

Accompanying the development of huge tract home projects and the creation of entirely new towns in the Jet Age is the revitalization of the cities; and that is more what this book is all about. In every large city in America restoration, rehabilitation, redesigning, and rebuilding (the Four R's) are ongoing. To name a few I have visited: Charleston, Richmond, Atlanta, Newburyport, and of course, Chicago, where I am currently involved in restoration work. For the first time in our history the care and concern for architectural greatness has been taken *out* of the museum, the foundation, and the government and is being controlled by the citizens, mostly with reference to their own homes. Let us hope that such work will continue through bad as well as good economic times.

So while the Jet Age architecture, like much of the Jet Age, is crass, commercial, and lacking in aesthetics, the countermovement of restoration is afoot that will help future ages to use and enjoy their heritage.

REMODELING SINS

Buried Architectural Pieces

Just about anything you can name has been buried in the process of remodeling. Doorways, windows,

and fireplaces are the most typical. Sliding doors that have become nonoperating have been buried in doorways behind molding. Windows have been buried behind drywall from the inside and behind siding on the outside. Frequently, all that has been removed is the trim; the glass is usually intact. When fireplaces became unpopular, nonfunctioning, or just in the way of more wall space, the mantels were removed and the opening covered up.

In your restoration you may well want to leave some of these things behind walls. If, however, you are a faithful restorer, you will want to uncover them. But first you must discover them. How? A chimney seeming to come from nowhere must come from somewhere; find out where. Once all the wallpaper is steamed off, plaster cracks may well outline an original doorway or window. Old photographs may show currently missing windows and doors.

For example, a Gunderson house in Oak Park had three lovely but buried stained-glass windows, one in the back parlor and two in the dining room. A carpenter was able to unearth them, fashion new trim, and with a good cleaning they were as good as new. Now they permit the light and beauty to enter the room as they originally did in 1907.

Covered Pieces

A favorite covered piece is the paneled door. It is disguised as a flush door with painted veneer, Masonite, or even plywood glued over it. Why was it covered? Removing the panels may provide you with the reasons. The old panels may be split,

This lovely top of the five casement windows in the west bedroom of the Frank Lloyd Wright Home and Studio lay buried between plaster and wooden shingles for many years. Now it forms the arched head of a five-section Palladian window. Of course, it is new glass and molding; the original was discarded when the opening was closed up.

The window opening after plaster was removed. You can see 2 × 4 supports for plaster lathe and wooden exterior shingles. Note the stencil design that was covered by the large oak woodwork piece in the first photo.

An exterior view of the "new" window. It is receiving a primer by Saturday volunteers, members of the Frank Lloyd Wright Home and Studio Restoration Committee. The porch roof on which their ladders stand was removed a week later, all part of the plan to restore the landmark to its 1909 design. Photos by Edwin Johnson

broken, or water damaged. It is also possible that this was an attempt to "modernize." Who knows?

What you can do is remove the covering material and the mastic or glue. Mastic is usually subject to removal with a mineral spirit solvent, and most glue will wash or strip and wash off.

Recently I was asked to restore a twenty-four-light French door in a lakefront condominium built in 1911. It was covered on both sides with veneer—simply nailed to one side over the original finish. However, it was glued over a sublayer of veneer on the other side, and the twenty-four glass panes and muntins had several coats of paint on them. At first restoration was not considered. Instead, replacement was sought until 1981 millwork estimates reached nearly a thousand dollars.

So I restored it for about one third of that amount. Soaking the veneer proved ineffective. Much could be pulled off and the rest removed with a coarse eighteen-inch rasp. Sanding smoothed the mahogany surface and stripping removed old finishes, including the paint.

Moved and Removed Pieces

Frequently, built-ins are moved or removed. Dining room sideboards were removed from their wall by the thousands when they were no longer considered fashionable. Columns, fretwork, and sliding doors were another favorite item to remove, the former because they separated two rooms the owners wanted to make into one, and the latter because it wouldn't stay on the track and they didn't know how to repair it.

Indications of removed pieces are pieced woodwork, particularly baseboard, woodwork with slightly different color, usually lighter where it was covered up with something, plaster defects like cracks, ridges, patches. You might also consult the former owners.

Such pieces as back staircases were also removed to provide for, typically, a downstairs powder room or a pantry. If you are bent on a faithful restoration, you may want to put these pieces back. This may entail having a reproduction made by a cabinetmaker, a costly thing today. Or you may want to hunt through old woodwork suppliers for a similar item (see Chapter Four). But what did the original really look like? Forget photographs, since few indoor ones were taken in the old days. If there are houses like yours in the neighborhood try to get into them and do some research.

Outside, everything from onion turrets to verandas have been removed. Widow's walks, wooden stairs, and bay windows have all been removed, dismantled, and carted away. Sometimes this was done to modernize; other times such elements as these rotted or burned and had to be removed, rarely to be replaced. Though major architectural parts may be costly to replace, as for example a turret, less costly trim can and should be replaced and painted over to match what survived.

HOW TO DATE A HOUSE

House dating is a science reserved for recognized authorities, a select group among whom I don't count myself. Therefore, I suggest that you contact your local landmarks group or your state group for the name of such an authority. While you wait for him or her to arrive, however, you may want to do a little snooping yourself. Here's how.

There are two classes of criteria. The first are construction details, and the second are a rather loose assortment that includes records, former owners, neighbors, the neighborhood, construction style, and materials.

Records are the most obvious source of dates. Deeds can contain just about everything you'd like to know. The problem is that many are not complete.

Former owners, particularly if the building has been held by only a few—better yet just one family, and best if it is from this century—are another approach. It is good, too, if you can talk to these people regarding remodelings, removals, and restoration, if any.

Older neighbors are sometimes a wealth of information, and there is at least one historian in every neighborhood. Hurry and get to this person before he or she is put into a nursing home. Often one's home is part of a "development"; all homes in your block look pretty much alike. Here, all you need do is get the date of one, and you have yours. Helpful, too, is noting carefully the exteriors and interiors nearby to determine just what *has* been done to your place.

The style and its revival period are important too. Having read this chapter, you should be able to put approximate dates on your house by tracing it back to the basic style. This is tricky, though. In places like Charleston some pretty good copies came along later than the original houses from which they were copied. Remodeling and modernization also cause problems. In Sister Bay,

Wisconsin, the oldest house looks a lot like others in town. However, underneath part of the clapboard exterior is a smaller log house, a former Indian trading post and the oldest house.

Materials are also an indication of the house's age. As no wooden house could be built in Chicago city limits after the great fire, a wooden house surviving to today within the old limits must have been built before 1871. Log houses in Wisconsin are much younger than log houses in New England, yet they are much older than clapboard ones in either place. Houses built of rubble brick near San Francisco have been built since 1906, because rubble brick was made from the rubble of the 1906 earthquake.

A final dating device from my bag consists of events, like the San Francisco earthquake and the Peshtigo, Wisconsin, fire of 1871. Another event was the Great Depression, which, when combined with material shortages in World War II, meant that very few houses were built between 1930 and 1946. Therefore, your house almost has to come either before or after those dates.

The construction details authorities look at are nails used, the hinges, the door panels, hardware like wrought-iron thumb latches, cast-iron thumb latches, Norfolk latches, wood screws, and hand-sawed lathes. As this gets quite complicated, I suggest you send to the American Life Foundation Study Institute, Watkins Glen, N.Y. 14891, and buy a copy of "A Glossary of Colonial Architectural Terms." The second part of this booklet deals with the dating of old houses.

Well, no matter what the exact date of your old house is, I can pretty much guess that it *is* old. Otherwise, you wouldn't have bought this book and read this far. And that undoubtedly means that you have some woodwork and trim repairs to do. So let's turn to the next chapter, in which I hope to help you with most of them.

Chapter Four

How to Repair
Woodwork and Trim

The woodwork and trim that you intend to refinish can have many necessary repairs, although at this early stage of your restoration project you are probably not aware of them. Perhaps that's because you haven't really taken a good look. Once you start stripping, you will have the opportunity for close inspection, because you and your trim will become very well acquainted. By then the most opportune time for repair has past; the key is to repair first.

Defects include holes and gouges, loose panels, splits in solid members, loose veneer, breaks of all kinds, warped doors, rotted pieces, and even missing architectural pieces. This chapter is meant to help you solve these defect problems. In this repair process you'll discover that repair is not only aesthetically sound but functionally sound as well.

Repair is easy if you keep in mind and follow three simple rules: properly prepare, use glue, and clamp. Woodwork and trim repair is a lot easier than furniture repair. Besides the three rules it sure helps to be patient, to note all defects and correct them at one time, and to carefully note how the element you're fixing was assembled and what it should look like when repaired.

Taking care of woodwork and trim casualties of time and Mother Nature should come before the stripping and refinishing stages. The reason for this order is that glue residue and surface damage caused by repairs can be corrected in the stripping process that follows repair. Why? Well, synthetic glue is water soluble and will be effectively cleaned off during the stripping of the cleaning operation. Any damage to woodwork incurred, such as crushed corners from clamping, can then be sanded and when stripped will blend in with adjoining surfaces.

THE REPAIR PROCESS

As in any procedure one has to use the correct tools, materials, and techniques. Since the only material is glue, I will substitute the word "glue" for the word "material." First, though, let's check out the correct tools.

Tools

Tools used for woodwork and trim repair are simple hand tools, unless of course you intend to manufacture millwork. Clamps come in two basic

Tools of the woodwork repair trade. At the back are pipe clamps, cauls, and wood glue. Front, from left, are thin crowbars, spring clamps, and a variety of C clamps. Photo by Dina Johnson

Here, the separation is being widened somewhat and glue is inserted. It is important to thoroughly cover all surfaces to be glued.

configurations, the C clamp and the pipe clamp. C clamps can be either wood or metal construction; wooden clamps are designed for furniture work, are heavy and expensive, making them unnecessary for most trim and woodwork jobs. Metal C clamps are more practical, though far from cheap. You should have a good selection ranging from two-inch to eight-inch openings. Pipe clamps are generally purchased without the pipe; they are the two ends, the clamping and the holding, and fit any 3/4-inch pipe. Buy pipe the length you need and have one end threaded; I suggest several two-foot lengths and several three-foot lengths.

The rest of the tools required are probably already in your toolbox. They are: a wood saw (crosscut), coping saw, wooden mallet, hammer, crowbar, several putty knives, and a pair of pliers.

The trim piece "in traction." Small clamps are C clamps and they keep the oak piece flat up against the pipe clamps. This process forces out excess glue which must be cleaned off the surface. Later, a piece of 1/4" × 1" × 12" oak was glued and doweled along the end facing the camera to ensure the gluing would hold. Photos by Edwin Johnson

A separation of boards which make up this 1" × 12" × 12' oak trim piece occurred, requiring repair. This large trim is at the top of the Palladian window in the west bedroom of the Frank Lloyd Wright Home and Studio and has been in place since about 1910.

Glue

Glue is the material designed to hold wood together. There are several kinds of glue available to the craftsperson. My choice has always been Elmer's, a water soluble, synthetic adhesive. The original white glue has been improved, and a special furniture repair formula colored yellow is really quite satisfactory.

The other popular glue is what I call traditional because it is touted by the old professional repairmen. It is a hot glue made by heating a cake of powder glue and applying it hot. Although there is currently a glue controversy raging, I think the old hot glue has been overrated. I am constantly repairing work in which it was the only holding material, and it failed to hold.

A sort of in-between adhesive material that combines holding power and ease of application is the hot glue gun. Its advantage is that it glues items that can't be clamped; you simply hold the assembly until it sets, which happens very quickly. So for small trim pieces and tiny sections of veneer, try the gun.

Techniques: Repairing with Glue

Woodwork and trim splits, breaks, and looseness should be glued and rarely nailed or screwed together for efficient repair. In my opinion there are two kinds of repair people, handymen and craftsmen. Handymen nail things together and craftsmen glue and clamp.

You see, the trouble with most nails is they don't hold over time because metal wears wood and separation occurs; metal splits wood, especially old, brittle hardwood that has had years to dry out. So I suggest that you be a craftsperson and use glue.

While gluing and clamping should be the principal means of repair, wood dowels can also be used in place of nails and screws where additional holding power is needed, clamping is impossible, or both conditions exist. To dowel, drill through the pieces to be joined and pump glue into the hole. Take a three-foot length of dowel the diameter of the hole, cut diagonal glue grooves in it with a rasp, cut a piece a little shorter than the depth of the hole, put glue on it, and slowly pound it into the hole with a hammer. Stop when the dowel end is flush with the surface and wipe off excess glue with a wet cloth.

In a somewhat similar fashion one can glue in pieces of wood to fill large gouges and holes or to hold two pieces of wood together in mortise fashion. So this can either be a patch or a holding device. For a good job try to match the wood species, color, and grain direction. Cut a patch piece the size you intend to use. Trace its outline on the woodwork or trim and cut a slot for it following the outline using a chisel, saw, rasp, or drill or all four. Put glue into the hole and on the patch piece. Then push the piece in and clamp if possible; otherwise, nail a caul over it using brads. When set, file or sand so that its surface is level with surrounding surfaces.

But I'm getting ahead of myself by discussing doweling and patching. First we should learn about the techniques of gluing.

Techniques: How to Glue

In general, you can repair successfully with glue by following a five-step procedure. The steps are:

1. Pull the pieces apart or widen the split.
2. Remove all old glue.
3. Apply plenty of glue to all surfaces.
4. Assemble all parts.
5. Clamp, clean off excess glue, and leave set.

1. Pull apart. Pull the loose pieces, the splits, and the breaks apart using appropriate tools so that sufficient glue can be applied to the total repair surfaces if possible. For example, separate the veneer at the door bottom from the core wood where looseness already exists by using a butcher knife, or take the loose staircase baluster out of its dovetail or dowel joint.

One should also widen splits so that plenty of glue can be forced in. Do this with a sharp knife, being careful not to damage adjacent surfaces. Sometimes it is necessary to insert two putty knives into the split for protective purposes and then force a thin crowbar between the knives to widen the split.

Cautions: Refrain from too much muscle which can cause a complete separation. Also beware of hidden nails and screws. Often, prior handyman repairs entailed nails, so if a break or splits resists your initial efforts you can bet there's a nail somewhere. Find it and remove it!

2. Remove all old glue. This is a necessary task because new glue will *not* stick to old glue. Glue is designed to stick to wood. So get the old glue off and out by scraping, using a rasp, and sanding flat surfaces. In jagged breaks or uneven splits there is the danger of taking some of the wood too and thus accenting the defect. Careful use of a small rasp, riffler, a sharp knife, sandpaper, or a drill for dowel holes can be tried. Recent glue repairs probably used synthetic glue, which you can try to remove by soaking or washing with hot water. You know the old glue is gone when the wood feels rough and porous and when it appears dull rather than shiny.

3. Apply glue. To simplify this task, I put glue from the gallon bottles in which I buy it in small plastic bottles having a long pointed nozzle like honey containers. Glue is then squeezed into splits, breaks, dowel holes, and onto surfaces. For rather long narrow splits a sharp knife blade is ideal for pushing in glue that has been squeezed along the surface. In tight places apply glue with an old ice pick or a long nail, or use the hot glue gun. When working with a wide expanse, as in regluing a large section of veneer, use your hand to evenly spread the glue you've squeezed on the surface; remove excess glue with a paint paddle or similar utensil. Here the trick is to get just the right amount on the problem area; too little material and the veneer will separate again, and too much will result in a lumpy look when everything has dried.

4. Assemble all parts. Put the baluster back in its joint, put the panel frames together, and place the bracket pieces together. It is not necessary for wood to touch wood at this point. However, you should be thinking where you are going to let the pieces set and how they are going to be clamped, because that's the next step.

5. Clamp, clean off excess glue, and leave set. Clamping or holding in some manner is absolutely necessary for efficient repair. Clamps not only prevent the repaired parts from moving but also apply the necessary pressure to force glue into wood pores.

It is helpful to work out the repair system in advance, as noted. Choose your clamps, determine where they will be placed, and get your woodwork protection blocks ready. Such blocks, called cauls, are small pieces of wood that go between metal clamps and the woodwork to protect the latter from clamp marks.

Occasionally you will find it impossible to clamp, as I once did in repairing veneer that had separated from the curved bottom riser on a staircase. Temporary nailing did the trick. I applied glue under the veneer on the core wood, laid the veneer back over the repair, covered the area with a piece of plastic sheet, and nailed several flexible paint sticks over all that to hold the repair until it set. After setting, the holding device was removed, excess glue sanded off, nail holes filled, and the patch was refinished with the rest of the staircase. Had less pressure been required, I could have used my hot glue gun.

Since it's a lot easier to clean off excess glue when it's a fluid, do this as soon as clamps are in place. It's a good idea to put waxed paper over the glued area, then cauls, then clamps. While this prevents complete cleaning of excess glue, it keeps the cauls from sticking to the patched area. In addition, some glue is picked up by the waxed paper and leaves when the paper is later removed.

COMMON WOODWORK AND TRIM DEFECTS

Defects commonly found in trim and woodwork are breaks, splits, loose pieces, rotted pieces, stuck elements, veneer problems, warpage, gouges, and missing architectural pieces. We're going to take a look at each of these in the pages that follow.

Breaks

I don't have to tell those of you who live in an old house that trim and woodwork elements break. You already know *that*. Frankly, as there are often too many and they can occur anywhere, it's a tough decision as to which ones I should illustrate and discuss with you. Well, let's look at window sash bottoms, quarter round, staircase balusters, and brackets.

Most such breaks not only *should* be repaired but *can* be repaired. I'll always remember a customer who showed me a curved oak quarter round that graced a lovely curved bay of six windows. It had been broken by her husband (a

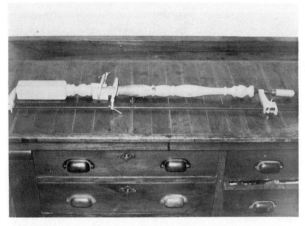

Put glue on all joining surfaces, fit the parts together, and clamp both across the breaks and the length of the baluster to apply pressure. Leave clamped twenty-four hours. Note the use of cauls to protect baluster surfaces against clamp marks. Photos by Edwin Johnson

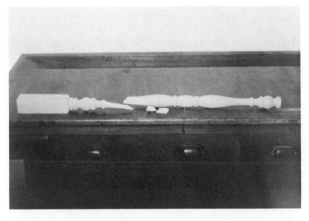

A broken staircase baluster is a common repair problem. How can it be solved? First, put all the parts on your bench.

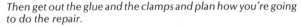

Then get out the glue and the clamps and plan how you're going to do the repair.

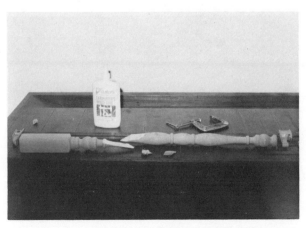

handyman?) when he attempted to remove it. She wanted to know whether or not to throw it out. "Throw it out," I exclaimed, "never!" I reminded her that considerable skill and cost had gone into getting that piece to fit the curve (there were vertical cuts made in the back of the piece to permit bending it). The replacement would have to be fabricated in the same way. So I repaired it.

First, I stripped off the paint because it had not been previously stripped and the baseboard had. Then it was repaired in place by applying glue to the breaks and nailing the parts back using the same nails and nail holes. Residue glue was carefully washed off to permit good stain coverage. The result was glued joints so neat that no filling was required.

Breaks are repaired using the principles of proper preparation, gluing, and clamping. As an illustration take putting a broken staircase baluster back together. Remove the two (or more) pieces from their positions, probably dovetail joints in the handrail and the stair tread. If they seem stuck but loose, look for hidden nails. Sometimes balusters are nailed, screwed, or fastened by doweling, so you might check for them, too.

Take the broken parts to your worktable and lay a sheet of waxed paper under them to prevent their sticking to the table surface in the gluing process. Get a pipe clamp long enough to hold the entire length of the baluster and several C clamps to hold it to the tabletop and keep it straight.

Apply glue to the broken ends of each segment, lay them on the waxed paper, using the edge of the table as a straightedge, and clamp them lightly to the table. Then lay a pipe clamp along the other side of the baluster and begin to tighten it; at the same time begin to tighten the C clamps. Wipe off the excess glue forced out of the joined areas as you apply minimal force to longitudinal tightening. Determine that it is straight and let it set overnight. In the morning you should have a perfectly good baluster, and probably an irreplaceable one at that!

Another common break is in the bottom of the upper window sash of a double-hung window. This element takes a real beating from ordinary use let alone rotting caused from condensation. To repair this, the best procedure is to remove the sash (often a neat trick in itself). See how to do it later in this chapter. If the joint is viable, insert glue and clamp. Rotted joints can be filled with a piece of wood and dowels used to hold the sash together. When the sash can't be removed in any way, try to get at the repair by removing the bottom sash, or attack the defect from the outside. Use dowels to hold; in very desperate situations glue and nail or use a screw to hold until the glue sets.

Broken exterior ornaments like brackets, fascia gingerbread, portieres, fretwork, and pediments can be best repaired if the piece can be removed and fixed in your workshop. Repairing them in place is the alternative.

Fortunately for you, such architectural elements are visually less critical than interior woodwork, as they are seen from a great distance. Combine this with their usual overly painted condition and it is clear that repairs need not have to be as carefully done as inside your home. Nonetheless, you do want the repair to hold; climbing to the top of that onion dome, for example, to repair the ornament is something you don't want to repeat—ever!

Splits

Splits are wood separations caused by drying out. Though they can be filled, it is best to try to repair them first, as filling is a temporary measure. And if your repair attempt fails, you can always fill with wax, lacquer, colored putty, or plain wood filler. Woodwork and trim pieces subject to splitting are panels, solid members, and glued members.

Panels are present in wainscot, doors, cabinets, and other built-ins. Such panel splits are the victims of time and carelessness. Sometimes splits occur because the element was removed and sent to a commercial stripping establishment where too much soaking and subsequent drying were the culprits. Generally, it is the lack of humidity that does it, though.

Splits take a little practice and know-how to correct, but they are not impossible. First, you should remove the panel from the door or the wainscot. Typically pull off the molding around it and the panel comes out. Sometimes the panel is recessed in a frame, and one or more sides of the frame must be disassembled.

Lay the sick panel on a flat plane, such as your worktable top, after placing a piece of waxed paper underneath. Get plenty of glue in the split and pull the panel together with a clamp at the edge where the split is the widest; if the split is in the middle,

Here is an oak bathroom door in the Frank Lloyd Wright Home and Studio with splits in three panels in crucial places.

Carpenter's glue was squirted into the splits and spread evenly with a knife blade.

The awl was then pulled downward, which forced the loose bottom half of the panel upward, pushing out excess glue. Small finishing nails were hammered into the panel at a downward angle in three places, catching the other side of the rail and holding the split together.

Two small scratch awls were hammered into the line separating the panel from the rail.

Excess glue was cleaned from the panel surfaces, nail holes were filled, and the split given twenty-four hours to dry. Here is the repaired door. Photos by Edwin Johnson

place a clamp over it in the middle of the panel. Pull the split together and wipe excess glue from it. Then clamp the panel to the bench top so it is perfectly flat; the split surfaces should be perfectly level. *Caution:* If the split has been previously repaired, or filled by a handyman, old fill and glue must be removed; otherwise, what I've told you won't work.

Splits occur in other woodwork pieces like door and window trim. Here, in addition to a dry environment, improper nailing is the probable cause. Then, too, painted surfaces inside your home are not the best protection from dryness. So if your woodwork is painted, it probably has a lot of minor splits (we call them checks). Unfortunately, they are not too visible under paint and make their appearance after the paint has been stripped. There is a need, therefore, to carefully scrutinize the painted surface for defects. Any you note are probably larger under the paint.

Trim splits can be repaired by first removing the nail or nails that may have caused them. Nails that resist pulling can often be driven through the woodwork and into the wall in back of it using a nail set. Another approach to nail removal is to remove the sick piece of woodwork and pull the nail through from the back with a pair of heavy pliers or nail pullers. Then squirt in the glue, clamp, and let it set.

Solid woodwork and trim members are especially susceptible to splitting because they were probably not quite dry in their centers when they were installed many generations ago. Staircase newels and veranda posts are good illustrations. To correct the split, try shoving and piling as much glue in the split as you can. Then start some fierce clamping beginning at the *narrow* end of the split and work your way toward the widest part of the split. Use as many clamps as you feel necessary to close the gap, and don't forget cauls.

Glued members differ from solid in that they achieve their mass from a number of glued pieces. Splits in these pieces usually occur where they were initially glued together. A good repair job here entails not only proper gluing and clamping but the removal of all the old glue. Try to get the old glue out with sandpaper folded with the working side in contact with the old glue surfaces. Wide splits, of course, permit the use of rasps or knives. For really bad splits it is best to pull the

piece apart, clean off old glue, and glue and clamp again. Otherwise, follow the directions for repairing solid members.

Loose Architectural Pieces

Less obvious than breaks and splits, loose elements in your woodwork and trim are more likely to be overlooked in your restoration repair plan. So you will have to make a special effort to detect them. It is helpful to keep in mind that just about any piece of woodwork or trim has the potential of coming loose, although those in heavy human and Mother Nature traffic areas are more likely candidates. I suggest that you go around and wiggle, wobble, tap, and pound. If anything moves, tag it for repair.

Stair balusters, both inside and out, and porch balusters seem to have a looseness problem; at times they are so loose they fall out. Careless owners and tenants have, in that case, simply thrown the piece out or else set it aside for later repair and lost it. Does any of this sound familiar?

Balusters fit into tread dovetail, mortice joints, or dowel holes and, as noted earlier, into the handrail fastened with dowels, nails, or screws. Tread joints are generally covered with molding, usually nailed and sometimes glued into place. Some balusters are part of the string, too. Spacers often separate balusters on the underside of the handrail.

To repair the loose baluster, remove it, clean out the old glue, dirt, or paint from both the baluster and the element to which it is fastened, reglue, and replace. In general, use old nail holes because they have enough holding power until the glue sets and because new nail holes may be *very* difficult to make.

Loose panels in doors and wainscot are another source of annoyance, but fortunately, you can generally tighten them without removing them. To do this, move the panel as far as it will go in one direction. Run a strip of glue along the exposed edge, push the panel by hand or carefully with a pointed tool, expose the other edge, and lay a strip of glue along it. Try this in the vertical direction, too. Then center the panel in its frame or molding and clean off excess glue.

If there is any danger that the panel may move

Some handyman repaired this loose casement window frame with a corner brace both inside and outside. It was more properly repaired by opening the window, drilling two 3/8-inch dowel holes through the edge of the frame, putting glue in the holes, inserting glued dowels, and letting set. After setting twenty-four hours both (ugly) corner braces were removed and the screw holes filled.

before the glue sets, tack a few brads in it, one on each side and against the frame. Leave the heads of the brads exposed so you can pull them out easily after the glue has dried. Fill the small brad holes with colored putty after they've been removed.

Still another looseness problem that comes to mind is the built-in sideboard drawer. Dining room sideboards have in many cases become the catchall of family treasures for years, really giving the drawers a beating. This habit has resulted in the drawers and their supports becoming quite loose. To test for such looseness, just in case you haven't already noticed it, take out each drawer, empty it, and set it on the floor on its back side. Now try to move it from side to side. If it's loose, it'll move all right! Loose drawer supports are evident when you are unable to slide the drawer in once it is out, or out once it is in. In addition, the drawer front should be parallel to the carcass in a sideboard in good condition.

Most likely, your drawer is nailed and glued together, but no matter if dovetail construction was the mode. You can disassemble it on your worktable by hammering it apart from its inside using a wood block to prevent hammer marks.

After figuring out how to clamp the assembly or at least how to put pressure on it if clamps are unavailable, put glue on *all* points of wood contact

and assemble the sides, back, and drawer front. Slide in the drawer bottom last and nail it with a flat-headed brad to the back. Place the assembly on a level surface to set, first making certain that it is all square.

Loose drawer slides and supports on the built-in carcass should be pulled or screwed off and any old glue scraped off them. Apply new glue to both the slide and the carcass where the slide fits and renail or rescrew using the *same* holes as before to assure perfect alignment of components.

Window shutters, another item that frequently needs repair, are really worth an attempt to fix. If you doubt this, price new ones. Paneled shutters are a lot like paneled doors, but to remove the split or broken panel, you'll have to knock the frame that holds it apart. Repair the panels as noted before, replace them in the frame, and reglue them.

As dampness and rot frequently attack old shutters, new frame parts, wood fills for mortice joints, and even new panels may be in order. I recommend making new frame pieces and filling deteriorated mortice joints with wood cut to fit and glued in place rather than using wood filler. Then fasten the frame together with dowels.

Rotted Architectural Pieces

The foregoing leads to this subject. Even some inside trim has been subjected to extreme environmental conditions. Recently I inspected some windows in a 1930 vintage apartment building that had been converted into a condominium. It was a cold March day and water condensation was literally running off the glass and onto the rotted sash bottoms. The owners had two alternatives: repair the sash or try to buy new ones.

New window sashes, especially if they are to be custom millworked, are very expensive. One of my customers had new sashes and interior frames installed in a two-story hundred-year-old building in 1978. The price quoted for wooden windows was about $15,000; aluminum windows ran about half that figure, so he settled for the latter. You may decide to try repair after you get such estimates!

Though some inside woodwork has been exposed to Mother Nature, *all* exterior trim has been zapped by her. Old and antique houses have had to deal with moisture and the resultant rot since Plimouth Plantation. So what fire didn't destroy, the elements did. It is really surprising so many old homes are still standing and relatively intact!

In this section we will look at what rot has done to window sashes and sills, door bottoms, staircase risers and treads, and porch posts.

Window sashes and sills are subjected to considerable moisture under ordinary conditions; however, under extreme humidity and lack of care they can really go bad. Usually, it is the bottom of the lower window sash and the bottom frame of the casement window that are either partially or completely rotted. For sills the same techniques that follow are applicable.

Small rotted areas can be cleaned out and filled with wood filler or colored putty, preferably after the wood has been sealed. Larger rotted areas will require wood patches, the installation of which has been already noted.

A completely rotted sash bottom should be removed and replaced with a new or older replacement one. In old home windows, sashes are usually held together with mortise and tenon joints, so you will have to take the entire sash apart to get at any rotted members. Removing double-hung sashes is tricky, but easy once you read the section later in this chapter on window sash cord replacement. (You are also referred to the last section in which replacement parts are discussed.)

Separate the frame by first laying it on the

This windowsill is so badly rotted I could stick my chisel three inches into the opening! As the exterior trim was going to be painted, it was heavily filled with wood filler, sanded, primed, and painted. Photo by Edwin Johnson

bench top. Take a small piece of one-by-two, place the end against the frame in one corner, and strike it with a hammer away from the center. Any mullion strips will also separate. Be careful of the glass, as it is probably the original, which makes it very brittle. You may only be able to separate the sash where the rotted piece is, but that's what you want. Right?

Replace the rotted piece with the new one the right length and configuration. Glue and clamp. Oh, yes, I nearly forgot. Most all window sashes are pine, and though new pine won't match in color or grain pattern, it will have to do. And color can be corrected, as we shall see in Chapter Six.

Door bottoms, especially those of outside doors, are also subject to the weather. In addition to the elements, your doors may have had to contend with people's feet and animals' claws.

Paneled doors can have their bottoms replaced with new wood frame pieces if a serious condition exists. Considering the high cost of new paneled doors, particularly exterior models, repair is clearly the less expensive alternative. Patching with wood or other materials, outlined earlier, may be sufficient and should be your first attempt unless otherwise indicated. Finally, if your door bottom is structurally sound but looks awful, you can always cover it with a brass plate.

To get at the bottom of the door, it will have to be taken off its hinges, generally by removing the pins. Older doors sometimes lift off when swung open. Lay the sick door on sawhorses so you can make the repairs at a convenient height. Check for other looseness at this time. First try to separate the bad frame bottom with the wood caul and hammer technique. If this fails, you will have to cut through the mortise and tenon joint. As this holding device has been destroyed, either cut new mortise and tenon joints or hold the replacement piece in place with dowels put through the side frame.

If just the veneer of a veneered door is rotted, it can also be replaced. (For veneer tips see the section later in this chapter.) For a rotted core, cut it out and replace it with anything that is the correct dimension—plywood, for example. Clamp it to the present core wherever possible; the old veneer or the new will do the rest of the necessary holding when glued in place and set.

Staircase risers and treads are subject to much abuse, especially those at the bottom of the stairs and at staircase platforms. Here ordinary use and frequent washing or other water-related problems may have caused rotting. Fortunately, most instances of partial rotting are next to the floor, platform, or tread, so one can cover them up with quarter round or some other type of molding.

In the case of completely damaged risers or treads the solution is their removal and replacement. If your stairs are to be carpeted, matching wood grains and species in replacement parts is not critical, but for bare wood decor you will have to shop around for the correct material.

You may have difficulty getting the rotted tread or riser out of the staircase, for it may be locked in by other risers, treads, the staircase string, or molding. If the piece in question is badly rotted, break it out. Cut the replacement part a little short of its desired length so you can tuck in one end and force the other one into place. Then move the new part around before nailing it into place so that no gaps show. If any gaps remain, you can always cover them up with decorative molding or, if barely visible, colored putty.

Exterior stairs are generally less critical because they will probably be painted later. Damage can be more extensive, however, and a decision may have to be made as to whether or not the whole staircase should be replaced. Try to resist replacing it with cement, the seemingly common cure. Remain faithful to the original!

Porch posts that have rotted may be replaced or repaired. Since those with any turnings may be difficult to find, I suggest you attempt repair. Do this by cutting off only the rotted part, typically the bottom, and attach a new turned or carved piece with a wide-diameter dowel. Try making your own replacement part. Start with a 4 × 4-inch or larger piece of Douglas fir. Create turnings with a rasp, and carving with a chisel and gouge. Smooth with sandpaper, working first with coarse grades and last with fine ones.

A casement window frame in the Frank Lloyd Wright Home and Studio is pulling apart. To repair it, the window frame must be removed, carefully pulled farther apart so the mortise joint is exposed, glue inserted, and then pulled together and clamped across the two vertical pieces with a pipe clamp. Photo by Edwin Johnson

Stuck Architectural Pieces

I need hardly ask if you have any stuck windows, doors, built-in drawers, or interior shutters. Living in an old house, you probably have a lot of stuck items.

Windows in many older homes have been painted partially or completely closed over the years. A quality woodwork refinishing job requires that both the bottom half *and* the top half of double-hung windows and all casement windows be movable. Otherwise, how are you going to strip off *all* the old finish? Some of it is hiding behind sills, stops, and sashes.

Perhaps you're thinking that you never lower the top half of your double-hung windows, or that certain casements like the one in the front hall closet is never opened anyway. Okay, stop reading, go to one of your double-hung windows that opens, raise the lower sash, and take a good look at the side of the upper half sill facing you. Ugly, isn't it, with all its decades of dirt, paint drippings, and crud. You can add to that the residue that later finish stripping will deposit there. It *is* necessary, therefore, to be able to move the upper sash, isn't it?

The problem with stuck windows is generally on the outside, so if you're removing paint from your trim, the problem will be partially solved. However, if this is strictly an inside job, you'll have to go outside with a ladder, a hammer, a window loosening tool, and a rigid flat paint scraper.

Hammer the scraper between the window sash and the frame cutting through layers of old paint all the way around the stuck sash. Then go inside and loosen the sash the same way. With great care hammer downward on the bottom of the stuck upper sash, using a block of wood to protect it. *Caution:* Since this is often a weak member, be gentle. When the top of the sash frame appears from behind the stop, insert a crowbar and pry up until there is enough opening for your fingers. Then use your hands to pull down.

For stuck bottom halves pry upward from the outside with a large crowbar. Push up on the underside of the sash frame top. Once the sashes have been opened, try to move them up and down a little. Of course, stripping old finish from them later on will restore them to their original mobility.

Casement windows can be made movable in essentially the same way. Hammering here is done in an outward direction (if it swings out), although a crowbar inserted between the inside frame and the vertical side of the sash can be effective, too. Above all, use care so you do not destroy the antique window frame or the old window glass with its air bubbles and other antique defects. After all, the wood is probably dry and brittle and may be developing a case of rot.

In the master bedroom of the James J. Glessner House, H. H. Richardson, 1886, one notes a broken window sash cord. Photo by Edwin Johnson

Window Sash Cord Replacement

Do you have any double-hung windows that you have to prop to keep open? Well, that's because the sash cord or chain has been broken and removed, leaving the pulley in the frame and the weight in its cavity.

The time to connect your sash once again to that ingenious device hiding in the hollows of your window frame is *now*, not after you've refinished. To make the sash connection, remove first of all the sash stops, although you may get away with taking off only the one on the pulley side of the frame, and slip the bottom sash out of its track. Large windows often have two cords per sash, only one of which is missing, so you'll have to swing the sash so you can disconnect the good cord or chain. Cords are held to the sash by being knotted and nailed into a cavity in the side of the sash, whereas chains are generally fastened with a screw.

Locate the weight cavity/s, remove the panel covering it, take off the deteriorated old cord from the weight, and attach the correct-length new cord. Take the free end of the cord and pass it upward through the pulley, tie a knot in it, and nail the knot into the cavity in the side of the window sash. If you have difficulty getting the cord through the pulley, remove the pulley, pull the cord through the hole, then through the pulley now in your hand. Screw the pulley back in place and proceed to fasten the cord to the sash. Swing the sash back into its track and nail the stop or stops back in their original place. If possible, use the same nails and nail holes to assure a good alignment.

Doors stick, too, don't they? Cabinet doors may need nothing more than some cool candle wax rubbed on them. Room and house doors may have to be removed, planed, sanded, and replaced for them to work properly. As with everything else so far, the time to do this is now, not after refinishing them, because that process includes door edges as well as their fronts and backs. Very old houses that have extensively settled necessitate all kinds of door shaping, even adding pieces to tops and/or bottoms to make them work properly. *Caution:* Sometimes doors swell and stick when humidity is high, only to shrink when house heat is on. Try not to remove too much wood; it's hard to put back!

Sliding doors have often stuck in the open position in between the walls; sometimes they have even come off their track. One way to attack this problem is to remove the woodwork around the door cavity carefully and look in to see what the matter is. Often the problem is woodwork that has swollen, making the opening through which the door must pass smaller. Scratch marks on the sliding door not only indicate that this is the case but tell you where the molding is out of line. Plane off excess wood from the molding, and before you replace it, rub some cool candle wax on the surface next to the door. If the door is off its track, try to get it back on now that you can reach it. Sometimes the hardware has become loose and needs tightening. And once in a while you will find that there is no door there at all! Surprise!

Loose Veneer

Veneer is the thin wood material that dresses up ordinary wood. Contrary to common opinion, veneer is not a sign of inferior quality, as much valuable eighteenth-century furniture will attest. However, as veneer is often very thin and has been glued, it can pose a problem that should be corrected now.

A typical veneer problem is that of contemporary doors. And a favorite place for the veneer to loosen is at the bottom of the outside door, since it is exposed to considerable moisture, an enemy of wood. Such loosening works from the door bottom upward.

Here is how to fix that before it becomes looser and chips away. Take the door off its hinges and lay it in a convenient work place. Insert a sharp knife under the loose veneer to probe the extent of the damage. Apply Elmer's furniture glue to your knife blade and work it into the farthest excesses of the looseness. Go along the entire bottom of the door in this manner, prying already loosened and even potentially loose veneer and distributing the glue between the core wood and the veneer.

Now to clamp this, get two pieces of wood the length of the glued area and as wide as the depth of the repair (3/4-inch plywood will do nicely). Clamp one piece on one side of the door and the other over waxed paper on the repair side, placing a C clamp about every six inches or so. If both sides have a veneer problem, you should also put glue under the loose veneer on the other side at this time. Granted this may be a rather large area to glue, but don't worry about the glue drying too quickly. Depending on conditions, you could take an hour to distribute the glue and properly clamp the entire door bottom.

If veneer is loose in the center of the door, raise the separated end, insert glue under it, and put a weight on it overnight. Looseness also takes the form of a bubble or blister. For relatively new doors first try heating the bubble with a hot iron wrapped in a rag and placed on the blister until the glue is reactivated. Place a weight on it overnight to set.

You will have to slit the blister and insert glue in the slit if the iron treatment fails. Use a sharp razor blade and cut a straight line in the veneer parallel with the grain and through the center of the blister. Insert glue into the bubble with a sharp knife point, put pressure on it, and leave it set overnight.

Veneer repairs for paneling are the same as for doors, except that you may not want to remove the paneling to make the necessary repair, especially if it's a small area. Try using the hot glue gun; scrape away the residue while it's still soft, though. You may also want to try fastening a caul over the repair, using small brads.

When the veneer is missing, new veneer must be used to cover the hole. How to handle that will be discussed shortly under gouges. Just you wait.

Warpage

Let's say that you want to refinish your kitchen cabinets but hesitate because some of the doors are warped. Perhaps they can be straightened. At least it's worth a try!

Remove the problem door, panel, or other warped piece and strip the old finish from it, the topic in the following chapter. It is necessary to strip off the old finish so that the wood can absorb the right kind of moisture under the right conditions instead of the wrong kind under the wrong conditions, which probably caused the warpage in the first place. Put the warped piece concave side down on wet bath towels so that the entire surface is covered, having first placed the wet towels on a perfectly flat cement floor, driveway, or sidewalk. Weight the piece with cement blocks, pails full of water, or whatever you can find that is very heavy. Some authorities state that one must do this with a hot sun overhead, although I have accomplished dewarping in my basement shop where no sun shines.

Be careful not to let this process continue too long; otherwise, it will produce a reverse warp. So when the piece appears flat, remove the wet towels, turn the piece over, and place the weights on the formerly warped side, with the piece in the same spot on the cement floor. After a short while reverse the position. This drying-out process sets the door and should prevent further warpage.

Once you're certain the door or other piece is completely dry, refinish it and hang it. Above all, avoid leaning it against a wall; lay it flat if you must wait before returning it to its original place.

Gouges

Most memorable is the customer who asked me to touch up "scratches" in her kitchen doors. Scratches! They were gouges. Someone with super long fingernails had gouged the surface of practically every kitchen cabinet door near the pull, almost as if an animal had clawed those areas. My professional recommendation was that the cabinets be completely refinished, but she did not want to pay for all that. So each gouge was carefully sanded and touched up with colored furniture touch-up lacquer. If the gouges had been narrower, a filler like the lacquer stick would have been appropriate.

Gouges in veneer and missing veneer pieces can be corrected by replacement or borrowed veneer. One source of borrowed veneer is the back side of a closet door, assuming it's the same veneer. Attics, basements, and barns often contain a former door from which you may be able to

remove some veneer for replacement purposes. Otherwise, you'll have to buy new veneer from a local craftsmen's supply house, although some, like Craftsmen's Wood Service in Addison, Illinois, operate a mail-order department.

Trim the damaged area into a square or rectangle shape, using a sharp razor blade or a veneer knife. Then cut a replacement piece to match, fitting the patch by sanding its edges, until it matches the hole. Hint: Place a sheet of number 80 sandpaper on the tabletop and move the veneer patch edge over it. Once a fit is achieved, apply glue to both surfaces, the veneer and the core, and clamp or use a weight for pressure. If your veneer is not thick enough to bring the level of the hole to the level of the surrounding area, use two or more layers of veneer. After setting, if the patch is above the veneer level adjoining it, sand until the levels match.

Veneer gouges can also be repaired by sanding the gouged area smooth and feather-edging the broken, jagged edges around it. As the core wood has a different grain pattern than the veneer, attempt to copy that grain with a ball-point or felt-tip pen or a pencil. Touch up the color with a stain mixture, paint, or a commercial touch-up product.

Replacing Missing Trim and Woodwork

You're all ready to restore your dining room woodwork, for example, when you suddenly notice that ten feet of base and quarter round is missing. Or you covered up a doorway that had been cut in your circa 1895 home in 1934 when it was being converted into a rooming house. Naturally, the trim was thrown out shortly after 1934, and now you need three feet of base and quarter round. What can you do?

There are at least six things you can do. You can search the premises, borrow, shop house wreckers, consult old woodwork specialty supply places, buy new millwork, or make parts yourself. Let's discuss each of these alternatives.

SEARCH YOUR PREMISES. The first thing you should do in your attempt to replace missing woodwork is to explore your house, garage,

The bottom piece of frame trim was missing. A search, however, turned it up. Someone had "stored" it behind a radiator! Photo by Edwin Johnson

Missing balusters in the servants' staircase of the James J. Glessner House. It's a good thing Henry Hobson Richardson can't see it! Photo by Edwin Johnson

carriage house, and possibly barn. Attics were a favorite storage place for old doors. Basements, especially old coal bins, may house the base you need. Garage and barn rafters often hold just the trim you're looking for.

BORROWING. If you were unable to find the missing piece loose somewhere and hiding, perhaps you can borrow it. After all, it may well be that the best door in your house is that one on the maid's room closet on the third floor. In addition, that closet could also house the necessary base, door trim, or even window trim. So borrow the trim, or trade it, putting the battered woodwork where it matters least and the best woodwork where company will see it.

HOUSE WRECKERS. Still another source of old woodwork is the building wrecker. In urban areas your chances of finding something are much better than in small towns, because they're always tearing down something in American cities.

Of course, while the quantity is always there, the quality may not be. The chance that the wreckers' has just what you need is remote. Furthermore, merchandise is not displayed as at Neiman Marcus; you'll have to plow through a lot of junk to find what you need.

OLD WOODWORK SPECIALTY HOUSES. These sources are much classier and much more expensive than building wreckers. Although they too may not have exactly what you are missing, they are in a position to give you more individual attention and may well help you in your search.

One such house is the Renovation Source, Inc., in Chicago. They are said to have a large collection of decorative architectural elements like cornices, brackets, pediments, mantels, and fretwork. In Baltimore the city runs the Salvage Depot, which has available, so they say, scarce, irreplaceable, and valuable building materials.

The Old-House Journal publishes its "Emporium" section monthly in which suppliers advertise old and reproduction pieces for the restorer. Once a year this publication prints a "Buyers Guide," a much more complete source section.

NEW MILLWORK. This is a source that can produce what you need from original plans, photos, and sketches. You can probably get what you want, but the cost may be prohibitively high. For example, in the dining room restoration of the Frank Lloyd Wright Home and Studio in Oak Park, Illinois, a missing 4 × 8-foot scrollwork indirect lighting panel was produced by a specialist from architectural drawings for a reported cost of $5,000.

Despite such high costs, I understand that several such firms have gone broke! That should tell us something about the nature of the work involved.

In addition to high cost, new millwork will probably not match the old woodwork in grain and natural color despite its being the same species. After all, an old oak tree cut and converted to woodwork in 1982 is a much different tree from one of a hundred years before. In addition to natural differences, the intervening hundred years of exposure to the elements has made old wood and trim still more different.

The dining room in the Frank Lloyd Wright Home and Studio in Oak Park, Illinois, is an excellent illustration of millwork replacement and the problems it caused. This room had been allowed to deteriorate after the Wrights left, and much of the original elaborate woodwork had been removed. So when restoration began, new millwork was made and installed alongside the old.

The eighty-five-year difference in grain and color clearly showed. In the refinishing process I had to carefully finish the woods differently so that the new matched the old, even though all the material was oak. It was ironic when, after the job was done, it was discovered that the carpenters could have used more old woodwork from the cellar, where it was stored, but took the easier path of nailing up the new!

This is the famous Frank Lloyd Wright family motto, "Truth Is Life," carved above the inglenook fireplace mantel in his Oak Park home (1889–1909). Note how the molding to the right and above the motto has separated. A structural defect due to settling, this separation cannot be corrected without major work. It remains, therefore, today after woodwork restoration has been completed. Photo by Edwin Johnson

MAKING THE MISSING PARTS. A final approach to repair is to make the missing part.

You should be able to get the wood species needed. In major cities this is more likely than in Small Town, U.S.A. Naturally, interior woodwork replacement pieces are more critical than most exterior trim in that the latter will be most likely painted or dark-stained. Inside, too, subsequent painting relieves you of wood species match.

Exact matching becomes necessary where landmark restoration is to take place. Missing woodwork and trim can be made in your workshop, and though such machines as lathes for turnings are certainly helpful, they are not necessary. Much of what you have to do can be made by hand. After all, in olden times all millwork was crafted by the carpenter on the job. All the wooden planes you see in antique shows and flea markets were once carried by a cabinetmaker or carpenter. Each one has a blade with a different configuration designed to cut a different pattern—make a different molding.

Woodwork and trim, then, can be cut by hand. Use you hand saw and plane to remove as much wood from the stock as possible. Then wood-carving tools like gouges and chisels will remove still more material, followed by a rat-tail rasp. Finally, sandpaper, starting with a very coarse grade like number 36 or 50 and finishing with the fine grade number 180, will smooth it all out.

Simple electric hand tools like a saber saw for scrollwork, a circular saw for cutting boards down to the beginning stock size needed, routers for making moldings, and drills for making dowel holes are good to have and to use. The decision to invest in one rests with how much you think you'll get from using it.

A possible alternative to making the trim or woodwork is to buy an assortment of trims and moldings that, when combined, make up the configuration you're after. I suggest that you cut and combine until you get what you want. Some additional shapings may still be necessary, but the collage has taken a lot of work out of the job. Of course, for trim that will be some distance from the general line of vision, details are not as important as with, say, fretwork separating the front and the back parlors. A gable ornament three stories up can be a rough approximation and therefore much easier to duplicate.

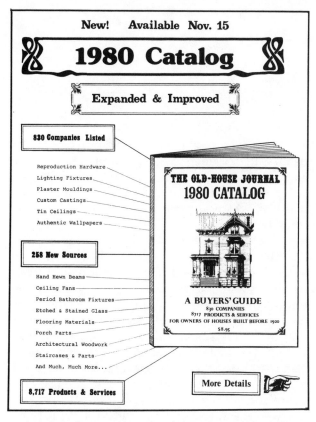
A source of restoration materials. (Courtesy of The Old House Journal, 69A Seventh Avenue, Brooklyn, NY 11217)

This is one supplier of restoration materials.

A source of restoration materials. (Courtesy of Renovator's Supply)

Russell and Erwin
Victorian Hardware
Catalogue 1865

A Treasury for Preservation and Restoration

A "bench-mark" of the Victorian hardware industry is what Lee H. Nelson, AIA in his new introduction calls this facsimile of the 1865 Russell and Erwin catalogue. With this catalogue, Russell and Erwin — "the oldest surviving name in the hardware industry" — established a standard for all other nineteenth-century hardware catalogues. This "inexplicable rarity" (which originally sold for $25.00 to the trade!) is a *one-volume treasury of preservation and restoration technology.*

Published by the Association For Preservation Technology (APT) and distributed by the American Life Foundation, this jumbo book has 470 pages and 3,300 engravings. Its table of contents lists 967 entries from A-Y: Axes, Brushes, Casters, Dishes, Escutcheons, Files, Gauges, Hammers, Irons, Jacks, Keys, Locks, Mauls, Nails, Ovens, Planes, Quoits, Rakes, Screws, Tongs, Urns, Vises, Wrenches, and Yokes.

There are also 16 pages of *lamps and chandeliers;* 21 of *cutlery;* 10 of *agricultural implements;* 7 of *silver plate and Britannia;* 9 of *bolts;* 14 of *bench planes and moulding tools;* 9 of *bells;* 2 of *coffee mills;* 4 of *hollow ware;* 14 of *hinges;* 9 of *scales;* 4 of *coffin handles;* and 4 of *sleighs and skates.*

Order from the American Life Foundation, Box 349, Watkins Glen, NY, 14891. Send $15.00 + $1.25 for book rate postage ($16.25). Send $15.00 + $2.00 for book rate plus Special Handling ($17.00) for faster delivery. *For deliveries in New York State, please add 7% NYS sales tax.*

An Encyclopedia of Victorian Ironwork

A few copies remain of *Victorian Ironwork: The Wickersham Catalogue of 1857* with a new introduction by Margot Gayle. Published in 1977 by The Athenaeum of Philadelphia and distributed by the American Life Foundation, this casebound book of 112 pages has been called, in an APT *Bulletin* review, a "veritable encyclopedia" —

Order from the American Life Foundation, Box 349, Watkins Glen, NY, 14891. Send $20.00 + $1.00 for book rate postage ($21.00) or $20.00 + $1.75 for book rate plus Special Handling ($21.75) for faster delivery. *For deliveries in New York State, please add 7% NYS sales tax.*

REPAIR CASE HISTORY

A luxury cooperative apartment building on Chicago's lakefront built in 1911 was converted to condominiums (what hasn't been converted lately?). There, in a ten-room condominium I first stripped and refinished the woodwork in the solarium. Then I stripped and refinished the built-in in the butler's pantry. Finally, I was asked to repair and refinish fourteen doors.

The doors were large, heavy, mahogany veneer elements which had been painted white sometime in the past. Before I got to know the owners, they had the doors taken to a commercial stripping establishment (I would have counseled against it). The strip joint removed not only the paint but some of the veneer as well. In addition, in their seventy-year history the bathroom doors had been subjected to much water by sloppy maids, and the cores were separating. My assignment was to repair them and replace missing veneer.

At first I thought that it would be necessary to patch with old veneer. So I borrowed some from an extra door in the condo storage room. When stripped, the old veneer looked much like my new material, which was much easier to use. So new stock was used.

Each door was removed and placed on two sawhorses. Small veneer patches, half an inch or less, were applied with the hot glue gun. Larger patches, sometimes five or six across primarily the bottom of the door, were held by Elmer's furniture glue and cauls and clamps. Glue was shoved into the structural splits and separations, then the veneer was put in place and the whole mess clamped! Once that was done, the excess glue was cleaned off where it had oozed out. After drying overnight, all the clamps, cauls, and waxed paper were removed and any surface irregularities sanded.

Chapter Five

Stripping Woodwork
the Easy Way

After making all of the necessary repairs, you're now ready to consider what to do with the old finish. Removal of old finish has been labeled stripping. It is a purely mechanical activity, and at the same time the most important preparation step. What I hope to do is help make your job easier, faster, and more effective.

We're going to concentrate in this chapter on interior woodwork. Because exterior trim is really another subject, it will be covered in Chapter Six.

TO STRIP OR NOT TO STRIP

You may be uncertain as to whether or not your woodwork finish really needs to be stripped. This is only natural, especially if the old finish looks good, because there is no point in making more work for yourself. Further, keeping the old finish, particularly if it's the original and in good condition, should enhance your home's value. I must confess, though, that I have seen few old house interiors that were well enough cared for that a completely new finish couldn't help. But, then, I've been accused of being too fussy!

Heavy layers of paint, alligator varnish, chipping, peeling, ugly runs and drips, dark shades, and inappropriate colors are all conditions that are clearly in need of correction. I guess it's the borderline "Should I strip or shouldn't I?" situations that are the most difficult of all to resolve. If any of these is your problem, first try washing a portion of the damaged woodwork. A satisfactory result should tell you, Continue cleaning. You'll recognize unsatisfactory signs. They signal, It's time to start stripping!

CLEANING WOODWORK

The cleaning process can take two forms: cleaning only and you're through restoring, or cleaning to prepare the woodwork surfaces for further refinishing. Woodwork requiring only a good washing appears to have a good, solid, and smooth coat. Though its color is appropriate, it looks a little dark, greasy, or streaked. The simplest and most effective method is to remove dirt and grease with a high-quality cleanser like Murphy's Oil Soap or Flax Soap (and carefully follow the directions on the jar). If using a rag, as the directions indicate, seems ineffective, try fine (grade 000) steel wool in place of a rag with the soapy water. Be careful to rub with the grain and apply even pressure so as to avoid scratching and to get a nice even color when this process is finished.

Cleaning woodwork in preparation for further refinishing necessitates a tougher cleansing agent. Here, mineral spirits like oleum, turpentine, or benzine are applied to the woodwork with fine steel wool. Dip the pad in a small pail containing the solvent, rub with the wood grain, and wipe with a clean rag.

If the finish now feels rough to the touch, sand it with a relatively fine sandpaper, such as number 180 production paper or grade 400 wet or dry paper used dry. A finish that is then still rough, streaked, or lumpy is a candidate for stripping; read on. However, if the result of this cleaning is a smooth and evenly colored surface, you're in luck. You need merely wipe it with a tack cloth (a specially prepared cloth for picking up all dust), turn to the chapter on refinishing, and follow the directions for applying a finish coat or a sealer and a finish coat. Now, this is really the easy way to strip, right?

SOME GENERAL QUESTIONS (AND ANSWERS)

Q. *Do you have to strip everything?*
A. So your woodwork flunked the easy or, better, the no-strip test. At this point you're probably girding yourself for a big project. That may not be necessary because some parts of your woodwork may be in better shape than other parts. For instance, ceiling beams and cove, because of their relatively inaccessible location, may have been spared the painter's or, worse, the handyman's brush. Consider yourself fortunate. Your task now, after you've stripped the bad finish, is to match the color and reflection characteristics with that of the old beams and cove molding. The point, therefore, is that one need not strip everything. That makes preparation easier; at the same time, it makes refinishing more difficult.

Q. *When is the right time to strip woodwork?*
A. The right time to strip is after all repairs and before any decorating. You see, stripping removes all excess water-soluble glue used in repairs. It will also remove wall paint and damage plastic tile and wallpaper. Newly sanded and refinished floors, even carpeting, can be damaged by chemical paint and varnish remover (stripper).

Now, if you've already refinished your floors, painted your walls, or hung the wallpaper, please don't despair. My work is living proof that one can strip woodwork without damaging *anything;* but remember, such work must be done with extreme care, often a painfully slow process. Later, I will tell you how and what to cover up.

Q. *Should woodwork be stripped in place or removed and stripped?*

A. The rule is to remove what can be very easily removed *and* replaced; strip in place what can't. Into the first category one can place most doors and casement windows. Some double-hung window sashes are easily removed, too. It gets sticky, though, in such areas as staircase balusters. Though balusters, to continue with this rule of thumb, can often be easily removed, especially if they're loose, getting them back can pose a problem and may require the efforts of a professional carpenter.

The advantage of stripping woodwork in place is that removal and replacement are often very time-consuming. When in place the pieces are held, freeing both your hands for stripping. Old woodwork is often very dry, making removal a possible source of damage and making renailing difficult, especially in very old oak. So the rule is doors yes, molding no.

Interior courtyard of Glessner House. The porte cochère, hall, *and kitchen doors enter from here.* Photo by Jim Kuba *(By permission of Chicago Architectural Foundation)*

Above, left, the landmark James J. Glessner House, Chicago. H. H. Richardson, 1886. Here the author stripped and refinished eleven exterior doors. Photo by Jim Kuba

Above, the familiar front door of James J. Glessner House. Stripping and refinishing it posed a difficult problem: one, it is fifty-six inches wide and requires three men to handle it. The wrought-iron frame is attached to tie hinges, making it a door support, and it was necessary to get under the frame to restore the piece properly. Finally, this building has many tours, all of which enter this doorway! Photo by Edwin Johnson (Courtesy of Chicago Architectural Foundation)

Left, here, both the door and the frame have been removed, and the author is applying stripper. Thankfully, not much finish remained on the outside of this ninety-six-year-old piece. Photo by Edwin Johnson (Courtesy of Chicago Architectural Foundation)

After the last application of stripper has been removed, the surface is wiped clean with a fresh Turkish towel. Photo by Edwin Johnson (Courtesy of Chicago Architectural Foundation)

The stripped door back in place. The dark marks are where the wood is still wet. In the next chapter we will see how this door was refinished. Photo by Edwin Johnson (Courtesy of Chicago Architectural Foundation)

Some Stripping Tips

As the odds are that you will not get off with so easy a task as simple cleaning, you better get ready to strip. To help you, here are some general tips. Though they seem simple, they've taken me several years to devise and to verbalize. They can now be yours immediately!

TIP NUMBER 1. Once you start to strip something, say a door, try to finish it. Certainly, never let stripper dry anywhere. It's not that you can't remove it later, but that you've invested a certain amount of time and effort plus expense to get where you're at. In order to assure completion of, say, a doorway, window, or ceiling beam, allow yourself plenty of time. However, if you must stop to feed your baby or to go to work, finish scraping off all loose finish and clean the area well with coarse steel wool.

TIP NUMBER 2. Strip at a comfortable work height. For vertical woodwork work as much as you can without ladders, stools, and steps. Reach instead. Strip removed pieces like doors and windows on sawhorses, low stools, or boxes. Lean them against walls. Never work on pieces flat on the floor, making you kneel, sit, or squat.

TIP NUMBER 3. While you're about the stripping task, get all of the old finish out and off at that time. Stick to your guns while the "gunk" (old finish plus stripper) is still soft. Remember, it's a lot more difficult to dig out when it's dry.

TIP NUMBER 4. Keep clean. Work with a clean brush, clean rags, and clean stripper. You can keep the stripper clean of old finish by: stopping to brush on more solution when you note your brush picking up dissolved gunk, work with a smaller amount of stripper in your pail at a time, dump thin and discolored stripper in your pail as it has stopped working, and clean your brush from time to time by wiping it on newspaper.

TIP NUMBER 5. Have music to strip by. No, I don't mean the Gypsy Rose Lee number, I mean your favorite kind of music. I carry my portable stereo everywhere; sometimes customers turn on their stereo so I can listen to the classics. Music, it seems, helps soothe the frustrations of woodwork stripping.

OBJECTIVES

Before we get into the nitty-gritty of stripping let's consider our goals. This is the most important preparation step in the restoration process; it is not the end, but a means. So we want to *completely* remove the old finish from the wood. This means not just *on* the surface, but *in* the surface. That's why mere scraping and sanding generally do not do a good stripping job and why one must use a chemical stripper. Even then, complete old finish removal, though our goal, is unachievable. Restored wood will never be the same as that newly arrived from the lumber mill. Old finishes and time have done their thing.

Our second goal should be to prepare the surfaces in such a way that they accept new finishes evenly. Of course, variations in wood color and grain prevent color homogeneity. What one should avoid is, say, a door panel that when completely restored is lighter where it meets the molding because of incomplete old finish removal. So one must strip relatively inaccessible areas, like corners, as well as areas out in the wide-open spaces.

Finally, our third goal should be to protect ourselves and all other objects that will not be stripped from the heat of the electric paint remover and the harsh chemicals in the stripper. Basically, this means to cover up. Cover your eyes, cover your hands, and your arms, and clear out the room or at least the immediate area in which you are working.

STRIPPING SPECIFIC FINISHES

There is a difference in tools, techniques, and materials used in stripping shellacked, painted, and varnished surfaces. Let's take a close look at each.

Stripping Shellacked and/or Alcohol-Stained Surfaces

As you will recall from the chapter on old finishes, all old homes having clear finish on their woodwork had at least some shellac applied. Generally, it was the sealer, but where it was the finish coat and that finish coat remains to this day, it can be removed with denatured alcohol because, of course, alcohol is the solvent of shellac. Further, in some homes an alcohol stain was also used, in contrast to the modern penetrating oil stains, which have a mineral spirit base. So if you are fortunate to have woodwork finished in this manner, it is worth your while to start stripping with denatured alcohol. Then experiment with a chemical stripper and see which works best for you.

To test for a shellac and/or alcohol stain, put some alcohol on a rag and wipe a spot on your woodwork. If the old finish dissolves rather quickly on the rag, you have shellac. To strip with

Principal woodwork stripping tools. Top left: electric paint remover, rigid three-inch scraper, flexible three-inch putty knife, one-inch hooked scraper. Lower left: long-handled wire brush and two-inch hooked scraper. Photo by Dina Johnson

denatured alcohol, apply it to the area to be stripped with either a brush or coarse (number 2) steel wool from a small metal pail. Some people have been successful applying alcohol with a small spray bottle, then wiping the surface with steel wool.

Keep in mind that alcohol evaporates rather quickly, so work with small areas. Also be aware that this substance will produce a new "high" if you do not have proper ventilation. So open some windows, even in winter in the North, and use a portable fan.

You will probably find that woodwork stripped with denatured alcohol will retain more of its original finish color than if it had been stripped with a methanol chloride stripper. If that original color is suitable, you need not stain it, but go right into the sealing and finish coat. How about that!

Stripping Painted Woodwork

You will want to strip paint from woodwork for one of two reasons. One, you intend to repaint it because it fits your taste or because it is the traditional finish. Two, you wish to completely remove all traces of paint never to see it again and stain, seal, and finish, or else just seal and finish, again because it is being faithful to the original or because it is your personal taste.

The reason I bring up these two alternatives is that your finishing goals determine your stripping activities. Stripping paint to prepare for a natural finish must be a superior job; stripping for repainting need not result in clear grain.

Stripping paint from woodwork has got to be the most difficult stripping job because of the tenacious nature of the material. If your woodwork has two or more coats of paint on it, the most efficient method entails heat. If, however, there is only one coat of paint over a previously sealed surface, or two rather thin coats, you can try "draw-scraping" it with a wide paint scraper. Take care to avoid making gouges in the surface by applying even pressure on the tool. This probably won't get all of the paint off, but the subsequent treatment with a chemical stripper will complete the task nicely.

Heat is the recommended technique for from two to ten coats of paint. And you have a choice of three devices for producing that heat: the torch, the heat gun, and the electric paint remover (EPR).

The propane torch has been around for years and is still used by some professional painters where the piece can be removed and worked on outside, thus eliminating the fire hazard. It is admittedly fast, but it can also cause serious scorching. Often such scorching cannot be sanded off and must be either covered by paint in the refinishing process or else professionally touched up. I have seen what it can do inside a home and therefore I absolutely do not recommend its use.

The heat gun is the newest wrinkle in paint removing. Looking and working very much like a hair dryer, it blows very hot air on a paint surface, softening the paint so that you can scrape it off. It is a good tool, but unlike its competitor, the electric paint remover, it does not heat up the painted surface as much. Thus, there is much less smoke and smell (less lead fumes, too, if lead paint is being removed). Both the heat gun and the EPR do the work at the same speed in experiments I have conducted. Disadvantages of the heat gun are: it's very noisy, it's heavy, it's three times as expensive as the EPR, and long strips of old (now hot) paint have a tendency of getting on the gun as you are removing them.

My choice of the heating tools is the EPR. It is lightweight, it's quiet, and it's relatively cheap. One can buy it in the local paint store for about twenty-five dollars; the heat gun costs about $60. Because of its weight, the EPR is highly maneuverable, too.

Besides these basic heating tools, one needs scraping ones as well. The most useful is the flat, rigid three-inch paint scraper; get one with a large wooden handle. In fact, get several. I generally work with four. A beveled, flat one-inch chisel is great for getting into corners; wire brushes with long handles do a good job in material removal; hooked scrapers with long handles and wide blades are also recommended. In buying tools try to get the biggest, the widest, and the sharpest. Avoid what I like to call the toothpick removal method—it will try your very soul!

Enough about tool description. Before we get into their usage, however, let's take a look at paint and varnish remover because it *can* also be used to remove paint. The reason I don't recommend strippers for paint is that they are slow, expensive, and messy. This places strippers in the usage category of removing varnish and what heat can't get off.

Nonetheless, you may have just a little paint to remove, or your heat gun broke down and the nearest supplier is a ninety-mile round trip, or you just don't want to use heat (like next to expensive, irreplaceable glass). Here are some tips for you. First, plan to use a lot of this material to remove paint effectively; and the more paint coats, the more stripper you will use.

Brush on the stripper and keep the surface you want to strip *wet*. Eventually, the paint will either get mushy, so you can scrape it off like whipped cream, or else begin to bubble—"perk," if you will—telling you it's ready to be removed. Scrape it off wide surfaces with a three-inch flexible putty knife, and off narrow ones with a narrower knife. Be sure it's ready for scraping, though. Premature scraping will result in much wasted motion and stripper.

Now, with this brief introduction turn to the section of this chapter entitled "Stripping Varnished Woodwork." There you will get the rest of the story.

HOW TO USE THE EPR. I will concentrate on this tool, as I highly recommend it for paint removal. All of what I have to say is based on my personal experience and does not preclude other effective procedures. You may want to experiment a little.

Stance and movement are important. Start stripping woodwork that you can reach while standing on the floor or standing on a stair tread if you are doing stairs. Hold your EPR so that it softens the painted surface, then move the tool up, down, or sidewise to the next spot you want to soften and scrape the first spot as clean as possible. Follow the EPR with your three-inch rigid scraper, moving the tools together. Now, you know the paint is ready for removal when it appears to swell or rise and perhaps smoke a little. When starting a job, you alone will have to determine how long to leave the EPR over a spot to do the job. Err in the direction of not holding it long enough; in this manner you will not singe or, worse, burn.

Depending upon the kind of paint and the number of coats you are removing, an overheated spot can either flame or just smoke and blacken. The flame can be quickly extinguished by blowing it out (much like a candle), though it will probably

leave a charcoal-like mark on your wood. To be safe, it is better to have a fire extinguisher or a bucket of water handy to prevent fire.

Flat surfaces are the easiest to strip with the EPR, so I suggest you learn to use yours on nice flat and wide woodwork. Avoid doors, as a singe mark in the center of a panel is a little hard to disguise in the refinishing step. Problem areas are, of course, recessed sections of moldings, like rosettes and window sash tracks, and decorative trim. Corners are also a problem. For recessed areas, melt and scrape the paint from the deepest sections first, leaving the surface paint on to protect that wood from scorching. The combination of the EPR and wire brushes is recommended, although one-inch hooked scrapers are also good. Don't worry about what you can't remove. In straight areas like the sash track, draw-scraping when everything has cooled and has become brittle will get a lot of old paint loose.

Corners are clearly the bane of woodwork strippers. Hold your EPR diagonally across the corner of, for example, the door frame and pull the

Stripping four coats of paint in one movement from an interior door frame using the electric paint remover. Here, the EPR is moving down, followed immediately with a rigid paint scraper. Note the paint coming off.

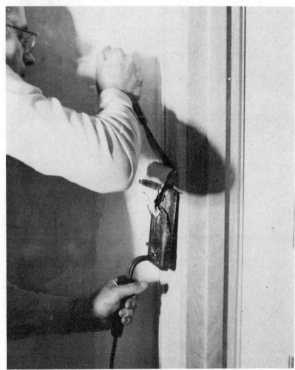

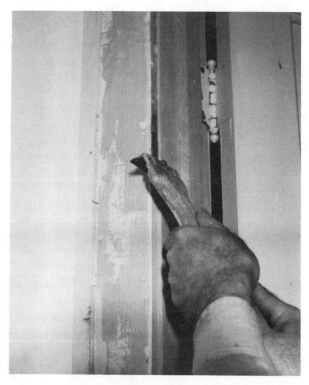

Moving up to the top of the trim piece, the scraper follows the EPR. Both tools move together as far as one can reach while standing on the floor. The horizontal frame was reached by standing on a two-step stool.

After the EPR on the main frame piece (note paint not removed), the joining frame corner is cleaned out with a sharp two-inch hooked scraper pulling down. Similarly, residue on the flat surface will be scraped.

Paint on the molding between the door panel and left vertical rail is removed with a wire brush, which closely trails the EPR.

Paint is being removed from the door panel. Note how clean four coats come off. This door was initially stained and sealed in 1920.

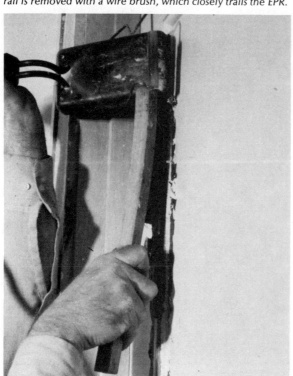

soft paint out from the corner with a hooked scraper. What paint remains, if any, can be scraped when cool with your diagonal straight chisel, pushing it into the corner. Corners of window sashes can be negotiated in a similar manner. Here, though, be careful not to put too much heat on the window glass because the EPR will crack it, especially on a cold day.

The residue of the EPR ranges from an ash to large pieces of dry brittle paint. At times this residue is very hot when it falls, so protect everything below. Plastic and paper, however, are not recommended because of possible fire. I use a heavy drop cloth, but the high temperature of some residue is attested by the singes and black-edged holes in my ancient and honorable drop cloths. The cooled residue, of course, can be easily swept up, collected, and dumped; just keep it out of the way of kids and pets. It may contain lead.

When not in use, keep your EPR on a metal TV table. The extension cord should have an electrical capacity to keep the EPR red-hot; try to use an electrical circuit on which other major appliances are not connected. Remember, the EPR grid must be red-hot to do you any good—glowing red-hot.

Now comes the stripper. Paint and varnish remover is brushed on the door frame with a clean two-inch bristle brush from a jar carried in a metal pail. Note heavy neoprene gloves worn by the author.

The residue of stripper, old varnish, stain, and some paint is being scraped using the three-inch flexible putty knife. Then it is dumped on newspaper on the floor.

Stripping Varnished Woodwork

The material to be used in stripping varnished woodwork, and painted woodwork *after* heat has been used, is paint and varnish remover, labeled stripper. There are two general varieties, light-duty and heavy-duty I call them. The light-duty has as its active ingredients acetone, toluene, and methanol. This makes for a compound that does a good job stripping woodwork that does not have a heavy buildup of material. The result is a wood that retains much of its original color, too.

Heavy-duty strippers, a must for removing the residue after EPR worked-over trim, and heavier buildups of varnish, stain, and varnish stain, contain methylene chloride and are both water-soluble and non-water-soluble. I prefer the water-soluble, as I can get a cleaner job with them; one washes off the final residue with clean water. The non-water-soluble strippers, once dried, permit the sanding of the final residue. The advantage of the latter is that damage by water is avoided, and

Brushing the surface, carefully, with a wire brush, which is especially helpful in removing residue from joining corners.

Washing tools: steel wool pad, old (but clean) Turkish towels, wire brush, pail of warm water, and stool on which to set the pail at work height.

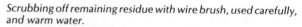

Scrubbing off remaining residue with wire brush, used carefully, and warm water.

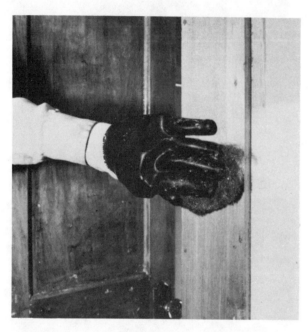

Steel wool further cleans the surface.

Wire-brushing molding—carefully, as this is soft wood. This cleans very effectively. By now, several applications of stripper have done their job. A last application is about to be washed off.

Steel wool pad with warm water further cleans wood grain.

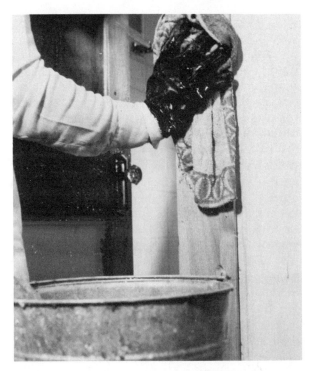

Turkish towel washes the frame. Then a clean dry towel dries it.

Sometimes stubborn paint remains through all the foregoing steps. Now is the time to dig it out. Here, a one-inch diagonal-cut chisel with a large handle is being used.

The finished door. All the top has been stipped. The bottom has been left painted for contrast. Note the beautiful wood grain that has been exposed. Foregoing photos by Dina Johnson

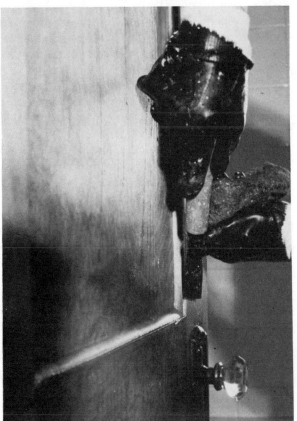

the areas of high humidity (anywhere close to water) permit stripping and proper drying for later refinishing.

So chemical strippers are the means for removing varnish. There are a few precautions we should discuss before turning to techniques. The first is, you *must* have adequate ventilation. Open windows and doors even in northern winters. Carry a small portable fan with you to keep the air moving. The active ingredient in strippers *is* toxic. Recently I heard of a guy who stripped the woodwork in about ten rooms of a fifteen-room condominium on Chicago's lakefront working long hours every day without even having opened a window in the four winter months he was there. He ended up sick and had to quit the job before he got to the fun part, the refinishing.

Second, since chemical strippers will strip the finish off anything in which they come in contact including your skin, cover everything you don't want stripped. Wear heavy neoprene gloves, long sleeves, old clothes, and a hat if you're working overhead. Protect your eyes. Cover all nearby furniture, floors, appliances, and walls not to be painted again with plastic drop cloths and newspaper.

You *can* protect walls next to the woodwork you're stripping by taping single sheets of newspaper right next to the trim and as far from it as you plan to splash. Then run a strip of wide masking tape over the paper and next to the woodwork. Do this on the ceiling over doorways and windows, too. It is important, however, that you remove all this *as soon* as you get through with an area, in any event at the end of the day. Otherwise, when you do pull it all off, with it will come paint, wallpaper, or both.

Similarly floors can be protected, first by avoiding large amounts of stripper and water in these places, and second by covering them well. Run wide masking tape along the quarter round on either the floor (if you have no carpeting) or the carpeting adjacent to the baseboard. Then lay a heavy plastic drop cloth along this tape and overlap it a little. Tape the cloth to the tape so as to seal out any possible seepage. Next lay newspaper over the plastic to absorb moisture. As the paper gets dirty and wet, just cover it with fresh paper; don't pick up until the end of the day. To help rid your house of the bad stripper smell, be sure to clean up *every* day. If, despite all your precautions, you do get

stripper on your carpeting, if it is water soluble it is quite likely you will be able to wash it out if you attend to it right away. Stripper seeped onto bare finished floors will remove the finish. I take care of such accidents when I am refinishing by rubbing in a little matching stain on the damaged floor, then seal and finish when the woodwork is being refinished.

STARTING TO STRIP. Devise a plan. Decide where you're going to start and where you're going to end up. Pick the easiest room to do first—and *finish* it. In a given room start with the easiest and most accessible place. And if two or more of you are going to work in a given room, work far enough apart so you are not in each other's mess.

The big moment is arriving in which you will finally see the true beauty of your woodwork. Start at the top: the top of the doorway, the top of the staircase, and the top of the window frame. The reason is that more of the mess from stripping falls down than splatters up. Buy stripper by the gallon, or by the case if you can get a better deal. Use a 2-, 2½-, or 3-inch China bristle brush with a long handle to give you reach. Pour the stripper into a wide-mouth jar or can carried in a small metal pail with a comfortable handle.

Be *very* generous in applying the stripper; use a lot. Let it work for you. Cover a workable area, small at first, and larger when you get the feel for the situation. Let it soak a few minutes. For example, on a ceiling beam a foot wide and twenty-five feet long, I would cover the whole beam's surface with four heavy brushings of stripper before starting to remove anything. On a flush birch door the whole side should be covered several times before starting to remove the residue. Really soak corners, decorative details, and recessed places. Keep all working surfaces wet.

For heavily varnished surfaces, watch for bubbling to signal it's time to start removing the dissolved varnish. For example, let's take an eight-foot French door made of mahogany in 1910 and containing fifteen lights (panes of glass). Three applications of stripper are brushed on one side of the door, which is sitting on two two-by-fours and leaning against my shop's wall. The old finish and stripper start to bubble; they're ready to bite the dust. I whip out my trusty three-inch flexible putty knife and easily scoop off the gunk on the flat surface all around the panes and flick it on the newspaper on the floor. Then, because this is soft, easily damaged mahogany, I clean the gunk off each mullion around each of the fifteen panes of glass with steel wool pads. I discover that this gets most of the old finish off. Two more applications of stripper get brushed on, and this time I get some on the glass so that it too can be cleaned.

Now comes the washing. The final coat of stripper is brushed on. Then I dip a coarse steel wool pad into a pail of clean warm water and clean off the entire door's surface. As the pad gets dirty, I rinse it and turn it. When it is too dirty to use, I take a clean one. After the steel wool, I wash the surface with a Turkish towel and dry it immediately with a clean towel.

If the door had been oak or even pine, I would have used long-handled wire brushes after the putty knife. Properly used—that is, without too much muscle and with the grain of the wood— these brushes are invaluable. And they can be cleaned. As they get clogged, I take a new one (I work with about thirty). Then at the end of the day I clean them all in a pail of warm water.

If this process seems like a lengthy one, remember that it is an important one. Good stripping opens the grain of the old woodwork so that it is really receptive to the new finish.

Cleanliness is a key to efficient stripping. So just as your stripper application brush should be clean at the beginning of each day's work, you should use clean rinse water, clean steel wool pads, and clean towels. The towels you use each day can be washed clean in your washer after a little soaking in detergent. It is better to dispose of dirty rinse water outside the home; it doesn't seem to hurt trees or shrubs, but it can hurt your plumbing, because it is full of steel wool shreds and wire brush bristles.

SUMMARY. In summary, here's how to strip using the chemical stripper:

1. Apply the chemical stripper with a wide paint brush.
2. Scrape off residue with a large putty knife.
3. Clean remaining residue off with first a wire brush and then a steel wool pad.

At Glessner House this door separates the home from the coach house. It is oak on the house side and yellow pine on the "barn" side. The vertical board design is typical of high-class stables. In its ninety-six-year history, the door had never been stripped. Hence it held layer on layer of varnish and stain. (Courtesy of Chicago Architectural Foundation)

Bert Ball, the author's helper, is brushing on water-soluble paint and varnish remover. Note the dark, dark stain color.

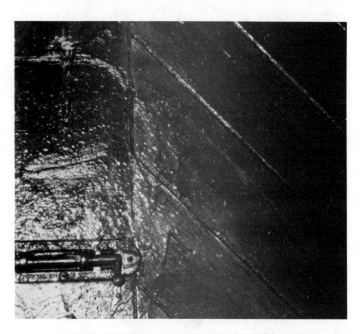

This shows the stripper at work. Note the bubbles indicating it is time to do the first scraping.

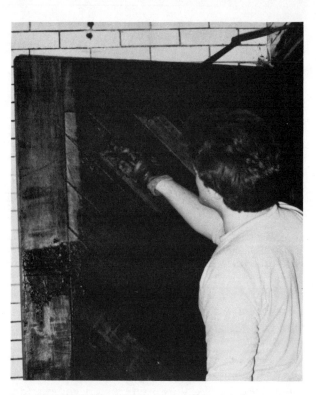

Stripper is being scraped off with the three-inch flexible putty knife. Bert is stripping each board with the grain. Next, he cleaned in the grooves separating the boards with a wire brush.

Another application of stripper was necessary. In fact, three applications were made before anything was stripped. This was subsequently stripped, and the third brushing was washed.

Steel wool pad cleaning off the surface before the "wash" application of stripper.

The wire brush cleaning with warm water gets residue out of all the grooves.

At last, Bert wipes the door surface dry. Notice the beautiful oak grain now visible after nearly one hundred years of hiding. Foregoing photos by Edwin Johnson

4. Apply more stripper and repeat (2) and (3) until the surface appears clean.

5. Last application of stripper (wash application); clean surface with wire brush dipped in warm water, then steel wool pad dipped in water. Keep wet.

6. Rinse with towel and warm water; dry with clean towel.

7. Evaluate: If old finish residue appears after drying, you washed the surface too soon. Use more stripper and follow the above steps again.

CLEANUP. Chemical strippers smell, so the room should be aired. I often use a portable fan to circulate the air. When you are through working in an area, pick up the wet newspaper and discard outside in a plastic lawn bag. Drippings of stripper on painted walls should be cleaned up (use old steel wool pads) to prevent paint etching. Wash stripper off window glass with your wet steel wool pads, rinse, and dry; it's much easier to clean it now than when it dries and hardens. Clean stripper and old finish off all hardware, such as door hinges, now too.

TIPS ON STRIPPING SPECIFIC ARCHITECTURAL PIECES

Now that you have a general knowledge and understanding of how to strip painted and varnished surfaces, let's look at how to work with specific items of woodwork.

Doors

Although it is best to remove doors from their hinges to strip them, they can be stripped in place. To remove them, though, take out their hinge pins using a hammer and screwdriver. Then either lay the door on a worktable or stand it against the wall. If you stand it, first strip the top half or so, then either turn the door upside down and strip the bottom half or keep the door right side up but place it on a low stool for stripping the bottom half. The important point is to keep it at a convenient work height.

If you can, remove the doorknobs and back plates for a complete job. Strip one side of your door at a time, leaving the edges for the last side stripping, thus making the door easier to handle when turning.

For paneled doors concentrate your initial efforts on the molding around the panels. If using the EPR, remove the paint here first; when using the chemical stripper, soak moldings and corners well before beginning to remove old finish. For moldings use the wire brush carefully. On flush doors apply stripper over the whole surface until it stays wet, then remove with a wide putty knife. Avoid using a wire brush on flush birch doors, as they are easily scratched when wet.

The photos of pages 91 and 92 illustrate stripping paint from a paneled door. Compare the painted door on page 91 to the stripped top half at the top of page 92. This door from the 1920s, impossible to replace, is reason enough to restore rather than remodel!

Windows

Now, there are windows, and there are windows. There are swing-in casements, swing-out casements, double-hung, and nonmovable. As I am presently refinishing a solarium in a turn-of-the-century house that has ten large swing-in casements, let's start with swing-ins. Since they swing in, their outsides become as important as their insides. The edges should also be refinished for a good job. Hopefully, your casements are as easily removed as those I'm doing. Take them off their frames, remove their latches, lay them on a worktable, and strip them one at a time, one side at a time. If the latches are also painted, soak them in a can of chemical stripper until the paint literally falls off. Then wire-brush them in a pail of warm water until they are clean, rinse, and dry them.

If you're removing paint, you will want to use your EPR. Because this tool is very hot, it can crack glass, especially glass that is cold. So don't touch the glass with the EPR, and keep a respectable distance from it, yet at the same time efficiently softening and removing the paint.

Corners of sashes and mullion strips are always a problem. Hold your EPR with the top diagonally across the corner and parallel to the glass. Scrape the softened paint toward you, then horizontally and vertically, while keeping your EPR as close to the corner as possible. When working with the chemical stripper, soak the corners well and don't try to get all the residue out until the wash application. In the meantime it is working for you. After rinsing poke a wet towel into the corners and then a dry one. Most of what's left can be flicked out with dry steel wool. The remainder is sanded, and what little stays in a good stripping job can be touched up.

For residue removal on the rest of the sash molding, use a wire brush, applying a light pressure because most sashes are pine and scratched easily, especially when wet. Since you will also be stripping the outside of the swing-in, you will probably have putty to contend with. Most of the paint can be gently stripped off the old putty; chemical stripper will also put aggregate into old putty cracks and seems to give it new life. If the old putty is in bad condition, however, now is the time to have it replaced.

Double-hung windows are much more common than casements. The first thing to do for double-hungs is to see that both the top and the bottom move. They should move so that (1) you can strip all of the sash and (2) you can remove old finish from the bottom of the top half that faces the room. If you can't get the top half loose, try to remove the bottom half by taking off the stop trim that holds it in (generally removing only one is sufficient), then take off the sash cords and slide out.

If both halves are movable, you should be able to strip both the upper and the lower while standing on the floor and raising and lowering each to work on them and around them. Here is how you do it. Brush the chemical stripper onto the window frame in back of the weight cords by holding the cords out with one hand. Then lower the top sash and apply stripper to the top two thirds of it. Raise the lower sash so that you can apply stripper to the remainder of the top sash, and brush stripper on the lower sash. Sounds complicated, right? Well, after the fifth or sixth window you will have grasped this system.

In newer homes such double-hung windows are completely removable. It is clearly to your advantage to remove them and to work on them on a worktable. Even in older homes the removing of windows, if it can be accomplished with little effort, saves time and energy.

Double-hung windows with six, nine, or twelve lights are very difficult and time-consuming to strip. Here you should work out a system to avoid a lengthy process. A recommended way is to first raise the sash to a convenient work height and apply the chemical stripper, making certain that corners are well soaked. Remove the dissolved residue with a wire brush; lightly does it. Strip all top mullions, then right side, left side, and finally bottom mullions. Next remove all you can with a steel wool pad, going around each light in a clockwise motion. Taking a clean pad, flick out residue from the corners, but don't worry too much about them. Repeat the process and then do the wash application and dry; remember, the glass should be cleaned now, too. Finally, flick out dried and loose residue with a clean and dry steel wool pad.

Swing-out casements are generally hinged, so they can't be easily removed. Further, since only one side and one edge can be seen from the room, that is all you need strip and refinish. Common to such windows is crank-out hardware. If it is painted, use chemical stripper to remove old paint. You may discover some nice old brass. Other than this, follow the directions for other window sashes.

Window frames, of course, should be stripped when you're in position to do the sashes. I prefer to strip them after the sashes, because they are reached more easily. All of the frame should be stripped including the very top next to the sash and the depth next to the wall.

When using your EPR, strip the most recessed areas first. Such areas are the deeply carved vertical grooves in frames, corners, plinths, head blocks, and sash channels. By doing them first, you don't scorch the paint-protected surface areas; then strip the latter. On some jobs you may have to really dig out paint. Use a diagonally cut chisel, a small hooked scraper, a wire brush, or all three. On some ornate pieces you may never get all of the old paint out. Don't fret. Later they can either be painted the color of the stain or else touched up.

In some very old houses paint and plaster on walls adjacent to window and door frames have mingled so as to blur or even obscure wood and wall division and/or molding detail. Here you have to decide how much of the frame you are going to restore without doing damage to the plastered wall. In conclusion you may use much of what was written about window frames to refinish door frames.

Stairs

Stairs can be bears. Rule number one is start stripping at the top of the staircase and work down. I will always remember my first stairs job. Starting at the bottom and working my way up, I couldn't understand why I was constantly messing up the newly cleaned balusters and handrail! Besides, I was always standing in a mess.

So, starting at the top of the staircase, strip balusters and handrail first, then the risers, the base, and last the tread, all within a workable area. Then move to a lower area and take the architectural pieces again in this order. If the treads are not to be stripped, cover them carefully with cut-to-size heavy plastic taped to the tread. Cover the plastic with newspaper to absorb dripped stripper, residue, and water. You may also want to cover walls, and floor and platforms below, as your mess *can* travel.

While square balusters are easy to strip paint from, providing you can get your EPR in between them, round balusters and newel and platform posts are another matter. Perhaps chemical stripper is easier to use, especially if there is much turned detail. If that is the case, *soak* the balusters with many applications of stripper, scrape what dissolved paint you can with a curved rug-cutting knife, and clean off the remainder with wire brushes and steel wool pads. An old rag may be helpful to really clean the surface before applying more stripper.

Stair carpeting can be protected from chemical stripper by laying wide masking tape on the carpeting next to the stringer. Then lay a continuous strip of plastic, available by the roll, and ideally stair width, and tape it to the previously laid tape. Then tell the kids to stay off the stairs until you're through.

The EPR is something else. Carelessly used, it will singe wool carpeting and actually melt some of the synthetics. You may want to pull up the carpeting and have it relaid when the job is over. In this way all the risers and treads will be stripped. After all, someday you may want to remove your wall-to-wall stair carpeting and the alternative to refinishing it all now is a half inch of paint next to the stair tread left as a reminder of how ugly it all once was.

An alternative is to disassemble the staircase railing and balusters and send everything out to a reliable commercial stripping joint. While it *does* save stripping time, putting back some railings is *very* difficult; old houses have a way of settling, commercially stripped wood can swell, and you may have to hire a carpenter to get it all back together. I know, I know!

Cove Molding

Nowhere is it written that cove should be stripped and refinished. Painted cove tends to lower your ceiling—visually, that is. Some cove has been painted for so many years that stripping for staining or natural finish is both difficult and unrewarding. Some cove is plaster; better check it out before you get your scaffold in place. Finally, cove stripping may either reveal ceiling plaster defects or even cause such defects if carelessly done.

If after this discussion you still want to strip your cove, here is what you can do. Cove is, by nature, curved. Let's assume your cove is painted. Using the EPR carefully to avoid scorching, soften and scrape paint from the *deepest* recessed areas first. Incidentally, you may find that the deepest recesses are plaster separating the picture molding from the cove; paint this a matching brown after completing the refinishing and no one but you will know the difference. After paint removal from recesses, remove it from surface areas.

For efficient paint removal you should experiment with any or a combination of: wire brush, heavy three-inch scraper in a vertical movement, butcher knife, wallpaper-cutting knife, or a tool you have fashioned to fit your cove's configuration.

When the time comes for chemical strippers, it is best to tape newspaper under the cove to protect about three feet of the wall area from drippings. Apply the stripper and wire-brush off the residual old finish; then wipe with a steel wool pad. Now follow the general chemical stripper process.

Ceiling Beams

While we're on the ceiling, let's talk about beams. As with cove the greatest challenge with beams may be getting at them for efficient work. Use two stepladders and an expandable plank. This gives you a good footing and also enables you to walk along and cover a larger work area. For large rooms use three ladders and two planks so you can cover the *entire* room width at once. A small scaffold on wheels is still another alternative.

Rule number one for stripping ceiling beams is start at the top (the vertical sides), then work on the beam bottom. The first beam to tackle is the one next to the wall where you want to start. Pick the least crowded part of the room so you can move fast at first. Work on the side and bottom of that beam and, if possible, the side of the next beam. Do the cove in between these two beams, then get down, move your ladders and planks, and strip the bottom and side of beam 2 and the side of beam 3 and the cove between beams 2 and 3. In this manner work your way down the length of your room, placing the plank between two beams instead of under one of them. Follow the recommended EPR and chemical stripper procedures, but be very careful of ceiling plaster adjacent to the wood. If the plaster is really unstable, it is better to leave a little paint on the beam, say, the topmost vertical edge, so as not to work-damage the ceiling.

To protect your furniture completely and to enable faster movement, it is best to remove all of the furniture from the room. In any event cover everything, because it is easy to splatter from ceiling height. Keep as many tools and supplies on the scaffold as you can, even your water bucket when in the wash cycle. I keep tools in a large pail.

Built-Ins

Not only were sideboards a favorite built-in in bygone days, but there were bookshelves, cabinets, and window seats as well. Frank Lloyd Wright, for example, disguised radiators with fake wooden cabinets. He also liked cozy fireplace nooks (such as his "inglenook") complete with seats. Ideally, these furniture items should be stripped and refinished if the room is being redone.

Take a sideboard, for instance. If it's in a late Victorian home, it is considered an antique by many and valued nearly as greatly as if it were mobile furniture. Consider also the replacement cost of that piece. Okay, you're convinced. You will refinish that, too!

Before you start stripping look for any repairs that have to be made. Often drawers are separating, drawer slides are broken, serving tops are split as are door panels, columns are loose, and parts are missing. Make all necessary repairs first, because stripping removes excess glue and tends to cover any repair scars (see Chapter Four).

Following repairs you can begin stripping off the old finish. If there is a lot of paint on the built-in, use your EPR tool and then strip it chemically. Should you strip the inside, too? If it's visible, and if it has a poor or painted finish, the answer is yes. That will more than double your work, though. You should at least do the inside of doors, both glass and paneled.

Wainscot

As with built-ins, wainscot takes many different forms. Sometimes it is merely the suggestion of wainscot, as with a chair rail or other trim. In more formal homes it is paneling: walnut, oak, rosewood, etc. In less expensive older homes it could be pine or cedar beadboard. Generally, fine paneled wainscot has been pretty well preserved. If it has not and you intend to refinish it, please follow the instructions for stripping paneled doors except, of course, for removal. Wainscot should be stripped in place.

For beadboard (tongue-and-groove) style wainscot, the problem is getting all the old finish out of the deep vertical grooves and tongue-and-groove fit. I refinished such wainscot in three rooms of a house in Chicago built in 1880. There were nine coats of paint covering it, one for every decade it had existed. First I used the EPR and literally dug soft paint out; this was followed by scraping surface paint off with the three-inch rigid scraper. Chemical stripper followed, with long periods to allow for soaking. Despite a fierce wire-brushing, some old paint remained. So, after refinishing was completed, I brushed paint mixed to match the stain into these areas and wiped the excess. The result was a complete success.

Base and Quarter Round

Moving downward toward the floor, we come to the base. Several problems accompany stripping base. One is your floor. The EPR, used with care, should not damage it, but chemical strippers will. So cover it up. Lay several layers of masking tape on your finished wood floor or on your carpeting. Lay heavy plastic drop cloth and tape it to the previously laid tape. This should seal out stripper; however, lots of newspaper over the plastic will absorb drippings and water and save your plastic for further use.

The next caution is the wall. In many older homes either the plaster next to the top or cap molding on the base is weak or else successive painting has created a paint buildup that has become either part of the wall or part of the cap. If you scrape too much of this buildup, you will find yourself with a plaster patching job. So leave a little paint on the cap next to the wall. Finally, if you are thinking of taking up your carpeting, by all means strip all of the base and quarter round now.

Base in older homes can be quite ornate and full of recessed areas. Frank Lloyd Wright put fifteen-inch-high base in his Oak Park house. As recommended with other pieces, strip recessed areas first. Typically, they are just under the cap molding. Cap molding, because of its curved configuration, necessitates one of the following tools, or a combination: wire brush, hooked scraper moved vertically, or a specially designed scraper. Following the cap, clean off the finish from the main part of the base and then do the quarter round. Do as much as you can reach in one kneeling position in that order, following the recommended EPR and chemical stripper techniques.

Kitchen Cabinets

If you have been wondering whether or not to strip and refinish your kitchen cabinets, have someone come in and give you an estimate on installing new cabinets. That should convince you to redo your old ones. Naturally, your decision will also hinge on their present condition. Such obvious defects as warped doors, split panels, or many, many coats of paint over unsealed wood are pretty hard to correct with stripping and refinishing. But if the wood is sound, little damage is apparent, and little paint is present, then it is certainly worthwhile to try a few cabinets and see how they come out. Then, after refinishing them you may want to put new hardware on them, and—presto!—like-new cabinets for a fraction of the "new" price.

Step one in stripping is to remove the doors and drawers and strip them on your worktable, having first removed the knobs and the hinges. Strip both sides of the doors and, of course, the edges. The insides of the cabinets need not generally be stripped; perhaps all they need is a good cleaning followed by sealing. Now, with both doors off and drawers out, strip the cabinet frame, using recommended techniques.

Second, replace the doors for refinishing, as they are generally easier to sand and refinish when they are hung and held. Drawers can be best refinished if they are stood on their backs on the floor so that their fronts are in a horizontal position.

Caution: If new door hinges are to replace the old ones be sure to get those which match the old configurations best. Even then rehanging doors is very difficult; new screw holes will have to be drilled, proper alignment is a tedious process and you may want to hire a carpenter. So, think twice before putting on new hinges.

It is generally advisable to refinish cabinet bottoms that show from underneath, though cabinet tops can be left as is.

WOODWORK CASE HISTORY

The Chauncey Williams House in River Forest, Illinois, was designed and supervised by Frank Lloyd Wright in 1895. Although it is a very large Normandy-style house, both Wright and Williams (they were friends of William H. Winslow, whose house Wright built across the river in 1894) were apparently cost-conscious, because pine woodwork and floors were installed throughout the house. Since then, oak has replaced or covered the pine floors, but pine woodwork and ceiling beams remain. Money was so tight, we are told, that Wright and Winslow themselves got big stones out of the river for Williams's house!

The Chauncey Williams House designed by Frank Lloyd Wright and built in River Forest, IL, in 1895. Hardly a Prairie School house, it does have some of this school's features: high casement windows, the ground-hugging, horizontal belt line course, and wide overhanging eaves. Photo by Nadine Johnson

I was asked to strip and refinish the living room woodwork. It consists of ten large ceiling beams, ceiling cove, three windows, five doorways, a large fireplace in an alcove, and high, elaborate baseboard. Fortunately, there were only three coats of paint over rather well refinished pine woodwork. Still, it was a major task and took 150 man-hours to complete.

The first task was to go through the entire 20 × 50-foot room and remove the paint with the EPR. Since paint over a sealer is always much easier to remove than paint over raw wood, removal of paint from the ceiling beams went rather well. The ceiling plaster was in very bad condition and was slated for replacement, so concern for old plaster was nonexistent.

The window woodwork went rather well, too, except that the casements were deep set with pine panels. Some scorching here caused a problem. What became the bear of the job were three doorways leading to the sun porch. Originally they were windows and the porch did not exist. When remodeling was done, newer pine was put in place and painted directly over raw wood. This made color match in the refinishing process difficult and stripping unbelievably hard.

Heavy water damage to the casements also promised less than satisfactory restoration. Recessed roll-up screens and the accompanying tracks made complete paint removal difficult. Two of the doorways had three-quarter round trim. The fireplace alcove had much previously damaged woodwork, splintered in some places. Two former fireplace seats (another "inglenook") had been removed, leaving the originally unfinished baseboard, giving them a two-tone appearance in the refinishing.

Once the EPR had done its job, the chemical stripper was applied. Using three ladders and two planks, I was able to traverse the width of the room. Remaining paint chips were scraped off, however, before putting on the stripper. Molding, joints, etc., were cleaned out carefully with wire brushes. A second stripper application was brushed all over the two beams I worked on at one time, and the residue wire-brushed off, carefully, with the grain. What remained was wiped off with a pad of number 2 steel wool. The third application of stripper was washed off with a wet wire brush and warm water, wet number 2 steel wool, and a wet Turkish towel. Then it was dried with a clean towel.

The fireplace was an unusual stripping job. Oh, yes, brick, tile, and metal are all subject to the power of chemical strippers. This particular fireplace had been covered with the same white paint as the woodwork. The paint was particularly difficult to remove from the mortar. Heavy wire-brushing was necessary to remove all of the paint. (The owners had the fireplace tile *repainted* afterward because they didn't like the blue tile. Actually, the tile covers the original Frank Lloyd Wright Roman brick fireplace. Someday someone will restore it!)

Roughly two thirds of the time to restore the Chauncey Williams House living woodwork involved stripping off the old finish. The remaining time was devoted to making it look pretty once again: refinishing, the topic of Chapter Seven.

Chapter Six

Stripping and Refinishing Trim and Siding

Your house may need some or all of the paint or stain removed from its exterior trim, siding, or both. This is a task motivated by both aesthetic and functional factors: aesthetic, because peeling paint looks awful; functional, because an unstable paint base will not hold successive coats of paint.

You know that old finish removal is in order mostly by looking over the trim and siding for signs of unstability and *not* by trying to figure out how many coats of paint are presently on your house. Flat trim and siding *can* hold countless coats of finish. After all, fifteen coats is only about ⅛-inch thick, certainly nothing to worry about.

Instead, it is signs of instability and ugliness you should be looking for. Physical signs denoting instability are peeling, buckling, splitting, "alligatoring," flaking, chipping, blistering, and looseness. Aesthetic signs are blurring of line on decorative molding, hiding of detail on figurative molding, and a "thick" look on such exterior pieces that are in close line of visual inspection such as front doors.

Some house exteriors can be restored, some cannot. The old Daubner homestead in northern Door County, WI, has been allowed to deteriorate too far to correct. Photo by Edwin Johnson

Another old Door County, WI, farmhouse whose exterior has been allowed to deteriorate to a point beyond restoration. Photo by Edwin Johnson

You know your siding and trim need stripping when you've got paint falling off. As Gregg Maholic says, "What are you going to do?" Photo by Jim Kuba

When the asbestos shingles were removed from this late Victorian home in Oak Park, IL, the owners found shingles, vertical boards, and siding in good condition. Only paint must be stripped. A scaffold tower is in place. Photo by Jim Kuba

THE WASHING ALTERNATIVE TO STRIPPING

As with interior trim and woodwork there may be the washing alternative to solving your exterior finish problem. Where there are few signs that the finish is unstable but the finish looks like heck, perhaps just a good scrubbing will do the trick. You know, people have been washing house exteriors in certain parts of Europe for centuries. Somehow, it just hasn't caught on in America. Perhaps someday it will.

To clean your house trim, mix a strong solution of Soilax and scrub your window and door frames, fasciae, and other areas. Then rinse off with a sponge. For your siding try using a brush on a pole to lengthen your reach. Start at ground level and work *up* to the roofline. Here, rinsing can be achieved by hosing down the wash water and wiping with a damp—and large—sponge.

If fortune has shined upon you, washing may be all your exterior requires. The next best situation, however, is one in which you can now proceed to paint a finish coat over the clean and dry surface. Finally, it is just possible that much of the exterior finish is in good condition, as revealed by the cleaning, and that only some of it is unstable and needs to be stripped.

Then, there is always the possibility that much or all of either the trim, the siding, or both needs to be removed. This being the case, you might well ask yourself, is it then worth stripping? Is it, indeed, worth it?

IS IT WORTH IT?

To help answer this question, I talked with several Oak Park, Illinois, residents who are in the process of restoring their house exteriors. For Cindy and Gregg Maholic there was no other alternative than to strip.

"When you've got paint falling off, what are you going to do?" Greg asked me. "Some of our neighbors had guys come out and put more paint over their peeling walls and trim after a little scraping, and charging them three thousand dollars for the job. In two or three years it was falling off again." For the Maholics it was clearly worth it.

Another do-it-yourselfer, Jim Shimon, when asked if his experience was a bad one, said yes. "Would I like to be through with it now?" he asked (he's 60 percent through). "Yes. Do I ever want to do it again? No. Do I have any advice for someone contemplating stripping the finish off their house? Yes. Don't!"

After Jim calmed down a little he confessed that he had achieved a great deal of personal satisfaction from restoring over half the exterior of his lovely, late Victorian, Greek Revival house. And considering the 1975 job cost estimate of $13,000, his is an economic accomplishment as well as a personal one.

Finally, there is my experience. I spent nearly forty hours stripping the paint from a trim called the belt line on the Cauncey Williams House, the landmark house designed and supervised by Frank Lloyd Wright in 1895. Previous coats of paint were so thick and so unstable that they had actually cracked open, making stripping the sole surface treatment alternative. The cost of replacing this eighteen-inch curved molding that separates the brick and stone base wall from the stucco upper wall and goes around this very large building is almost beyond calculation, since custom millwork would be required to produce it.

Despite these success stories, the question posed is still a valid one, and perhaps one that only you can answer. Today, many owners of frame houses are covering wood siding with aluminum; in the past asbestos and other types of shingles were nailed over siding. Some were covered with brick or stone. Distressed trim, some of it integral to the authenticity of the house as a widow's walk, was simply removed, never to be replaced. It would appear that one has many alternative solutions.

It seems to me that sensitive restoration as well as restoration that enhances the value of one's home calls for maintaining the wooden siding and trim as long as is humanly possible. As an example, one should note the eighteenth-century clapboard homes in New England that are still in excellent condition. To achieve this, providing a stable base for the next coat of paint is quite necessary.

The Chauncey Williams House, River Forest, IL. Designed and personally supervised by Frank Lloyd Wright in 1895, it had undergone extensive remodeling in former years, to be substantially restored today. The author stripped paint off the belt line around this landmark house. Photo by Edwin Johnson

Chauncey Williams House entrance trim, an arch so typically Wright. The author is stripping with an electric paint remover and a hooked scraper. The curved trim makes a putty knife rather useless.

Up, up we go, stripping eighty-five years of paint off the trim at Wright's Chauncey Williams House. Photos by Pamela J. Johnson

How do you know when your trim needs stripping? When it looks like this: seven coats of thick paint weathered from eighty-five years of Mother Nature. Photo by Edwin Johnson

Here's that same section of the belt line. The reader can count the paint layers. Photo by Edwin Johnson

A stripped section of belt line. Two ladders and a plank sufficed for "scaffolding" here. Photo by Edwin Johnson.

The belt line stripped of seven layers of paint. The color that remains was well covered with a primer and the finish coat of paint later. Photo by Edwin Johnson

PARTIAL STRIPPING

There is the possibility that only some or certainly less than all the exterior needs finish removal. You needn't feel bad about that, for though you may now be fired with ambition and really want to get *all* of the old finish off, those who have done just that have told me it wasn't *that* great an adventure. Exterior stripping, simply put, can be hard, tedious, time consuming work.

What you should do is to carefully examine your trim and siding to determine just *where* the old finish is a problem. Sometimes it is areas exposed to the sun and other times those the sun rarely contacts. Perhaps it is just the ornamental detail on the front gable or porch balustrades or brackets or the front entry that need old finish stripping.

I think it is sound advice to state that you should only concern yourself with surface problem areas. Because when you consider the age of your home and the environments to which its exterior is exposed, it is highly unlikely that you will ever be able to correct deficiencies "once and for all time." So take restoration one trip at a time, and when

your next painting is due, strip bad finish once again.

Perhaps you are thinking that Dr. Ed is becoming philosophical. Yes, I guess I am. Recently I read that the Cologne (Germany) cathedral, begun in the thirteenth century, has a crew of sixty full-time stonemasons who are constantly at work repairing and rebuilding what time has injured and destroyed. And that's stone! Granted your home may be only one century old instead of eight, the lesson to be learned is that home maintenance is a continuing task. So make it easy on yourself and your spouse and do mostly what you deem necessary for now and for the short-run future.

Professional house painters agree that it is perfectly all right to strip finish from a selected surface problem area, then sand it, prime it, and cover it with your cover paint. Don't fudge, though. It's important that you make certain your finish coat is going over a sound base. Therefore, if you have a generally overall bad exterior it means you'll have to strip all of it right down to the bare wood.

113

SOME GENERAL QUESTIONS (AND ANSWERS)

Q. *When is the right time to strip?*
A. The right time to strip exterior trim and/or siding is *before* you put any finish coat on a given side of the building. A possible exception is the stucco exterior, for any stucco repair and subsequent surface treatment may damage the trim restoration job. As to the right season, strip wood at a time of year when the weather allows you to cover the bare wood quickly. It should not be allowed to sit exposed to the elements.

Q. *Should exterior architectural pieces be stripped in place or removed for stripping?*
A. Because of the nature of most such pieces, stripping must take place while the piece is in place. There are some exceptions: shutters, fretwork and other rather easily removable and highly decorative-detailed pieces, and doors. Removing

doors is debatable, though. On their hinges they are held securely, vertical stripping allows the residue to fall free, doors in place keep the wind and the rain out, security is enhanced, and a manageable task for one person is achieved. After all, some exterior doors are extremely heavy and impossible for one person to move while off their hinges.

Q. *If any architectural pieces are removed, can they be sent to a commercial stripping place for stripping?*
A. Yes. Several considerations, however, are in order: make certain the place has a good reputation, do this only when there is simply too much paint or too much detail for you to cope with, and think about the time you will spend in piece removal, transportation, and putting it back.

EXTERIOR STRIPPING TIPS

In addition to the stripping tips in the previous chapter, there are several general considerations that should assist you in the removal of old exterior finish.

TIP NUMBER 1. Start on the ground. Begin removing old finish with both your feet on the ground, if possible. In this manner you will learn how best to handle your tools and do this particular job without the additional concern of ladders, scaffolding, and height.

TIP NUMBER 2. Be prepared for fire. Since most exterior finish stripping entails heat, the possibility of fire is always present. Keep either a

large extinguisher close at hand or else your garden hose ready to operate at a moment's notice.

TIP NUMBER 3. Work safely. A ladder as the sole means of reaching your work area is the *least* safe method. Two ladders and ladder jacks supporting a plank is better. Best is scaffolding. Always tie ladders and scaffolding to the building; they have a tendency to fall.

TIP NUMBER 4. Prepare well for refinishing. People I have talked to—amateurs and professionals alike—agree that preparation is from 75 to 90 percent of the job. So view stripping as a *means* and not the end.

KINDS OF EXTERIOR FINISH MATERIALS

Exterior finish materials consist of nothing at all in the case of rural primitives and handymen's specials to stain, varnish, shellac, and paint. And

there are a variety of paints; the most recent is latex, the most difficult to remove is milk paint, and the most dangerous is lead.

No Finish

In rural America there are houses from which the original paint, if indeed there was any, has long ago vanished. Such a house is great for two reasons: (1) there is nothing to remove, and (2) you are free to finish such a place as "natural." Their disadvantage is that Mother Nature had undoubtedly wrought some destruction, and repair or replacement may well be necessary.

The James Shimon family residence, Oak Park, IL. Two sides have been stripped, primed, and painted. Jim will have saved himself at least $13,000 (1975 estimate) by stripping and painting his lovely, late Victorian Greek Revival house himself. Photo by Jim Kuba

Stain

All or part of many homes has been treated with exterior stain. In contrast with interior stain, exterior stain contains a pigment to help it resist the elements. Therefore, it tends to have the same characteristics as paint; that is, there is a material buildup with successive coverings with subsequent chipping or flaking.

In common with interior stain, however, is its high absorption factor. This may well make complete color removal impossible, whereas surface material has been scraped away. Stain can be removed satisfactorily by draw-scraping—pulling a hooked scraper over the surface without applying heat. Draw-scraping is particularly useful when removing damaged stain finish from siding shingles.

Varnish and Shellac

Varnish and shellac are rarely used for exteriors, except for doors and door frames, so they will be discussed together. In more recent times, however, some gables and garage doors have been finished with stain, with shellac as the sealer and varnish as the finish coat. Some very old and relatively untouched (by painters) exterior doors may still have shellac on them, particularly if they are located in protected places, like a covered balcony.

The removal of old varnish, shellac, and the stain undercoat is best accomplished with a chemical paint and varnish remover, as described in the previous chapter. Refinishing a gable with natural varnish, after it has been stripped, is debatable in my opinion. An improvement is to use urethane in place of natural varnish. Still better, put two coats of exterior stain on the stripped wood, period. Though a stained and varnished gable on a fifties-style ranch house is being faithful to the original, in most climates it is asking for a maintenance problem. Exterior stain, on the other hand, is made to withstand the elements.

The southeast corner of the Shimon House showing the contrasting stripped and repainted south side and the paint-peeling east side. Photo by Jim Kuba

Paint

Paint is by far the most common exterior trim and siding cover, and for a very good reason. It has a superior ability to withstand the environment. But it is not all good. On the debit side are material buildup, cracking, chipping, flaking, chalking, buckling, blistering, peeling, and alligatoring. Moisture can get under paint and attack the wood behind it, let alone be in the wood when it is first painted. Sun fades paint colors and dries out paint. Hail can chip it and make noticeable dents in it; sandstorms can sandblast painted surfaces. And, of course, paint can melt, singe, and burn.

What's a person to do? Is there no perfect cover? No, there is none. Though paint is probably the best, figure on painting your house again in about seven years. And somewhere down the pike someone else is going to have to strip off another century or so of finish, despite your heroic efforts!

THE STRIPPING PROCESS

Let us assume that you have decided that some exterior trim or siding stripping—perhaps all of it—*is* worth an investment of from several months to several years of your time. How should you proceed with the task? In this section I will tell you.

The format is to discuss the task in its four principal parts: tools, materials, preparation, and techniques. The first topic, tools, can be further divided into hand and support.

Hand Tools

Many of the hand tools used in exterior paint removal have already been discussed, so some of this is review. Here they are grouped as heating, scraping, and sanding tools.

HEATING TOOLS. Heating tools soften the paint and heavy coats of stain so that they can be scraped from the wood surface. The three basic heating tools are the propane torch, the electric paint remover, and the heat gun.

The electric paint remover (EPR) is a shielded electric heating grid measuring about 4 × 6 inches attached to a handle. An extension cord connects it to a 115-volt electric outlet. It is important to have an extension cord both long enough to do the job and heavy enough to carry the proper current. For maximum efficiency connect the cord to a house circuit on which no other device is drawing electricity. You know it's working at top level when the electric grids are glowing bright red.

The EPR is cited by both pros and amateurs doing trim and siding paint removal as the best heating tool in both speed and safety. Considering the number of fires that have been started and the buildings burned to the ground during the paint-stripping process, one cannot stress safety too much.

The propane torch that you can buy in the hardware store comes equipped with a nozzle for paint burning. Though some paint professionals use tank propane torches, most use the small hand-held tool. Its advantage is speed; some say it is 50 percent faster than the electric paint remover but the EPR is best because of the combined speed and safety benefits. Most agree, however, that its disadvantages—scorching and fire starting—make it unsatisfactory for siding and attached trim paint removal.

No so for the architectural piece you can remove, however. Take off a shutter and place it on sawhorses in your yard away from house and garage, and the torch will work very well, they report. I say "they" because I've never used one. My work outside to date has been on landmark houses where even scorching is to be avoided. Therefore, I use only the good old EPR.

To return to the fire hazard for a moment. You see, the torch sends a terrific blast of heat up between sometimes very loose clapboard. In addition to the heat blast, hot cinderlike paint residue is also blown up between the siding and between trim and siding. And in older homes where there *is* insulation it is often a dry paperlike material; painters have told me of old homes with what looks like shredded newspaper serving as insulation. Both these forms of insulation either burn on contact or smolder and then burn. So it is simply not worth the risk the torch creates to those I've talked with, and that's good enough for me. How about you?

The third device is a relative newcomer. It is the electric heat gun. As I reported earlier, it looks and acts very much like a high-powered electric hair dryer, but of course, it is much hotter so that it can melt paint. The melted or softened paint is then scraped away. This tool's advantage is that because it is not as hot as either the torch or the EPR, the danger of lead fumes from lead paint is less, as is the fire hazard.

Those who have used the torch, the EPR, and the heat gun tell me that the heat gun is not only slower but also much heavier—too heavy for eight hours on the scaffold. It's slow because it heats a much smaller area than the EPR. All things considered, I recommend the EPR.

SCRAPING TOOLS. Scraping tools come in two styles, if you will. There are the pushing tools, which are all a variation of the putty knife, and the pulling tools. Both seem to have their place, so you should plan on purchasing both kinds. My preferences are a three-inch-wide, wood-handled, heavy, and very rigid putty-knife-style scraper for pushing and hooked with "("-shaped blades for pulling. The former tool I never sharpen, preferring its rather square-cut scraping edge; and for the hooked scraper I keep a hand grinder on the job site for frequent sharpening.

One veteran amateur paint remover felt that a triangular-shaped two-inch blade connected at a right angle to a comfortable handle is the best paint-scraping tool known to mankind. He is unique; most prefer tools similar to what I recommend. Preference has a lot to do with what you have learned to use *well*, I suspect.

Finally, there are custom-made scrapers. At times it is to your advantage to make your own tools from good scraping quality steel to do special paint removal jobs. For example, portico columns and pilasters often feature fluted vertical cuts. Getting six coats of paint out of these buggers with a straight-edged putty knife or wood chisel will gouge the column plus take an inordinate amount of time. Better technology can solve this problem. On your grinding wheel cut a rigid putty knife

blade or old butcher knife blade to fit the configuration of the flute. Cornices or any trim configuration other than straight can be stripped much more efficiently with a custom-made scraper.

SANDING TOOLS. Sandpaper is a material and will be discussed later. Here, let's consider the belt sander, the disc sander, and the grinder-router.

Though I will not recommend electric sanders, either belt or disc, for most interior woodwork refinishing, I readily recognize their efficacy in exterior trim and siding restoration. For though the danger to interior trim is increased by using these machines, it is diminished for outside trim simply because one does not have to be as careful outside. Moreover, outside there is much more space both to cover and in which to maneuver.

In general, the belt sander is recommended over the disc, as there is less chance of damage to wood surfaces with it. Thus, when sanding 2¾-inch exposed siding on a thirty-foot-high plank suspended from ladder jacks, it is possible to miscalculate and gouge with a disc sander. Why, just today I noticed disc-sanding gouges on the siding of the 120-year-old house in our neighborhood—a combination of "handymen" and a dangerous tool.

A third tool new to me is a sort of grinder-router that uses sharp blades to remove what the EPR and scraper did not. The couple who reported it showed me photographs of the end result. There, exposed, was the raw pine siding, so raw you could almost smell the fresh pine!

It should be stated here, although I will get ahead of my story, that any sanding work at all is debatable activity. One house stripper stated that he managed to get down to bare wood with his EPR, that it was smooth, and that it required no further treatment. My experience is that there is some residue left after heating and scraping, especially where the old finish was very thin. That, plus the roughing up of the wood surface that this process can cause, leads me to conclude that *some* sanding is probably necessary. For flat surfaces a belt sander is recommended; where it is not, hand sanding is called for.

Some final words on all tools: Buy and use the widest, largest, and sharpest tools available. Don't be like some who buy too few tools, too small tools, and tools that are too dull. This advice applies to the EPR as well. Get two, because on the average siding job you'll use at least that many. Then you're prepared for a burnout which often occurs the day the paint store is closed or you're thirty feet up and thirty miles from your supplier. You see, time is worth money—even *your* spare time.

Supporting Tools

Reach is a far greater problem when one goes outside to strip and refinish. Older houses with their third-story gables and turrets all perched on high foundations are a challenge. Therefore, one needs all the help one can get.

That help comes from ladders, ladders with ladder jacks and planks, and scaffolding and planks. As noted earlier, a single ladder limits one's reach and one's safety. Thus, its usage is, or should be, limited also.

Extension ladders holding ladder jacks—L-shaped steel bars that fit on ladder rungs to hold planks—are my second choice. They are a kind of compromise position between a single ladder and scaffolding. They work well for moderate stripping, say, window trim, fascia boards only a story high, and fretwork between porch columns. Their advantages are lower cost, greater mobility, and simplicity in setup, take down, and storage. Their disadvantage is that for high places you have little to hang on to. In addition, they are useless for wide eaves that extend way out beyond house walls, and they provide little on which to hang tools, extension cords, and water hoses (in case of fire, remember?).

If you are planning to undertake a siding stripping job, the scaffold is *most* highly recommended. People I've talked with said they at first thought they could do it without the scaffold, only to discover later that they couldn't. Their jobs would have taken much less time if they had started out on a scaffold.

Scaffold can, of course, be rented—planks and all. Their advantages are safety, tool-hanging convenience, and added reach. For example, you can put casters on a 5 × 5-foot scaffold tower and place it on plywood sheets on the ground. The plywood provides both a level place and mobility. Then place eight-foot-long 2 × 12 planks on the horizontal scaffold supports. Now without bending or standing on your toes you can reach a vertical

area of about four feet and a horizontal one of about eight feet, or a total area of thirty to thirty-five square feet, without moving either planks or tower. That's reach, isn't it?

For efficient use of the scaffold tower move your planks up four feet when the bottom thirty square feet are stripped and strip the next higher thirty or so square feet. Keep one plank about waist high in back of you to give you protection from falling and on which to put tools. If you keep tools in a container like a pail with a handle, they are more portable, they won't fall to the ground, and they are in a position for easy grabbing.

Of course, you can work with two scaffold towers and string longer planks between the pair. That's really great reach. But remember, safety requires that the towers be tied to the building.

Shimon's scaffold tower has a plank, plank hangers, and ladder extension necessitated by the lack of room in his neighbor's yard. Photo by Jim Kuba

Materials

In the materials category are chemical stripper, brushes, sandpaper, rags, tack cloths, primers, thinners, paints, and stains. Chemical stripper, as noted in the previous chapter, should be a water-soluble variety. It is used for stained and varnished doors and door trims and is therefore limited in exterior stripping.

It is possible that you will need a few long-handled wire brushes to clean paint out of decorative trim, molding, and panels as well as to clean your EPR. The use of scraping tools for most decorative trim is awkward and inefficient, hence the recommended wire brush. I heat an area and then brush out the soft paint. Because this process clogs the brush's steel bristles, I work with a number of brushes and let the clogged brush cool while I use a clean one. Later, when all the brushes are full of paint residue, I clean out the cooled and brittle paint particles by brushing over a hooked scraper.

Sandpaper of all grades can be used on the job. The general rule is to begin sanding with the coarsest grade sandpaper you can use, then to continue sanding until you use the finest. For example, on an exterior pine molding just stripped of seven layers of gummy paint, begin sanding with number 36 or 50 grade production sandpaper, then use number 80 and 120 and finish with 180, not spending *too* much time with any single grade.

Steel wool is another smoothing material. Again, start with a coarse grade, say, number 2 or 3, and finish with grade 00. Steel wool is more flexible for detail and curved surfaces than is sandpaper. On the other hand, it is also dirtier.

Dirt leads us to rags, which are certainly necessary for both dusting and cleaning. If old T-shirts are not available, you should be able to buy a five-pound box of clean rag material from your paint store for about a dollar a pound (1980 price). And if you don't get the rags too filthy, you can recycle them via your washer.

FINISHING MATERIALS. Even if you do not strip down to the bare-bare wood, you will certainly have exposed some raw or near-raw wood in the stripping process. Therefore, the wood will have to be primed. The correct material is oil-base primer, because it puts oil back into the

Safety first includes proper footing for your scaffold. Here, Jim has properly leveled his tower. Note the rope holding the tower to a ground stake. Photo by Jim Kuba

wood. Latex primer, on the other hand, puts water into the wood. This should be avoided, as water is generally considered to be an enemy of wood.

The finish paint should, in my opinion, be oil based as well. This recommendation is based not only on my personal opinion but on that of exterior house restorers, professional painters, and a leading paint company consultant I have talked with. Though oil-based paint requires more work and more skill for correct application than latex, it is far superior in coverage and protection.

For color accent on decorative trim, moldings, and other exterior details you can use latex paint. I say this not to placate any latex adherents reading this, but as good advice from a friend. Decorative trim, as that frequently found on late Victorian houses, is difficult enough to cover, so why should you make it still harder by using oil-based paint? Both application and cleanup are made easier with latex.

Preparation

Preparation, as we have already learned, can take from 75 to 90 percent of your efforts. And most of your efforts will be in removing unstable paint and stain base. Nonetheless, before we get into the actual stripping, there are preparations we can make. Perhaps the first is to plan the job.

PLAN YOUR JOB. Decide what you're going to do, what you'll need, when you're going to do it, and how you will proceed. First, note what *has* to be stripped. Perhaps all you will have to do is take a single ladder around to a few places, strip the peeling paint, and prime it.

On the other hand, paint may be falling from your home like leaves from the trees in the fall. In this case a more detailed plan is necessary. I believe that you should start in the most accessible and easiest possible place. Then, if and when the going gets rough you are in good condition; you have both a lot of know-how and a lot of momentum to carry the task through to completion.

Decide what you're going to need. Make a list of tools and materials. Call several scaffold rental firms for prices, availability, and delivery. Try to get a good deal on supplies; buy sandpaper by the sleeve and paint by the five-gallon container.

Decide when you're going to do the job. At this writing it is the first week in January, there's over a foot of snow on the ground here on the shore of Lake Michigan, and the temperature hasn't gone over zero for three days. It is hardly the time to strip paint outside. And if you live in Houston, you will want to avoid this job in the middle of summer, because the job is hot enough without Mother Nature's assistance.

Set up some sort of a work schedule and try to stay with it. As with interior woodwork stripping, *fewer* blocks of *longer* work periods are preferable to the opposite because of the time involved in getting in the mood, changing clothes, setting up, getting out the tools, getting the garden hose in place, and climbing the scaffold. Then afterward there is the cleanup. If you have pets and/or children, don't leave paint chips lie around, for they may contain lead. And, finally, *you* have to clean yourself.

Those members of the vast army of strippers I've talked with tell me they spend about thirty hours a week on their projects in late spring, summer, and fall. It has taken one person three years to strip and refinish 60 percent of his 2,800-square-foot three-story house working on this schedule. A couple also working thirty hours a week in good weather has stripped and refinished about 85 percent of their three-story 3,200-square-foot Queen Anne over a four-year period. The thirty-hour week breaks down into sixteen to twenty hours per weekend and five-hour evenings twice a week.

It's a good idea to plan on completely finishing one side of your house at a time, trim and all. That is, do it all when your scaffold is there. When stripping is completed, prime and paint. Not only is heavy equipment movement facilitated but you will get a most welcome break from paint stripping. There is the added advantage of seeing the end result; that may serve as a much-needed incentive to continue.

MISCELLANEOUS PLANNING. Are there any trees in your way? Perhaps they best be trimmed. Now. Or cut down. Now. The same goes for trellises, vines, and shrubs.

Does your house restoration consist of removing add-ons that destroy its aesthetics and authenticity? It seems best to pull them off now so you can get at the surfaces behind them.

Conversely, are you planning to put back on a porch that was removed in 1940 in an attempt to make a colonial out of your Queen Anne? Why not do that first? Then, any carpenter's damage can be corrected when you refinish.

Stripping Techniques

Your goal in the stripping process is not to strip, but to strip so that the new exterior finish coat will go on over a stable base, and look just great. So what you're really doing is preparing your trim, siding, or both so it will make a terrific reception for the new coat.

HEAT AND SCRAPE. Stripping exterior paint and heavy stain can be reduced to a rather simple formula: heat and scrape. One can heat and scrape two ways: heat the surface and remove the EPR and then scrape, or else heat the surface and move the EPR in a straight line to the adjacent spot while scraping the spot just heated.

Heating a spot and completely removing the EPR while scraping is the method most mentioned to me in my research. It certainly gives one more flexibility in scraping and does not require as much muscle as the other technique. To me, however, it is awkward and slow.

My procedure is to follow the EPR with a three-inch rigid flat paint scraper in a pushing manner. On siding the right and left hand unison movement goes from right to left, and on vertical trim the movement could be either up or down. Thus, for me the EPR is always ahead of my scraping, heating up the *next* spot to be scraped. This not only is faster but keeps the scraper from getting gummed up with old finish so fast.

Of course, the scraper eventually does collect melted paint and loses its effectiveness. As I work

Up two and a half stories, Jim Shimon is starting to strip the north wall of his house. The job, which took him three years to complete, gave him a lot of personal satisfaction. But his advice, after stripping the six columns on this house, is "Don't do it." The author doesn't take him seriously. Photo by Jim Kuba

Jim Shimon is starting at the top of his Greek Revival's north wall. The process he uses is "heat and scrape." Jim recommends an electric paint remover to soften old paint and a triangular (three sharp edges) scraper, fastened at a right angle to a large comfortable handle. Photo by Jim Kuba

with a half dozen scrapers, when one gets gummed up, I put it down and use another. When all six are out of commission, I stop and clean them off, using one scraper to clean the others. By this time the paint has dried and cooled and become quite brittle. It is generally easy to clean off.

After you've scraped a given "unit," like the trim around one window, there may still be some residue left. Just as with the old finish on your tools, this residue has become brittle. You can draw-scrape this with a hooked scraper and *no* heat. That should really clean the surface and not require any chemical stripping.

Curved molding is often a problem for most people. For me, however, it is not, because I use my wood sculpture gouges. They are all one-inch blades and have different-diameter curves, one of which is bound to fit the molding's configuration. The gouges, however, cannot be used with the sharp cutting edge necessary for sculpture work. I change the beveled edge to a right-angle one on the grinding wheel. Artists' supply stores have such gouges. Of course, you can customize any paint scraper to fit the curve of molding.

To remove paint from detailed, decorative molding, simply change the "heat and scrape" formula to heat and brush. This may not be as effective because of the melted paint sticking in the detail, so if making the design crystal clear is crucial, you will have to get the rest of the paint out with a chemical paint and varnish remover.

It should be obvious that the precautions one has to exercise in using the EPR on interior woodwork are unnecessary on the exterior, particularly for trim well out of the normal line of vision. Here, some gouging and even scorching is permissible. But again, watch out for fire.

And be careful about splinters. You can create some mighty large and long splinters in this heat-and-scrape process. Splinters are especially fond of entering one's fingers at the end and lodging under one's fingernails, a particularly painful process. Wearing work gloves will afford some protection, but if one attacks you, be certain you pull all of it out. Once part of a splinter left in my right middle finger traveled half an inch toward the palm, even turned direction, and came out six months later at the finger's first joint.

TEN STRIPPING PROBLEM AREAS. Let's look at the stripping process in more detail by examining ten problem areas. Although these will probably not exhaust the problems you are likely to encounter, you should be able to deal creatively with most encounters.

But first, here are some general rules:

- Heat *while* scraping.
- Your EPR should be a brightly glowing red-hot tool.
- Use plenty of physical support.
- Get some emotional support, too.
- Don't be too fussy.
- Use the largest tools possible; avoid the "toothpick approach."

1. Window sashes. They are a problem because they contain glass and putty. It is very easy to break glass with heat, especially when it is cold. So never use a torch on window sashes, and be darn careful with your EPR.

Putty cannot be successfully stripped. Chemical paint solvents have a tendency to also dissolve the putty, and torch and EPR heat is of no avail, since putty is next to glass. Generally, solid putty lying snug up against both glass and wood can be painted over. If your putty is neither of the above, I suggest that you remove it—carefully so as not to crack the glass. To do this, try renting an old putty softener from your paint store. Then replace it with new putty, caulking, or glazing material.

2. Balusters are a problem because there are usually so many of them and because former painters in order to really cover them laid a lot of paint on them. They are often so close together that it is difficult to get at them with the EPR; their turned and/or carved configuration is of no assistance to effective paint removal, either.

I would be half tempted to remove them and send them out to a dependable commercial stripper. Another solution is to remove a section of them and burn off the old paint with a propane torch while the section is resting on sawhorses. The cindered residue can then be cleaned off with a wire brush and steel wool.

3. Columns. Though columns are round, one can efficiently scrape paint from them with a straightedge. You can start out scraping horizontally and finish with a vertical scraping for more smoothness. Just be careful; avoid muscle that, combined with a sharp edge, can make curved surfaces flat.

Columns with flutes require a specially shaped scraping surface. It will certainly pay to make several custom scrapers. And, as columns are made of a number of pieces of wood glued together, avoid too much heat when removing paint from them. A painter friend of mine caused two large columns to separate when he overzealously used his propane torch for stripping off years of old finish. Fortunately, his customer was very understanding, forgave him, and bought two new columns.

4. Pediments are classified as a problem more because of their location than because of their configuration, although that, too, makes stripping them difficult. Pediments have a habit of being located on the highest point of the turret roof, the gable, or the roof itself. When pediments hang, they are way out on the corners of eaves or else under the peak of the highest gables.

This makes pediments (do you call them finials?) nominees for a one-hand-stripping operation; with your other hand you hang on, right? Right. I would certainly consider stripping a pediment with the chemical solvent. Slosh it on the piece with a brush and keep soaking it until bubbles appear on the surface. Then, with your long-handled wire brush—keep hanging on—reach out and give it a good scrubbing. Repeat until most of the old finish is gone.

5. Fretwork, too, was placed in relatively inaccessible spots at times. It may be a good idea to take it down, because you can strip it more easily off the building *and* because it may need repair. After all, it is probably the most delicate part of your exterior trim and it is a hundred years old. Fortunate enough is the fretwork that has survived, let alone remained in perfect health. Saw through the nails holding it in place rather than risk injury from your crowbar.

6. Dentils. Strip the interior space and sides between the dentils with your EPR first, and then strip the end that's exposed. The reason for doing it this way is that you will burn the stripped, exposed end when you apply enough heat to soften the paint on between the dentils. You're fortunate if your house does not have any dentils; they're pretty but they're a pain.

7. Corners. There are all kinds of corners and you will probably encounter each and every one of them in your stripping job. Paint and stain have a tendency to build up more in corners, because that's generally the spot the painter hits first with his brush full of paint or stain. From there he brushes out. That's good painting technique, though it makes paint removal more difficult.

As you are approaching a corner, say, where the edge of a window frame meets the siding, move ahead with your EPR and dig the paint out of that spot, then return and continue heating and scraping into the corner. Doing it this way will help you avoid scorching uncovered wood.

8. Eaves. Eaves are a problem because they are so high, they frequently extend way beyond your house's walls, and you have to work over your head. In addition, because eaves are generally not too exposed to the elements, the paint has stuck to them and often it's good and thick.

Here it's especially important to work at a really good height *for you*. You may find that kneeling or even sitting is more comfortable. If it is, arrange your scaffold and planks so you can kneel or sit. Even lying down may work better. Never forget, that's the position in which Michelangelo painted the ceiling of the Sistine Chapel!

9. Doors pose a problem in that they have probably been painted more often than any other exterior architectural piece. And for good reason. They are also exposed to more physical abuse, making them a candidate for repair.

Generally, it's advisable to repair a door before you strip it. Even though you may not really want to tackle a door repair right at this point, get a price on a new front door from your local lumberyard. You will probably not only want to repair it but strip it, refinish it, and use it in the future with more care and respect.

Because a door, especially your front door, is highly visible, you may well want to strip it with much greater care than, say, the fascia boards. If that's the case, then I recommend that you very, very carefully remove most of the paint with your EPR, then use a chemical stripper à la your interior woodwork.

10. Shutters, especially movable ones, not only are a lot of work to strip but frequently need repair, as they are highly susceptible to rot. It will surprise you when you begin to remove your shutters to find some literally fall apart in your hands. If the shutters were not part of the original design, you may want to just leave them off. Otherwise, repair or replacement is necessary.

Stripping old finish off them is said to be a tedious process. It can be speeded up by using the propane torch, but please do it on wooden horses and not on your house.

Sandblasting Wood Surfaces

A final word on paint removal concerns a caution on sandblasting. There's only one word for it: don't. A sandblasted wood surface is porous and the hard heartwood grain is exposed since the softer grain has been blasted away. So the result is a 3-D look at a pitted, porous surface. This is clearly unsuitable for refinishing. Both the pros and the amateurs warn against letting someone talk you into sandblasting your old house surface, be it wood or even stone. That's always been good enough advice for me!

THE REFINISHING PROCESS

This is it! This is the goal toward which you've been working so diligently. Refinishing is the payoff. It can be divided into three steps: sanding, priming, and finishing. First, let's look at sanding.

Sanding

Admittedly, exterior trim and siding do not need to be as smooth and former-finish-free as interior woodwork does. In addition, it will be painted once again, so neither clear grain nor absolute smoothness is necessary. So from a functional point of view exterior trim sanding can be kept to a minimum. Let your own personal taste together with your time objectives govern the extent to which you will sand.

I personally feel that intelligent use of production sandpaper makes the belt and disc sanders unnecessary for most jobs. For wide areas fold an 8½ × 11-inch sheet into quarters; for narrow areas fold a smaller piece into either quarters or halves. Start with the coarsest grade, number 36 or 50, and using a window sash as an example, make ten passes at it. Then use number 80 for seven or eight strokes, number 120 for five strokes, and finish with three strokes with number 180 grade paper.

You see, the number 50 and 80 are doing the bulk of the material removal. The remaining grades are just smoothing the grain. Sanding this way is not a big deal and does not require a lot of strength.

Several sanding tips are in order. Use the paper until the pores look clogged; then switch to a clean sheet, because the paper you're working with has worn out. Oh, some say you can clean out clogged pores, but that takes time and anyway the paper is probably worn. To cut the cost of sanding, buy production sandpaper by the "sleeve"—one hundred sheets in finer grades and fifty in the coarser. Wear work gloves to protect you from both wood splinters and raw fingertips. And wear a paper sanding mask to protect your respiratory system.

After sanding, dust off all surfaces with a clean, dry cloth. Brush out corners with a clean old paintbrush, and vacuum dust and paint particles from sills and other areas the brush can't reach. For a really neat job, wipe all surfaces to be primed with a tack cloth just before priming.

Priming

The purpose of the primer, used before applying paint, is to seal out moisture and seal in natural oils. While primers come in both oil-based solutions and latex, everyone I've talked to concurs with me and recommends oil-based primers.

Brushing on primer entails more concern for coverage than concern for brush and lap marks. So just make certain you cover everything well.

Primer paints can be tinted. It is especially important to make primer colors close to the finish paint color if the finish coat is to be a darker color. Other than tinting, it is generally recommended that you use the primer just as it comes in the can (although some professional painters thin primer a little. And if two coats of primer are necessary, they add a little enamel to the second coat to give it body.).

If you are planning on staining your trim or siding instead of painting it, don't use a primer. Instead, put on two coats of exterior stain, allowing the first one to dry before applying the second.

The Finish Coat

It's a good idea to plan the finish coat. You may want to use a traditional color; you may choose the original color determined by paint chip analysis; or you may want to go untraditional. After all, it's your house! But maybe you should get some help.

Help is often available from experts attached to a local restoration project. For example, several architects connected with the Frank Lloyd Wright Home and Studio in Oak Park have consulted with local owners of landmark homes on paint colors, among many other aspects. There are several nationally recognized paint analysts who, for a fee, will advise you.

It may well be that you have a knowledeable and dependable paint supplier who will give assistance, particularly if you appear to be a good potential customer. But whatever color or colors you choose, it's a good idea to determine in advance how much paint or stain you will need, buy more than you need all at once, and store it where it won't dry out or freeze. Why more? One can always misfigure or have an accident and spill a few gallons. Why buy it all now? That is your assurance of having exactly the same color to cover everything, *and* you may get a better price.

Before you begin brushing on the finish coat, make sure the surface is cool, dry, and smooth to the touch. If priming has raised the grain a little, sand the surface lightly with 400 grade wet and dry sandpaper used dry.

Start your painting at the top and use a *good, clean* 3½-inch-wide China bristle brush. If you are painting trim and siding, paint them at the same time; that is, take both trim and siding paint and brushes up with you—paint up to the trim, then cut in with the trim paint even if it is a different color. Wipe off any excess paint and splatter on work to be painted below.

This procedure of painting trim and siding while one is in a given place *can* cause lap marks where the siding brushing stopped and started up once again. To avoid this, first try to end siding painting at logical places—a window or door frame, a corner, a piece of ornamental trim. End the stroke with a relatively dry brush. Then, when you return to the siding, start a few inches from the end stroke and brush into it with a relatively full brush, making certain that you do not overlap too much. On very wide and unbroken expanses try not to end your brushing of each piece of clapboard in exactly the same spot. Instead, vary the ending spot to form sort of a zigzag down the building.

Plan your painting so you can complete an open section of wall before quitting time. Otherwise, there is the danger of obvious lap marks where you start out the next day.

To get the proper coverage, note not only the paint color but the light reflection of the painted surface as well. Missed spots or too lightly painted spots will show up as not reflecting as much light as properly painted places. So work with a strong sidelight if possible.

If when you start to apply the finish coat it seems to be soaking in too fast, as noted by a somewhat faded color or a poor light reflection, it is quite likely that you need another coat of primer. It is generally better to apply two coats of primer and one coat of finish in this instance than one coat of primer and two coats of finish. It's also cheaper.

As noted earlier, trim colors such as those applied to decorative moldings, fretwork, and other decorative details can be latex paint brushed on over either the primer or the finish coat. Otherwise, use an oil-based paint. Experiment with trim colors until you get exactly what you want, even if you have to waste a few quarts of the material to do so.

You know, when you consider that you have a great, great deal of time invested in the proper preparation of your trim, siding, or both, it stands to reason that you should take your time at this stage. This is especially true of trim. Don't get paint on the window glass—take your time. Don't paint the brick next to the front door frame—take your time. Your goal should be to work just like the first-class professional painters!

CONCLUDING COMMENTS

It's the night before New Year's Eve 1980 and I am sitting in the back parlor of Cindy and Greg's Queen Anne home. A fire is burning in their lovely tiled Victorian fireplace framed with oak columns and topped with a large mirror. We are drinking beer and reminiscing about their exterior restoration project begun in 1976 and now 85 percent completed.

My tape cassette is about full, so I have to bring my interview to a close. I ask, "Is there something you'd like to say to someone thinking about an exterior surface restoration job?"

Greg thinks a moment before he answers. "Yes . . . It's something the whole family has to get involved in. Especially bad is where one person is attempting to do something and the other person is always discouraging him. I think you'll never do a project like this without the support of both the couple. There's just *too* much for one person to handle."

Cindy adds, "I agree with Greg. And you can't let your peers deter you. You have to ignore people walking by, looking and commenting when you're not so sure yourself if this is what you want to do."

I agree.

Chapter Seven

Refinishing Your Woodwork:
The Fun Job

By now you've probably put a lot of hours into removing all of the old finish from your woodwork. Since that is a considerable investment in time and effort, not to mention money, you will want to follow through in good form to make your project a complete success.

That this is the critical stage in woodwork restoration is attested to by many of my customers who have bogged down at this point and called me in to finish their job. Why did they hesitate at this point? Were they burned out? That's part of the explanation, but more likely it was a lack of refinishing knowledge, and that in turn resulted in indecision regarding alternative materials and methods.

Well, in this chapter we'll be discussing the decisions to be made and the techniques to be used so that you'll be able to continue your woodwork restoration through to a successful completion. After this stage you will finally see the fruits of your labor. It can't come soon enough, you are probably saying!

REFINISHING OBJECTIVES

Now that all of that old ugly paint or alligator finish-varnish has been removed, your fun job really begins. What should your objectives in the refinishing step be? Your goals should be (1) to achieve color evenness throughout, (2) to achieve your desired color, (3) to achieve a furniturelike feel to the wood.

Ideally, the color should be about the same tone throughout the job. Of course, this is an impossibility in that wood itself has intrinsic color differences; these are natural and therefore acceptable. We do not want to add to these, however, because of poor preparation or poor refinishing.

The desired color is the color you had in mind perhaps even before you started the whole project, or anyway once you got into it. One must take into consideration the color differences of different wood species. Obviously pine will strip much lighter than walnut, and there is nothing you can do to make walnut woodwork as light as pine, but you can make pine match walnut. The first finishes applied to your wood also pose a color limitation because they always, to varying degrees, stay with the wood. So one chooses one's colors with these limitations in mind.

Finally, your front door, or any other piece of woodwork, should feel just like your furniture when you're through restoring it. This is entirely possible unless the wood is badly damaged. Proper refinishing preparation, refinishing, and follow-up should ensure such woodwork as your windowsills being just as smooth as your best table.

West bedroom casement window staining, Frank Lloyd Wright Home and Studio. Once these windows opened out, as Wright felt all casements (the only kind of window) should. When were they changed to open in? Photo by Jim Kuba

Staining casement windows at Frank Lloyd Wright's home. The color was carefully chosen by a committee to match the original when this was a late Victorian residence. Photo by Jim Kuba

CHOOSING THE COLOR

Some folks can't go beyond choosing a color because it seems an insurmountable task. To assist you here are some considerations:

- Your decorating taste
- Your present home furnishings
- The home furnishings you intend to acquire after restoration
- The style of your home
- The use that will be made of the room
- Timelessness over trendiness
- How your woodwork was originally finished

Your decorating taste should prevail; even over an interior decorator's. How do you want it to look?

Did you see a photograph in a magazine of a room that appealed to you?

If your present home furnishings are more formal, more Mediterranean, or more old English, darker tones are called for. If, on the other hand, you are modern or have a lot of primitive furniture or you collect Art Deco, you will want to use lighter shades.

Perhaps you intend to throw out all your early attic and refurnish to fit your restoration plan. Then, a room with Victorian furniture can wear a darker shade like fruitwood very well.

The style of your home should carefully influence your woodwork color choice. If yours is a Queen Anne-turned-Colonial and you are restoring it to a Queen Anne, a golden oak color is recommended. As most Prairie School homes were built when Mission Oak furniture was popular, the dark tones of that wood seem appropriate.

Consider the use that will be made of the room. Perhaps kitchens should be lighter so one can see the bugs better. Just joking.

The extremes in color seem to have a trendiness characteristic to them. So if you are looking for a more timeless color shade, more moderate or middle tones seem in order.

Finally, and especially if yours is an important house, you should duplicate the original color with which your woodwork was treated. That color is probably somewhere: the maid's room closet, the frame of a covered-up window or an original door, removed and stored in your attic.

Natural Finish vs. Stained Finish

Woodwork color can be achieved in two ways: the "natural" wood color arrived at by sealing and finishing, and the stained color achieved by staining first and then sealing and finishing the woodwork. The big question is, Should you stain the wood, or should you finish it natural?

By stain is meant an oil-base composition made in a variety of colors and in several pigment densities which will give the wood a color. Staining has the advantages of giving you the color that you want, making color coverage more even by ironing out the slight color differences between wood, say, framing a door, and it even covers some defects.

A good example of stain giving you the color you want is in mahogany refinishing. Mahogany, when stripped, shows its natural redness, a color most people don't especially like. To compensate for the red, I stain mahogany with a dark brown-green stain (Fuller O'Brien's English Oak). The result is a very pleasing dark brown with just enough red left to positively identify the woodwork as solid mahogany.

Another example is pine. This species doesn't have much color, so one is rather free to do what one wants with stain. The control over color that stain gives one here is a decorator's dream!

Besides the color-control feature of stain, you should consider that much old woodwork is shopworn and damaged from sometimes unkindly years. Patches, bruises, nicks, and even gouges all cover up much better when stained.

Finally, you may discover upon completion of the stripping job that several kinds of wood were used by the construction carpenters way back in 1878. Bless their hearts, they often used what was around. This was especially true if the original woodwork was to be painted. Even if all the *original* woodwork was made from the same species, there may have been lighter and darker pieces. Recently I inspected a fifteen-room condo built as a co-op in 1923 and loaded with Art Deco style birch woodwork. Originally painted, the dark heartwood pieces made no difference; today, stripped, they really show.

Many old homes, too, have been extensively remodeled, entailing different wood species or, at times, awkward combinations of old and new woodwork. Restored old homes are often put back together with doors and woodwork from salvage houses, sometimes even from a distant city. Here, as in the other situations cited, stain gives you control; it puts you in the driver's seat.

Natural finish, in contrast to stained, takes the natural color of the wood after stripping and after sealing. This color is really not the natural color of the wood, because the original finish on it puts into the wood either a stain color or a paint pigment, some of which is retained despite stripping, sanding, and even bleaching.

The question of natural versus staining can quite easily be resolved via the color check. The color check that determines how the woodwork looks natural is to rub some mineral spirits on the prepared wood. *That* is just about what you would get by sealing only. If you like it, all you have to do is skip this section on staining and begin reading about sealing your woodwork.

Sometimes the color check results in dramatic color changes, as with walnut. For most pine, however, sealing produces very little change. Now, there are advantages to natural finishes. They save the time spent in staining, and the grain appears clearer in that no stain pigment or color masks it. The disadvantages are that in the natural finish you lose control of color, woodwork defects like old nail hole fillings will show more than if stained, and shaded woods before sealing will remain shaded afterward.

Just to illustrate the natural process, I recall doing a woodwork job in a circa 1905 dining room

Beginning the staining of one of four ceiling grilles for the vaulted playroom ceiling in the Frank Lloyd Wright Home and Studio. Hand cut in 1981 from oak plywood from drawings of the originals, which were long ago rotted and discarded, the curved grille stain color is a mixture of three standard colors to match the color of the original room woodwork. Photo by Edwin Johnson

The finished grille. It has been stained with a penetrating oil stain, specially mixed. Sealing was with thinned polyurethane on both sides. The surfaces were sanded and the finish coat of full-strength polyurethane was brushed on. With this kind of refinishing, the new grilles will last longer than the original, which the author feels were sealed and finished with shellac. Photo by Edwin Johnson

that featured oak beams, oak trim, and a built-in oak sideboard. When it was stripped of an ugly green paint, the woodwork had a lovely color of its own, there was minimal damage, and no foreign woods had been used. After testing for the natural color, a natural finish was requested by the customer. The completed refinishing was beautiful. Much more common, however, is the need for stain to achieve color cover-up, color evenness, and color control.

REMAINING OLD FINISH

Despite your dedicated stripping, some old finish may remain, particularly in recessed areas, decorative carvings, and corners. You should try to get some of it out without expending too much effort and without being destructive to the wood. Digging and scraping are the two recommended methods.

Digging

Digging entails using one or a combination of tools and techniques. Tools include special digging tools, screwdrivers, ice picks, butcher knives, and chisels. Try any and all but keep in mind for efficient work the necessity for using as large and as sharp a tool as possible, and the need for a time limit. As you will learn later in the chapter, stubbornly remaining old finish can be painted or touched up to look like the finished woodwork.

Scraping

Scraping is the technique for last-minute fast removal of overlooked residue before sanding. As with digging, a variety of wood scrapers is available. Use the largest and sharpest and scrape with the grain, avoiding roughing up or otherwise damaging the wood.

Bleaching

Sometimes bleaching can clean woodwork that still has some old finish in it, or woodwork that you wish to lighten up a little. While dramatic effects can be had from bleaching, generally the wood is no different before or after this process. So don't expect miracles, but it is worth a try if you have a problem.

The easiest way to bleach is to brush Clorox brand laundry bleach on the problem wood and rinse it off with clear water on a rag. Use Clorox full strength and be sure to cover up anything you don't want bleached, like you and your clothes.

SANDING THE WOODWORK

A careful and conscientious stripping of relatively smooth woodwork may well result in little need to sand. In fact, one should attempt to remove the old finish with as little grain raising and damage to the woodwork as possible. That caution coupled with complete removal of the old finish should result in very little sanding activity.

The necessity to sand is illustrated here. Baseboard in the foreground has been sanded; that in the background is stripped but unsanded. Photo by Edwin Johnson

When to Sand and When Not to

Sanding wood surfaces accomplishes two things. One is smooth grain, which was raised in the stripping process, the passing years, or both. Sanding also lightens the wood color. Your first objective in sanding should be to make the surface smooth to the touch for both aesthetic and ease of care reasons. After all, woodwork is easier to clean when it is smooth. Your second objective is to obtain uniform color in the end. Too much sanding in one area and too little in the adjacent one will result in nonuniform color even though you stain. So don't overachieve your first objective to the detriment of your second!

Perhaps a couple of examples are in order. I refinished a dining room that has an oak bay consisting of three large windows and a large oak window seat. Over the years the seat had been used for holding plants, and (you already guessed it) the plants had caused water rings, which were later covered up by paint. Once the paint was stripped, dark water rings of different diameters appeared everywhere. To carelessly sand out these marks would have resulted in a number of light smudges. So with great care only the dark ring marks were sanded until the color match was nearly perfect. This was achieved by first using number 80 production sandpaper following the complete ring and sanding both with the grain and against it. Then I used number 120 grade, followed by 180 grade. In an instance such as this, one may not only sand out too much wood color but also remove too much wood, thus causing depressions in the wood, or the "dishing effect." When faced with a particularly deep stain, one has three alternatives: sand it out completely and take out too much wood, leave it alone, or leave it alone and attempt a touch-up after sealing the wood. I favor the latter.

Hand Sanding and Belt Sanders

I was called in to complete a staircase refinishing job begun by a young couple. They had removed all the white paint with the EPR and had started to strip chemically. Then they started sanding before completing the latter task. Using a belt sander, they had oversanded the newel, a square Mission-style piece, hence easy to sand. There was, however, no way the same results could have been achieved on the stair risers, locked in as they were by the string. My suggestion was that I complete the chemical stripping and hand sand as much as possible, then lightly stain the newel so it would match the color of the rest of the staircase, following the "natural" refinishing method. The customers rejected the suggestion, with the result that they now have a nearly blond newel and a light brown staircase!

So if you plan to use a belt sander on a job where some hand sanding is called for, do not oversand with the machine. The result, unless compensatory staining is done, will be uneven color tone.

How to Use Sandpaper

Use a good brand of production sandpaper, such as 3M, and let it work for you. Start with the roughest grade sandpaper you dare to use and sand by hand.

If you stripped off the old finish and if you use the hand sanding method properly, there is really little need for mechanical sanders. For larger surfaces like doors take a full sheet and fold it in quarters, place the palm of your hand on it, and sand parallel to the grain. Tearing the sheet in quarters and folding the quarter in half seems to be a good sanding surface for small areas. Keep switching sanding surfaces as they become clogged, finally cleaning off each surface with used sandpaper and using that sheet again. Save some old worn sheets for sanding smoother surfaces later.

You should initially sand parallel to the wood grain, but you can also sand across the grain, if it appears necessary, with finer sandpaper grades. For example, the tops and the bottoms of panels in paneled doors often need more sanding than the rest of the panel. Here you can carefully and lightly sand across the grain with 120 grade or finer. In general, however, sand with the grain, starting with a few passes of coarse grades, 36, 50, or 80, if the surface is bad, then sand more with 120 grade and still more with 180. For most surfaces 180 grade is fine enough.

Buy your sandpaper a dozen sheets at a time, as most stores will give you two for nothing; sleeves are still cheaper. If much sanding is called for, buy and use a mask to prevent inhaling much of the dust. And remember, for an easier project rely on stripping to remove the old finish rather than sanding.

STAINING YOUR WOODWORK

By nature stain is a color pigment mixed with a carrier, such as oil. It is designed to penetrate wood rather than lie on the surface, as most paint does. It is not, however, designed to cover much of anything. Thus, the wood under stain must be not only clear of other finishes but free of anything that will hinder stain penetration. Stain needs to be protected; thus the need for sealing it.

Stain Varieties

Stain varies as to material, pigment, and color. Let's look at each variable.

MATERIAL VARIETIES. Stain manufacturers produce primarily penetrating oil stains, although plastic latex stains and water-soluble stains are also available. Penetrating oil stains are by far superior for most purposes.

PIGMENT VARIETIES. Stain brands differ in their pigment content and therefore their covering qualities. Some brands, like Pratt and Lambert's Tonetic, expose much of the wood grain, whereas others, like Fuller O'Brien, have greater grain-covering ability. Still other brands, like Benjamin Moore's Benwood, have even greater grain-covering features. None of these brands is necessarily recommended, however; woodwork that has more defects and less attractive grain would require, in my opinion, the greatest grain-covering ability of Benwood.

COLOR VARIETIES. Much more extensive than pigment varieties are the color varieties in stains among the various producers and, alas, among different lots by the same producer *and* over the years by that same producer. Thus "fruitwood," a popular color name, of one stain producer is not likely to be the same color as "fruitwood" of another, and the fruitwood of 1971 will not match that of 1981, even though made by the same firm. So choose a color by one manufacturer only, and buy enough for the entire job, which may include your whole house over the period of a few years.

Choosing a color is another matter. Stain color charts are unreliable enough so that you should supplement them with actual testing on your woodwork. Several variables preclude accurate color representation on charts. Stain charts are based on color photos of that producer's stain on raw, never-before-finished, *new* wood. Consider that even new wood varies in color. That coupled with your old and, at times, *very* old woodwork necessitates testing.

MIXING STAIN. You can mix stain. To be safe mix only those colors made by the same manufacturer. But why mix? You mix to achieve *just* the color you want, for while a company will produce, say, ten shades, the shades *you* can achieve are infinitely variable. Just be sure to mix only the shades of one given manufacturer.

When I began in this business, I was much like the old Henry Ford, who told his customers that they could have any color car they wanted so long as it was black (only I usually recommended fruitwood). And most of my customers went along with my recommendations until I was given the Frank Lloyd Wright Home and Studio dining room woodwork restoration job in 1978. The challenge was to determine the original color of that woodwork (ca. 1889) and then mix an exact match for it.

First, we found the color on the inside of an old cabinet door. I cleaned up the surface to expose the true color and then produced a number of stain mixes, each applied to samples of the

Mixing the stain color for the front door of the James J. Glessner House. The oak door had to match the mahogany stain color of the house's entry. Conceivably the entry has the original color applied in 1886.

Testing the stain mixture color by dabbing a little on the front door frame and comparing the color with the entry. Several attempts were made to get a perfect match.

woodwork in that room. Another problem was that some of the oak woodwork in that room was new, having been put in place as part of the restoration by carpenters in 1978. A panel of Wright authorities then chose the best color. Now I am an authority on mixing stain colors.

How to Stain

PREPARATION. Before staining, the dust from sanding as well as all of the stripping mess should be cleaned up. Dirt and dust are the enemies of any good refinishing job. Highly recommended is the use of a tank-type vacuum cleaner to get all of the dust out of corners, cracks, outside windowsills, and the floor next to the quarter round. Finally, wipe all surfaces with a tack cloth, an old furniture refinisher's dust-collecting device. It is a piece of cheesecloth that has been treated so that it has a tacky quality, thereby enabling it to pick up most dust and dirt. You see, your paintbrush will pick up any nearby dust and commingle it with the stain; a stray breeze coming in your window will blow dirt from the outside sill on the inside sill. Such particles will make the finish rough no matter how much you try to sand it later.

BRUSHES AND BRUSHING. Stain should be brushed on the woodwork surfaces with as large a brush as possible, and the last brush stroke should be parallel to the grain and blend in with the end of the previous stroke. For flush doors a 3½-inch brush is appropriate, and for many windows a 3-inch brush can be used, although a 2- to-2½-inch brush may be better when nine- or twelve-light window sashes are encountered. Tapered brushes are best for most woodwork, as they permit easy access to corners. Ideally, your brushes should be *very* clean, long-bristled, and flexible. They should be high-quality China bristle for maximum efficiency; considering the cost of your project so far in terms of labor and materials, an expensive brush may really be cheaper because of its results.

Wiping stain instead of brushing it is unnecessary, time-consuming, and may leave lint. Likewise, wiping stain off the woodwork after brushing is generally unnecessary providing you choose the correct tone in the beginning. Still another stain-

application technique is using a paint roller, as some "professionals" do, and brushing into corners with a paintbrush. It may be effective, but I have never found it necessary.

A little stain, you will find, goes a long way. Though the amount of stain required does vary with the porosity, age, and dryness of the wood, it takes less stain to cover a given interior area than it takes paint. To avoid stain runs, work with a relatively dry brush. Start staining in corners with a full brush and work out in one direction from them. Stain pieces in the same location to prevent unnecessary motions.

For example, for windows start in the upper right hand corner of the sash next to the glass and brush that molding, then the sash, then the frame under the sash cord, then the trim holding the sash in place, and finally the frame from top to bottom. Following that, stain the top sash next to the

Brushing stain on the front entry of Glessner House.

A three-inch China bristle brush is being used to brush the stain on the nearly hundred-year-old oak trim. Stain requires complete brushing out with a minimum of material on one's brush. No wiping of stain is necessary if done correctly and with the right color. Photos by Jim Kuba

sealing, you discover them. Too late? No. Just more work.

Staining other architectural pieces follows the recommendations laid down for windows and doors. For built-ins, however, it is best to refinish the inside, then go outside. Shelves should be removed if possible and stood around the wall of the room. In staining of staircases start at the top but watch for stain drips on unfinished rails and balusters below; wipe them from time to time because such drips will dry fast and leave their marks.

Your stain job can have its tone lightened in three ways, if you so desire. Of course, getting the right tone in the beginning is the better alternative. But let's assume that as you get more stain on, your woodwork looks a little darker than you thought it would.

The first lightening trick is to wipe the surfaces with a very clean, lint-free cloth. Now, for the remainder of the staining you can work with stain that has been thinned with paint thinner. Or you can lighten your stain color mix by adding a lighter shade. This shade must be substantially lighter, however, like platinum. And a lot is needed. Remember, it's much easier to *darken* a stain mix than it is to *lighten* it.

Main hall at James J. Glessner House, H. H. Richardson, 1886. The circular door at left has been stripped and refinished by the author. Stain, mixed to match hall paneling, was followed with a sealer of thinned polyurethane and a finish coat of full-strength polyurethane. Photo by Jim Kuba

window glass, the sash, the inside of the frame, and then the frame itself. Stain the left side in a similar manner, then the bottom of the sash (make sure you stain *behind* the top of the bottom sash and on top of it). Get off your ladder and stain the bottom sash of the double-hung window, raising it to get all of the sash, then the sill and under the sill.

Doors should be refinished in place, hung on their hinges. In this way they are highly manuverable and at the same time held by something other than you. For paneled doors brush in the panel moldings first, then the panels, and then the frame. In staining flush doors apply the stain horizontally and complete with vertical finishing strokes from top to bottom. Watch for runs on flush doors, for sometimes heavy grain will disguise them at first and three days later when you are about to begin

Glessner House kitchen door following a coat of penetrating oil stain mixed to go with the other exterior doors but with reduced redness. Photo by Jim Kuba

The author staining the coach entrance doorway at Glessner House. Note drop cloth. Stain is in a fiber container in a small pail. When the job is over, the fiber container is emptied and disposed of. Photo of Jim Kuba

The "18th Street" door at Glessner House. It has been stripped of old finish, and a new bottom rail has replaced the old (1886) rotted rail. A locksmith put oil in the locks, which has leaked down the right side rail. Both are refinishing problems. Note original bottle glass in the door window. Photo by Jim Kuba

A pair of lovely balcony doors over the "G" entrance at James J. Glessner House. They have been stripped, stained, and sealed by the author. Photo by Jim Kuba

Starting the staining of the front door at James J. Glessner House. It has been removed by three husky men and placed in the coach house. A temporary plywood door complete with ADT alarm contact was built and installed the four days this piece was being refinished. Here, the author is sanding. Photo by Jim Kuba

Following sanding, a good wiping with a tack cloth is a must. Photo by Jim Kuba

The same stain mixture used on the front entry frame is being brushed on the Glessner House front door. Photo by Jim Kuba

Brushing stain requires a good brushing out of the material for even coverage. No wiping of stain is necessary. Photo by Jim Kuba

DRIPS AND RUNS. Drips and runs of stain can ruin your job. While working it is a good idea to keep watching for run areas. After staining a piece go back and wipe up drips and runs with a rag or a dry paintbrush, taking care not to remove too much stain. Of course, it is best to avoid runs by working with a drier rather than a wetter brush, by working stain into the wood, and by wiping excess stain from your brush as you go along.

If perchance a run should occur and you miss it and it dries overnight, it's not the end of the world. It can probably be wiped off by vigorously using a dry rag or gently using a rag with mineral spirits on it.

SEALING YOUR WOODWORK

The purpose of the sealing coat is to protect the wood (if "natural" finish) and the stain (if you stain) against the environment. If you decided earlier to refinish your woodwork "natural," then sealing will be your first refinishing process after sanding. Be sure you read all about cleaning the surface and the work area after sanding. If you stained your woodwork, this is step number two for you.

Of all the steps in the woodwork refinishing stage this is usually the simplest and the fastest, because all you need do is brush on the sealer. Make sure that the stained surface is clean, especially if it has been a few days since you stained. In that case dust up with your tack cloth.

Sealing Materials

The sealing materials you can choose from are shellac, natural varnish that is mixed with paint thinner, and polyurethane, also mixed with paint thinner. Others much less commonly used are lacquer (*only* to be used when lacquer will also be the finish coat) and special sealers used only in conjunction with natural varnish.

Sealing the "G" entrance door at Glessner House. Note light reflection the sealer provides. This helps in assuring complete coverage. Photo by Jim Kuba

SHELLAC. Shellac is by far the most ancient and venerable of sealers. It was once all that was available for the finish coat as well. The advantages of shellac are that it does not cause stain bleeding and that it dries quickly. The reason bleeding does not result is that shellac has an alcohol solvent while stain has a mineral spirit solvent and the two solvents simply do not mix. Shellac is deficient though, in that it will discolor with age, often turning dark when in contact with moisture.

NATURAL VARNISH. This is a traditional, longtime favorite that seems appropriate when it is to be used in full-strength for the finish coat. To use this material as a sealer, thin it according to the manufacturer's directions. The principal disadvantage is not so much its use as a sealer as it is using natural varnish as a finish coat, for it does not provide a hard enough finish for most woodwork. More of that later.

POLYURETHANE. For several years now I have been using polyurethane, properly thinned (25–30 percent paint thinner) for wood absorption, as a sealer. Its advantages are that it flows, it dries rather quickly, and it is the only sealer one can use with polyurethane as the finish coat. By stating it flows I mean that there are no brush marks, no material buildup, and that it has a hand-rubbed appearance. As to fast drying, under ideal conditions of temperature and humidity one can seal and brush on the finish coat in a medium-sized room in the same day. Polyurethane can also be purchased in spray cans and sprayed on removable pieces such as muntin strips.

The principal disadvantage of polyurethane as a sealer is that when it is thinned it can cause the stain to bleed. By bleeding is meant the commingling of the polyurethane solvent with the stain, which has the *same* solvent. One can prevent most if not all bleeding, however, by leaving adequate time for the stain to dry, not brushing on too much stain, preparing the prestained surface for adequate stain absorption, and by not "working in" the sealer. If bleeding occurs, it will both thicken and color the sealer, so one should add more paint thinner if this should happen. Too much color in the sealer may spoil the job, so it is well to discard that batch, clean the brush, mix some more, and continue sealing.

OTHER SEALERS. There are other rather exotic finishing substances mostly geared for furniture work, such as wax, beeswax, and tung oil. I feel that most of them are designed for furniture refinishing and should not be considered for your woodwork. Tung oil and other oils not only require many applications for proper refinishing but are somewhat sticky, causing them to attract and hold dust, and are more expensive than the materials recommended in this chapter. Further, tung oil really does not seal, at least in the sense that shellac and polyurethane do. Finally, such materials are not as durable as polyurethane for such high-traffic areas as your windowsills.

Sealing Techniques

THINNING THE SEALER. Most polyurethane and varnish manufacturers give specific instructions for thinning their products for sealing purposes. It is best to follow them, at first anyway, until you get a feel for your particular job conditions. Too much thinner will result in unsatisfactory sealing of the stain and wood; too little thinner will result in improper wood absorption of the material.

Giving the Glessner House kitchen door the finish coat. Good brushing should start at the top. Photo by Jim Kuba

SOME SEALING TIPS. At the risk of being too elementary, I think it is necessary to tell you what sort of container you should use for your sealer, and how to prevent contamination of your polyurethane inventory. As to container, I have found that putting my sealer mix in a two-pound metal coffee can and carrying it in a four-quart (number 5) metal pail is most convenient. But why a can in a pail? It prevents dripping.

You will probably buy your polyurethane by the gallon because you will need a lot and a gallon is cheaper than four quarts. Mix *just* enough sealer for the job at hand; if you run out, mix some more. Then throw out what's left. Do not put it back in the gallon because it will contaminate an otherwise fresh batch. Lest you be concerned that your Scotch ancestors will roll over in their graves if you waste anything, I will remind you that dirt is the enemy of good refinishing. And after a few hours of sealing, your sealer will have everything in it from paint chips to bread crumbs to cat hair. So chuck it.

Brush care, too, deserves mention. Clean out as much sealer (or stain) as you can by scraping the bristles on the edge of the metal container. Then wipe out the remainder by squeezing the bristles between newspaper. Do all this before you dunk your brush in paint thinner, because it saves thinner. Of course, back in the days of forty-cents-per-gallon thinner this was unnecessary. And while it's okay to soak your brush in thinner to put it "on hold" for the finish coat, make sure the thinner is fresh and clean. Soaking a brush in dirty thinner will help make the finish coat very rough.

BRUSHES AND BRUSHING. Although spraying sealers is a possibility, as in the case of lacquer to be followed by lacquer, there is usually too much preparation necessary and too little surface to cover to warrant that process. Generally, a paintbrush will do. So, as with staining, use a top-quality, *really* clean China bristle brush, and one as wide as possible. Tapered (pointed) brushes, in my

141

opinion, are the best, because there are so many corners to cover in woodwork.

Apply a generous amount of sealer, but since it runs because of thinning, you should not start at the top of a piece of woodwork, but down a ways. Then work your way up and then down. Brushing sealer on ceiling beams or other predominantly overhead pieces can be sloppy, as sealer runs through your brush and down the handle. You can be neat by constantly wiping excess sealer off your brush onto your paint pail and by wiping the metal part of your brush and the handle.

As the sealing stage does not require the care of staining or applying the finish coat, a few runs and drips are permissible, providing you scrape them off before the finish coat. Such runs can often be removed with your fingernail as you sand the sealer after the job.

PREPARATION FOR THE FINISH COAT

Before you can brush on the finish coat, there are a few more things to do. Sorry about that. Those tasks are sand, touch up, and fill. First, let the sealer dry. Drying time varies from a half-day to several days depending on humidity conditions.

The front door of Glessner House has been sealed and the sealer given a day to dry. Here, the author is lightly sanding with number 600 wet/dry sandpaper used dry.

Sanding

Okay, you've sealed your woodwork. Good. Now feel the surface. It's rough because sealing raises the grain of the wood. This must be sanded, but ever so gently, so use wet or dry sandpaper, dry. If your woodwork is very rough, grades 320 and 400 are best; if it is slightly rough, use grade 600. Fold a sheet in quarters and rotate sides, and for smaller areas use a quarter sheet folded in half. There is no need for heavy sanding at this point. Just pretend you are dusting the wood.

A white residue or dust will result from this sanding, so again whip out your tack cloth and dust the surface. Also, if any dust or dirt has accumulated on, say, the floor next to the quarter round or around doorways, vacuum it up and use your tack cloth, because when your brush touches the floor it will pick up any and every thing.

Touch-Up

Old house woodwork is usually damaged; baseboard outside corners, for example, get chewed up from foot traffic and from vacuum cleaners.

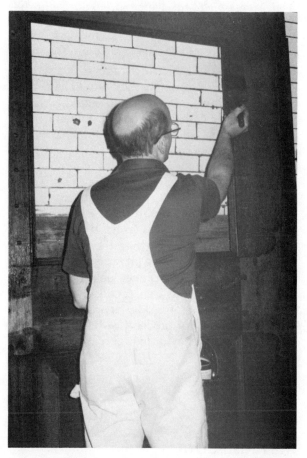

Sanding is followed by wiping with a tack cloth. Note that the outline of the wrought-iron suspension system could not be removed by stripping and there was no need to sand it out as it was recovered with the original wrought iron.

Now the final step: the finish coat. This is full-strength good-quality polyurethane being brushed on. Photos of Glessner House door by Jim Kuba

Bottoms of old doors have nicks from kicking. Because of these defects, you may not be able to remove all of the old finish, and because of their depth, you did not wish to sand them out. Touch-up is the solution to this problem.

Window trim is often ill-fitting in older homes; gaps have developed into which enthusiastic painters have brushed seventy years' worth of paint, perhaps in the vain hope that it would fill the gap. That is impossible to remove. Often old-fashioned wood filler, plaster, or Spackle were stuffed into cracks and defects by professional painters. Again, the solution is touch-up.

The best touch-up material is a lacquer or alcohol stain, because it dries quickly and goes on over mineral spirit solvent materials. There are several prepared colors and brands available in hardware and paint stores, though I use a profes-

sional furniture retoucher's kit with fifty colors in powder form which I mix with any one of three alcohol-based solvents. With a custom color I go around the woodwork after sealing and sanding and touch up not only all damaged areas but those that did not take the stain too well. Typically, one such area is the inside corner of base, especially if the base was heavily painted before refinishing. (More of this in the next chapter.)

So one strips the best one can and then touches up by brushing a vertical line in the exact corner of the base, the beam, the window sash corner, or the stair baluster. Quickly wipe to avoid a painted look, and enough will remain in the corner to cover up the color defect. This process also has the effect of sharpening up or defining the intersection of two boards.

Another touch-up material and one much

more accessible to the average weekend refinisher is paint. Yes, paint. For example, a dining room ceiling beam refinishing job I did with rather elaborate trim on the beam's horizontal surface left ugly white paint a half inch above the surface. Digging it out in a room that size would have been a very time-consuming task and would have left large gaps where the old wood had separated. So after sealing and sanding the pecan-stained beams, I brushed in specially mixed and matched semi-gloss paint, carefully wiping the excess off surface areas with an old rag. The result was an even color appearance.

Paint was the best touch-up in this case because there was extensive covering necessary and paint goes a lot further than lacquer and alcohol-based stains and a lot faster. Furthermore, there was no wood grain cover-up problem in that the paint residue was in a recessed area. Paint's disadvantage is that it is slow drying. Thus, in this instance I could not proceed with the finish coat but had to wait a day or two.

Nail Holes

Nail holes are another problem to solve before the finish coat. *Never* fill nail holes until your wood-work is sealed, because fillers have an oil base that prevents the wood from properly absorbing stain and sealer. In addition, until the woodwork is sealed you will not know its final, true color, and this prevents correct color match of the putty. So fill nail holes with colored putty to match, and do this after sealing.

Old nail holes were filled once upon a time with various substances some of which are strippable and will take stain, and some of which will not. For those filled holes that did not take the stain, or which did not look good after sealing if you used the "natural" approach, you can just touch them up. Why waste your time digging out the old nailhole filler and then replacing it with colored putty? Use the recommended touch-up materials instead.

THE FINISH COAT

The purpose of the finish coat is to protect and enhance all that you've accomplished to date, so its importance cannot be minimized. First, let's look at materials again.

Finishing Materials

SHELLAC. Shellac applied at near full strength is generally not satisfactory because of its water absorption characteristic. In addition, it dries so quickly over a shellac sealer that brush marks may appear and remain.

NATURAL VARNISH. A coat of semigloss natural varnish has the advantage, in my opinion, of a somewhat softer appearance and feel than polyurethane. Its disadvantage is less resistance to water, sun, plants, etc. However, if you plan to take good care of your woodwork, do not hesitate to use this material. Most of my townhouse has

natural varnished oak woodwork; all of our lake house has polyurethaned oak woodwork. They are both very lovely, but the polyurethane is wearing better under somewhat more difficult circumstances.

POLYURETHANE. Properly used polyurethane is a most satisfactory finishing material. It not only wears well but dries quickly, reducing the time in which it can pick up foreign materials that can spoil your refinishing job. A disadvantage is that poly *can* get a plastic, hard look if it is not applied and sanded properly. Further, it scratches more easily than natural varnish.

The committee at the Frank Lloyd Wright Home and Studio that administered the restoration of the dining room was uneasy at first over my recommendation that polyurethane be the finishing material. They feared a plastic look. After they inspected some of my refinishing with polyurethane, they felt relieved in that it had a hand-rubbed appearance. The end result of the dining

The completely refinished front door of James J. Glessner House, Chicago, Henry Hobson Richardson's last design, built in 1886. Door, glass, wrought iron, and lock are all original. This was the first time in nearly one hundred years that the door was completely removed and refinished. Photo by Jim Kuba (All photographs of James J. Glessner House door courtesy Chicago Architectural Foundation)

room in that historical site was a very durable, hand-rubbed-appearing finish. Now all the woodwork in Wright's Oak Park home has a polyurethane finish; we think Mr. Wright would approve.

Techniques of the Finish Coat

In general, the techniques are similar to those outlined in the sections on staining and sealing. Exceptions will, however, be noted.

BRUSHES AND BRUSHING. Brush with the grain, looking into a sidelight source to avoid misses. Carefully brush out lap marks. Watch for runs by going back over your work from time to time and wipe wet-appearing areas with a dry brush or your finger, as they are potential runs.

LIGHT SOURCES. On a dark day or in a dark room use a portable lamp placed slightly in back of you and either to your left or to your right and work toward it. Electric light sources are especially important when finishing windows, as they more than compensate for the light coming in the window.

RUNS AND MISSED AREAS. Runs are more likely to occur at the tops of doors, doorways, and window frames, and missed areas will more likely be just out of your line of work vision. So inspect more carefully such tops, and get above and below your normal line of vision to spot misses. They show in that they are not wet-appearing. Day-old runs can be removed with your fingernail. After scraping them off rub the area with paint thinner on a rag.

ANOTHER FINISH COAT. Usually one finish coat of near full strength polyurethane over the correct sealer coat is sufficient. After all, you want to avoid the heavy, thick varnish look that you may have spent so much time to remove a ways back. At times, however, the woodwork is so old and so dry that it readily accepts and absorbs not only the sealer coat but the finish coat as well. The way to tell if you need a second finish coat is to look at your woodwork, after the finish coat, in a strong light. Does it have an *even* sheen? If so, your job is finished. If not, lightly sand the woodwork with 600 grade wet or dry sandpaper, wipe with the tack cloth, and lay on another coat of urethane, only this time a little thinner than the last.

FINAL SANDING. Following the last finish coat, *lightly*—oh so lightly (sand like you're dusting)—sand the surfaces with *worn* 600 grade wet or dry sandpaper. This should give you a furniturelike touch.

So now you have achieved your refinishing goals: the desired color and the desired touch and the desired protection and preservation. You deserve *much* credit, for this is perhaps the most difficult and time-consuming of all decorating projects!

What to Do If You Goofed

Let's say that you stained, sealed, and finished the woodwork in a room and after all that work you didn't like the color. Is this the end? Must you live with it forever? Is stripping it the only way to make a change?

The answer to all these questions is no. And I don't mean by that, that you can paint it all over again.

I learned the way to solve this problem the way I learned practically everything else in this book, the hard way. What happened was that I stained, sealed, and finished two of four ceiling grilles for the Frank Lloyd Wright Home and Studio in my Wisconsin shop—in other words, away from the color standard. The result was a distinctly lighter color for these 3 × 6-feet curved, pierced oak panels.

What I did was mix Cal-tint, a universal colorant, with 20 percent thinned polyurethane until I got the correct shade. The particular colors in this instance were raw sienna and burnt umber. Cal-tint comes in plastic bottles with pouring spouts on them. So what you do is squirt a little color in the polyurethane solution mix and test on the finished surface until you get the color you want.

But before you can brush this solution on, sand the old surface to remove the apparent gloss. Wipe with a tack cloth, and brush on the new color. What you will get is a stable finish that, unless it is quite dark, will not cover up the wood grain.

Still another problem that has recently surfaced is that of a Prairie School house in Oak Park in which a previous refinisher stripped off the old finish, sanded the woodwork, and rubbed in two coats of tung oil. It created a very orange color the owner (and I) thought was poor and not in keeping with the tradition of that architectural style. How does one remove tung oil? Do you have to remove it in order to stain?

Answering the last question first, tung oil need not be removed, at least completely. It does not seal, but is absorbed into the wood. Therefore, you should sand the surface, and wipe it clean with alcohol generously poured on a cloth. After that, you can feel free to use a penetrating oil stain, a sealer, and a finish coat.

Chapter Eight

Do Your Own
Floor Refinishing

This subject of floor refinishing has been saved to the very end of the restoration process for two reasons. The first is that your floors are the last thing to be restored. Yes, you should do everything else first, including all your decorating. If you doubt my advice, and you well may, look at this controversy the opposite way. That would mean that you remove old floor finish and refinish floors *first*. Then strip and refinish the woodwork, then paint walls and ceilings or hang wallpaper. Sounds ridiculous, doesn't it?

But, you ask, won't refinishing floors harm my other endeavors? Well, it will probably raise a little dust, but sanding can't hurt anything. Stripping off old floor finish, though, can spot adjacent surfaces if you are sloppy. There is, though, a whole lot less danger in refinishing floors last than first.

The second reason for letting this go to near the bitter end is that what one is to do with the floors in old house restoration is one of the more difficult problems with which you'll have to deal. Think about it for a minute. How should my floors look? How did they once look? What materials should I use on them? Finally, how should I care for them?

Regarding how your floors should look, I suggest that they should look just the way you want them to. I stressed being faithful to the original in woodwork restoration, but one must be a bit more practical with floors. They take a much greater beating than woodwork; original colors and materials like beeswax on unsealed wood are impractical. Boiled linseed oil over which wax has been applied may give you the antique look you want, but it requires a lot of maintenance.

Perhaps you want your floors to look just like new. Though that may seem entirely admirable and logical, it is probably impossible if you have an old house. Besides, it does not seem to me to go with an older building; you have an old floor, and in my opinion it should look old.

Materials should be the latest and best available. To use materials of a century and a half ago merely for the sake of authenticity is unnecessary, uncalled for, and asking for trouble. The question of materials came up when restoration of the Frank Lloyd Wright Home and Studio began in 1977. I recommended polyurethane and some purists disagreed. Cooler heads prevailed in the belief that if Wright were alive *he* would have recommended the best that technology can provide, because he was a most progressive and experimenting architect. Today, over four years have elapsed since the initial woodwork restoration. Not only has the original refinishing been highly stable under difficult conditions but it has retained its hand-rubbed appearance.

So in this chapter you will be helped in both the techniques of floor refinishing and some of the difficult decisions that must be made.

SHOULD YOU REFINISH YOUR OWN FLOORS?

The question of whether to do the refinishing yourself was not raised in reference to your woodwork, because the answer is obviously yes. The same does not necessarily hold for your floors.

Here, however, there are factors that point to having a good professional floor refinisher do the job. He has the equipment and the know-how, and his fee is certainly nominal.

The pros have not only more equipment than one can rent but better, heavier machines as well. A good pro will own a three-wheel eight-inch drum sander weighing two hundred pounds, high torque, 220-volt, which incidentally costs $4,000. Second, he has know-how; I am told it takes two years to fully train a good floor sander. Using the machines, the edger, for example, takes a lot of skill. The edger is really a takeoff from a large disc sander, a tool that can mess up a sanding job unless one has a lot of skill.

Finally, for what he does, the typical floor refinisher charges a modest fee. Today, in Chicago, one can get an average-sized room refinished for from $150 to $200. Why? Most floor sanders are pretty competitive.

As I see it after talking to a do-it-yourselfer who not only refinished all the floors in his seven-room house but helped a relative do his, there are three good reasons for refinishing your own floor. The first is you have control over the end result: the color, the fastidiousness, and the finish. Some pros *are* a little sloppy, his color (if other than natural) may not be exactly to your liking, and most pros prefer natural varnish to polyurethane because it can be put on over a fast-drying sealer whereas urethane cannot. Then, too, there may be no or few floor sanders in your town or near your rural dwelling. And finally, most floor refinishers today call themselves floor sanders. This means that they believe in finishing floors only one way: sand off *all* the old finish and start over. This approach, as we will see, may not be the one for you.

Things to Do First

As with the other restoration projects noted previously, it is important to make all necessary repairs first. This activity can range from eliminating simple squeaks, to nailing down loose boards, sinking all nails, and pulling bent and bad nails and tacks, to replacing bad floorboards or entire sections.

Two approaches to eliminating squeaks are to pour talcum powder in the spaces between boards or to fasten the boards better than they presently are. This fastening can be with nails from above the culprit or with wood screws from below, up through the subflooring. Go around with a hammer and a nail set and sink all protruding nail heads below the surface so that you can fill the hole later on with filler. Using a nail puller, remove bent nails and tacks left over from the carpeting-pulling job.

If board replacement is called for, one should try to replace with both the same wood species in the present floor and the same board width. In most homes built in this century we are talking of an easy task; in eighteenth- and nineteenth-century homes, however, custom millwork may be the order of the day. In one hundred-year-old home where I watched a professional floor sander work, the kitchen floor was maple, the living room pine, and the two bedrooms oak. So to be faithful to the original in your floor restoration, you may have to do a lot of searching. Nonetheless, do it first!

Though this goes without saying, I will say it anyway. Plan the floor job. Figure on moving everything out of the room and on not using that particular room for anywhere from a weekend to a week, depending on how many hours a day you plan to work and on how fast you are. A professional team of three can sand *and* refinish a four-room flat, entry, and pantry completely in five to six hours. However, if this is your first attempt at refinishing, I would plan on taking just a little more time than that.

SANDING VS. STRIPPING

Old floor finish can be removed three ways: sanding, stripping, and a combination of the two. Which method you choose depends on floor condition, room size, and aesthetics.

Certainly floor condition is important. A relatively new floor or an older floor in good condition need not be sanded. It can be stripped of its old finish. The same is true of floors that have been sanded so often that the boards have become dangerously thin. After all, if done properly, each sanding removes about 1/16 inch. In addition, some floors, such as parquets and old softwoods that have been covered over with hardwoods, have very thin hardwood boards exposed.

Examples of floors in bad condition are those with uneven boards due to settling and boards that are warped longitudinally and across the grain, called cupped. Deep gouges and heavily worn places like the bottom stair tread can also be helped by sanding. Finally, floors that have been mercilessly refinished over the years present a real challenge to a potential finish stripper and are candidates for sanding.

Room size is a second factor in the sand/strip controversy. Stripping floors the size of the armory on your hands and knees is an impossible task; even small rooms present a formidable task.

Aesthetics is a final consideration. Sanding *will* generally make old floors look new. All traces of the original patina are removed. So if you want a new floor made of old wood, sand it. If you want an old floor, strip it. There is a world of difference.

An old floor has character. Some of the original color is retained as well as all the care marks when it is stripped of its old finish. The boards are often mellow. Adjacent boards possess a slightly different color and wear. Sand and you'll lose this.

The original old floors in your home have been treated and used in such a way over the years so as to achieve a really nice patina. Many softwood floors were scrubbed daily with lye water, others were washed with soda, and some were not washed at all but dry-rubbed with a brush and hot sand. Some were occasionally rubbed down with clay or brick dust. Later on hardwood floors were bleached, still later sanded and stained dark colors like walnut. Add to all this the many feet that passed over the boards, the waxes, oils, and just plain dirt. What you may have is a great patina that seems a shame to destroy by sanding. So you should consider stripping rather than sanding.

THE WASHING ALTERNATIVE

Perhaps before you do anything that is as irreversible as sanding or stripping off old finish, you should really wash your floor. Give it a good scrubbing with soap and water. Better yet, use a good detergent and a bristle brush. For stubborn dirt apply full-strength detergent. If some spots still do not come up, they are probably either water, urine, or radio battery acid. Old water spots can be identified as a dark gray, urine is orange color, and old radio battery acid (they really used to have wet batteries in radios) is black. Water spots can be sanded out but urine and acid spots can't. Sorry.

Rinse off all the soap or detergent and wipe dry. Now, how does the old floor look? Can't tell? Wipe a little mineral spirit on several boards. Like that? Well, let the floor dry thoroughly. Then if it's a little rough, *lightly* sand it with grade 400 wet or dry sandpaper used dry, wipe with a tack cloth, turn to the section of this chapter entitled "Floor Refinishing," and read. If this didn't work for you, read on.

STRIPPING OLD FLOOR FINISHES

It is just possible that your floor is painted, so let's tackle that problem first and get it out of the way.

Painted Floors

As with painted woodwork and painted siding, old paint should be removed with the electric paint remover and wide flat paint scrapers. If you forgot

how to use the EPR after reading my cogent directions in Chapter Five, I suggest you return to that material.

Two techniques that may be helpful with floors is to first strip a group of boards in an area you can easily reach with moving your knees (use kneepads, incidentally). And in corners use a large (two-inch) hooked paint scraper very well sharpened and pull toward you, out of the corner.

Stripping Clear Finishes

Few of us are so fortunate(?) to own painted floors. Instead, ours probably have clear, or relatively clear, finishes. Be they stain, oil, varnish, wax, nothing but the dirt of the ages, or whatever, they can be removed with a water-soluble paint and varnish remover (stripper).

The two approaches are the kneeling and the standing. With either, start stripping in the corner farthest from the door through which you plan to exit, and work toward it. If you prefer to work on your knees, brush stripper from a small metal pail over an area you can easily reach without moving on your knees. As you will be working directly over the methylene chloride solution, I suggest that you keep the windows open despite the weather outside and place a large floor circulating fan on the floor so it blows the fumes away from you.

For large areas and in the center of smaller rooms you may try standing. Attach a three-inch brush to an old handle so that you can dip in a pail of stripper and brush an area of floor. Whether standing or kneeling, keep applying stripper until the old finish begins to bubble or liquefies. If you kneel, scoop up the residue with a flexible three-inch putty knife (or larger) into an empty gallon stripper can from which you have removed the top. From the standing position move the residue to the adjacent area with a long-handled floor scraper while trying to pick up some of the gunk and dumping it into the empty gallon container.

Apply more stripper, though less this time, and scrape the area clean. After the scraping use steel wool pads, number 1 or 2 grade, and wipe the work area clean. A third application of stripper should be enough. You can tell if it's enough by noting how clean the boards look. If they are not clean, scrape the residue and wipe clean with steel wool (change pads when they get full of gunk). If the work area is clean, wash off the stripper with warm water. For the standing position use a sponge mop and keep washing the area until all residue is cleaned up. And for you kneelers, clean up the residue with wet steel wool pads, then wet toweling followed with dry toweling. Try to use a minimum amount of water; in contrast to woodwork, water *has* a place to go in floors.

As with your other stripping it is necessary to experiment with how much stripper to apply, how often, how long to wait, how much to scrub, etc. Make it easy on yourself and apply as little as possible as few times as possible, and scrub as little as possible. Too much scrubbing, especially with the wire brush, will put deep scratches in the soft, wet wood, which you will later have to sand out. It is good, too, to overlap your stripping a little. Remember, stripping old finish over a floor is much more critical than off a four-inch-wide piece of woodwork. With your floor, uneven stripping may well result in uneven color in the refinishing process.

If you are stripping stair treads, be sure to start at the top and work your way down. And you might as well strip the string and the risers as well.

Because water was used to clean off the final application of stripper, much dampness remains in between the floorboards. So if your environment can best be described as humid, the house heat is off or nonexistent, it is going to take a while to dry for refinishing. If you are in a hurry, bring in a portable heater, a large floor fan, or both. But it must be dry; otherwise, your sealer (if you are going to finish "natural") or your stain and sealer (if you desire more color or darker floors) will stay tacky for a few days.

Since the wood grain has been raised in the stripping process, some sanding will be required before the floor can be refinished. Hand sand as suggested in Chapter Six. Start with a coarse paper, which will do most of the work. Fold 8½ × 11-inch sheets in quarters, hold in the palm of your hand, and sand evenly and with the wood grain.

SANDING OLD FLOOR FINISHES

Sanding is by far the more common method of removing old floor finishes. In fact, a few years ago it was the only method ever discussed.

Recently the greater emphasis on *restoration* over rehabilitation or, worse, remodeling, has dictated stripping as the alternative approach to old finish removal. We will look at both methods in this chapter.

Equipment

The main sanding tool is the drum sander, so called because sanding is accomplished by an eight-inch (or narrower) drum on which is fastened the strip of sanding paper. The drum rotates in a forward motion pulling the machine—and you—along with it. Most rental machines are low torque, 110 volt, with two wheels to help you balance the drum. You must, however, do the balancing by lifting the machine so that the drum makes just the right contact with the floor.

Though the drum sander removes the bulk of the material from the floor, it cannot get right up against the baseboard. To remove material from around the edge of the room (about three inches or so), one must also have an edger, or "spinner," as some call it. This is a heavy-duty disc sander also with two casters to help you get an even cut at the wood.

Finally, there are often instances when you have to sand under something, like a radiator. Professionals use a noser, a small disc sander with the rotating sanding disc on an arm extending a foot or so from the machine body. I don't know whether these are available from rental places. So much for the sanding machines.

In the floor finishing process the pros apply varnish with a floor polisher and a rotating steel wool pad that both spreads out the varnish from where it is poured on the floor and works it into the wood. This is a process much like waxing a floor with a buffer, a process some of you are already familiar with. Varnishing with a polisher, in contrast to waxing, is a neat trick, one that I recommend leaving to the pros. For most of us applying varnish or polyurethane with a three-inch brush will do very nicely.

Probably the only hand tool you will need if you sand is the two-inch hooked scraper. It usually comes with a long, wide handle so as to give you the scraping power you will need. Buy a blade-sharpening file with the tool and keep your blade razor sharp for maximum efficiency. The hooked scraper is the best tool for removing old finish from corners which the circular edger cannot reach.

The most important material is the paper. It comes in eight-inch-wide strips for the drum sander and in disc shapes for the edger. Grades range from the super coarse number 4 to 100-2/0, about the finest you will require.

Professional floor sanders often use number 1

fuel oil on the floor when sanding with number 4 paper to prevent clogging of the grit on the paper. The oil, I am told, is to be used *only* with high-torque 220-volt drum sanders.

EQUIPMENT SOURCES. One can buy floor sanding equipment, rent it, or borrow it from a friend. Drum sanders cost anywhere from a few hundred to four thousand dollars each at today's prices. Edgers, of course, are less expensive. One could conceivably use a good disc sander as an edger, but with great care.

Tool rental centers carry floor-sanding machines. I am told that they make most of their money selling you the paper, because the average person sanding floors for the first time will use a lot of it. It seems that the excessive amount of paper usage is caused by putting it on the drum incorrectly and using the machine improperly. So if your tool rental center is a long ways from your sanding job, I advise you to buy a lot of paper with the agreement that you can return what you don't use. The pros buy their paper in long rolls, so their cost is currently under two dollars a yard.

And you may be fortunate to know someone who will lend you a drum sander. If it is a good one and your friend comes with it, you are most fortunate. As with woodwork stripping it is good to have a knowledgeable friend to get the sander started.

How to Sand Floors

As I said earlier, it takes two years to completely learn this skill, so I feel funny trying to tell you in the space of a few pages how to do it. Though I wish you good fortune, my lawyer tells me I must issue a disclaimer at this point on your floor-sanding endeavors.

STEP 1. Put the paper on the drum sander so it will stay on and do the right job. Although the pros start with a coarse grade like number 4, you may be safer to start with something less coarse, like number 2. One amateur told me he felt "more comfortable" with number 2 paper. Certainly there is less danger of cutting too much material with a finer grade paper.

STEP 2. Try to connect your machine to a power circuit with no other operating appliance on it so as to get the maximum torque possible for your machine. If necessary, connect to the main electric box. Sort out the electric power cords so they won't be in your way.

STEP 3. Mentally divide the room in half. Sand with (parallel to) the grain of the boards doing about half the room at a time. Move the machine slowly; when you get to the end, raise the drum so as to avoid a dish or trough. The same goes as you approach the center of the room. Move forward from the room's center toward the opposite wall. Move backward over the same path to the center of the room. Move the machine over and cut another path.

Sanding across the boards in a *very* small room, like an entry, is permissible. Do it with care and do not remove all of the material. Then get down to bare wood with your edger, ending with a finishing stroke parallel to the boards.

STEP 4. Material removal should be nearly complete for the first forward and backward movement with your most coarse paper. The balance should be removed with the finer paper second pass. Pros will start with number 4 over a coat of number 1 fuel oil lightly mopped on the old finish. The second treatment is with number 2 paper, then 80-0 paper for a natural finish floor, and to grade 100-2/0 when a darker than natural finish is desired.

STEP 5. After each floor coverage with each of the foregoing paper grades, the paper must be changed on the drum. So when the machine is stopped, sweep up what dust the machine's vacuum didn't get. (I suggest you wear a good-quality dust mask and use a floor fan if fuel oil is used.)

For a really fine floor-cleaning job vacuum the floor after you are *all* through sanding. Especially get in all corners and under the molding and/or quarter round.

STEP 6. Go around the edge of the room with the edger using the same grade paper as the drum sander, that is, number 2 with number 2, etc. Operate the edger while on your feet. Keep your

The first step a professional floor sander takes is to mop on number 1 fuel oil. Note poor condition of this hundred-year-old maple floor. Photo by Edwin Johnson

back straight, bend your knees slightly, keep your feet wide apart to give you good balance.

The trick with the edger is to remove material, feather the edge left by the heavier, more powerful drum sander, while avoiding disc-sanding marks. To do this, keep the edger level and move in a left-to-right direction along the baseboard, then back and forth from the wall, followed with movement along the wall. This should do it for "natural" finishes. More critical darker shades require hand sanding along the line where the drum roller stopped just short of the baseboard. The edger cannot quite do the job well enough for the critical finish necessary for darker than natural shades. So hand sand to "feather." You will note that despite this there will be a slightly raised line like a beach where the drum roller stopped. This will be especially true if the floor has been previously sanded.

154

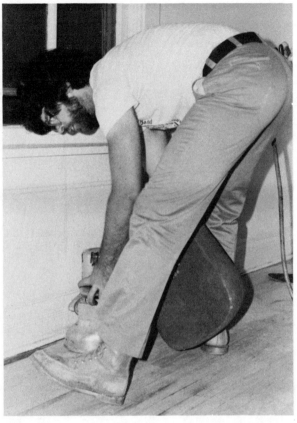

Above, left, using the drum sander, the pro goes forward and backward over one eight-inch strip once. As this machine has a strong forward pull, operator must hold it back. Note how much material one run has removed. Photo by Edwin Johnson

Above, after the drum sander has done its work, the edger is used to remove material along the edge of the floor. Note how this pro is standing and holding his machine. Photo by Edwin Johnson

Left, for areas neither the drum sander nor the edger can sand, a hooked scraper must be used, as on this sill. The pro demonstrates proper grip. Movement is to the right (operator's left). Photo by Edwin Johnson

A section of the pine bedroom floor in a hundred-year-old house sanded only with number 4 paper. Finer grades will be used next. Photo by Edwin Johnson

For smaller floor areas such as this entry hand sanding after the drum sander has coarse-sanded it is recommended. Photo by Edwin Johnson

After sanding, material not removed by the drum sander's vacuum is swept up with a dry paintbrush. Good jobs need a good floor vacuuming, too. Photo by Edwin Johnson

Sealer is being brushed on this small entry floor. A half hour later one can walk on the floor. After a light sanding with fine wet/dry sandpaper, used dry, this floor can be finished. Photo by Edwin Johnson

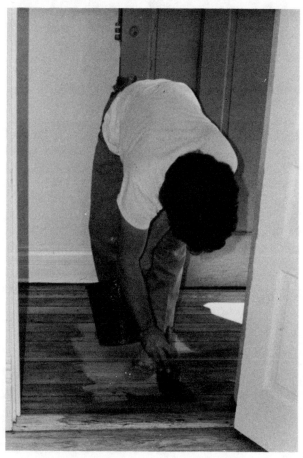

STRIPPING AND SANDING

Before we turn to how to refinish floors, perhaps a word on stripping *and* sanding is in order. Though this is generally not a "professional" approach, some do-it-yourselfers have found it works better than straight sanding.

Stripping and sanding is a possible alternative in material removal when there is an inordinate amount of old varnish with which to contend. Previous homeowners of your place may have varnished their floors every other year for thirty years with the result that a quarter inch of old varnish is lying there staring at you. Here, a rough stripping job may well be a faster way to operate.

By rough stripping I mean getting most of the old finish up with stripper and leaving the balance, once it dries, to be sanded off. This method also enables you to start with grade 80-0 paper, one with which you are less likely to do serious surface damage. So you may want to consider this sort of middle-of-the-road process.

FLOOR REFINISHING

After the old material has been removed either by floor sanding or by stripping, the finishing process begins. First let's investigate the finishes. They are: stain, varnish, polyurethane, and wax.

Finishes

Natural finish consists of a sealer and a finish coat. The pros generally use a good-quality lacquer-based sealer and a natural varnish finish coat.

They like the lacquer sealers because they dry quickly, in fifteen to twenty minutes under ideal conditions. This is a necessity because of the dust that is raised and because their time is very valuable.

Now, the only finish coat one can put on over lacquer is natural varnish. Perhaps you will recall all the pros and cons of natural versus synthetic varnishes when used on woodwork. The same arguments apply for floors.

I personally favor polyurethane and have used it on my own floors, like the staircase treads and risers. As you are planning to do the job yourself, you, too, can use polyurethane. It is quite unlikely that you will get a professional floor refinisher to use it, however.

Polyurethane natural finish, you will re-member, consists of a sealer of thinned polyure-thane and the finish coat of full-strength poly-urethane.

Darker finishes, as they say in the trade, require a stain, then a sealer, then the finish coat. Again, as in woodwork restoration, I recommend a penetrating oil stain. Many pros use the Watco brand penetrating oil stain; however the brands I noted in Chapter Seven for woodwork refinishing are perfectly okay. Darker finishes can be sealed with a regular sealer or can have wax applied when dry. The wax is put on with a rotating steelwool pad attached to a buffer. Wax is good because it gives your floor a hand-rubbed look and it's easy to apply. But it falls short of protecting floors from heavy traffic. Natural finishes and sealing stained floors are accomplished by brushing on a sealer. If you intend to use natural varnish as your finish coat, the sealer can be one specifically made for floor refinishing. As the professional floor sanders use a high-quality lacquer sealer almost exclusively, why shouldn't you?

If you want to use polyurethane as the finishing material, you must use polyurethane as the sealer. I recommend thinning it when it is the sealer (¾ urethane to ¼ paint thinner), although one amateur did his floors natural with two coats of full-strength polyurethane and he's happy with the outcome.

To avoid "bleeding" of the stain as well as bubbling of the polyurethane, be sure to let the stain dry out. Then brush on the sealer so that it flows; it is unnecessary to "work" it into the wood as you may have done when brushing out the stain.

Allow the sealer to dry. Under ideal conditions the lacquer sealer will be dry in a half hour. Thinned polyurethane can be brushed on in the morning and sanded and finished in late afternoon. Floor fans, turning up the house heat in winter and damp conditions, and operating the air conditioning with the fan on constantly under humid conditions will greatly assist in the drying process.

What comes after sealing? Remember? Sanding, of course. A very light sanding with number 400 wet/dry sandpaper used dry should smooth the grain raised by sealing. Wipe it with your tack cloth.

Brush on the final coat of full-strength polyurethane or full-strength varnish going with the grain—with the floorboards. Avoid lap marks by keeping your brush wiped of excess material and by brushing out all material.

Don't paint yourself into a corner; start there instead. Keep off the floor for at least a day.

ALTERNATIVES

One alternative to doing it yourself is to do *part* of it by yourself. Some floor sanders will agree to do just the sanding and not the refinishing. And since sanding is the "heavy" work, you might want to let him do that. In this way you still have "control" without the work and the mess.

Still another approach to this task is to refinish only part of the floor. I personally feel it is sloppy, but it might be the right approach to solving your problem. If you have rugs, you may want to finish only where the floor shows and not under the rug. That's the way my parents used to do it back in the late thirties; their floors always looked nice with a minimal amount of work.

One do-it-yourselfer I talked with said he stripped most but not all of the old varnish off by hand, then bought his own machine and sanded the balance. Felt it worked great for him.

HIRING A PROFESSIONAL FLOOR SANDER

Okay, perhaps I've convinced you that you do not want to do this job yourself. You live in an area where there are a few pros listed in the Yellow Pages. How should you go about getting a good one?

It's always best to get someone who is personally recommended. Short of that, what can you do?

Go through the Yellow Pages, call a few, and ask them to come over and give you a bid on the job. Get in writing what they will do; after reading this chapter you now understand the process a lot better, don't you? My personal prejudice is that you should get a union rather than a nonunion sander. In big cities there are a lot of guys out there working with floor sanders. Most of them are pretty good; some are terrible. As union sanders are better trained and paid, they will do better work.

Some pros do what is called a "clean it up" job. A realtor wants to sell a building, he gets a low quote to clean it up. I've seen that. You can see brush hairs embedded in the finish. Gouges, especially along the edge of the floor, are visible or can be felt. There are machine splices in the center of the floor; color unevenness is visible. You can feel roughness indicating dirt or poor sanding. Obviously, you want to avoid this kind of work.

After you get quotes, ask to see some of their work. It will be worth your while to spend a few hours inspecting. By this time you have assured yourself that this particular sander is competent.

CARING FOR WOODEN FLOORS

Although I am anticipating the next chapter, while I am on this subject of floors, I thought I'd point out a few things.

Just as dirt is the enemy of good refinishing, it is also the enemy of good finishes. Dirt is an abrasive, so dry-mop or vacuum your wooden floor at least once a week.

Do not damp-mop or use water-based cleaners. At the landmark James J. Glessner House in Chicago, where I was refinishing a dozen exterior doors recently, the porter wet-mopped the floors regularly. I shuddered each time I saw him "cleaning" floors designed by Henry Hobson Richardson.

You should protect your floors with regular waxing and buffing. At our lake house we use Bruce Clean and Wax with our buffer once a year with great results.

A streaky, dirty oak floor before cleaning and waxing. Photo by Edwin Johnson

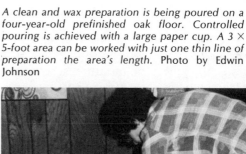

A clean and wax preparation is being poured on a four-year-old prefinished oak floor. Controlled pouring is achieved with a large paper cup. A 3 × 5-foot area can be worked with just one thin line of preparation the area's length. Photo by Edwin Johnson

Next, a home model floor polisher is used to work in the wax-cleaner solution. Photo by Edwin Johnson

The cleaning step should be left to dry. Here you will note the unevenness this step produces. Photo by Edwin Johnson

Perhaps it goes without saying that you should use your wood floors carefully. Rather than dragging pieces of furniture across your floors, pick them up, put casters on them, place cups under heavy furniture legs.

Accidents will occur, however, despite your greatest concern. Take stains, for example. Remove stains by quickly wiping up the spill with a soft cloth dampened with a little cleaner-wax. Urine is impossible and works fast to penetrate stain, sealer, and finish. Don't put dirty diapers on wooden floors. A quick washing with a soft soap like Murphy's may help, though.

You can remove chewing gum, tar, and candle wax by first rubbing the affected area with an ice cube. This chilling treatment makes the culprits brittle so that they can be gently scraped off. Then rub the area with your cleaner-wax. One trick for removing alcohol spills is to rub the stained area with fine steel wool (000 grade) dipped

Waxing and cleaning are followed by a buff brushing with fine-bristled brushes. For a super finish this step can be followed with a felt-pad buffing. Photo by Edwin Johnson

in mineral oil and finish off with cleaner-wax on a soft cloth.

Scratches will occur under the best conditions. Rub in matching stain and wipe with a dry cloth. Hey, wait. This is stuff covered in the next chapter.

Chapter Nine

Caring for Your Woodwork and Trim

The care that museums housing historic rooms and landmark houses from Salem to Sonoma give their fine antique furniture and woodwork include correct heat and cooling, proper humidity, no sunlight, and no people contact. Since none of us lives in a museum much less a landmark house, such tactics are impractical. Nevertheless, our newly restored woodwork deserves the best care possible.

Perhaps this is news to you. Taking care of woodwork and trim? Who in the world does that? Not too many, I'm afraid. But look at it this way—there's a lot of *you* in that restored dining room woodwork or refinished staircase, isn't there? And there's probably a lot of money, too. Ah, now you're with me. To continue.

If you're like a lot of my friends and customers, you're probably confused by the some-times conflicting furniture and woodwork care methods given by experts in newspaper and magazine columns, antique dealers, and by just ordinary people. Some say no care is needed; some say wax while others say don't wax, use cream. Still others disparage waxes and creams but praise oils. Television commercials tell us that there's nothing like Pledge or Liquid Gold or some other national brand.

Well, my purpose in this last chapter is to remove some of this confusion, tell you what the enemies of trim and woodwork are (so you can be on your guard), and assist you in patching surface defects after restoration. As a professional antique furniture and old house woodwork restorer I have my pet care methods. And as a married man I have my wife with whom to consult. We've put together our combined wisdom all for your benefit.

CARE OBJECTIVES

The owner of old house woodwork should have three objectives in caring for the trim and wood-work:

- to preserve
- to protect
- to prevent

I like to think of them as the Three P's. There is certainly in us the strong desire to preserve a bit of history, a part of the past. Wood products can last for ages, as ancient Egyptian tombs have demon-strated, if they are properly preserved. Just as we don't live in museums, we don't live in tombs either, so maybe bringing them up wasn't such a good idea. But in those old tombs there was no moisture and no handyman to paint on another color when someone got tired of the original finish.

Protection and prevention may sound a lot alike to you. The dictionary, however, reads that protection is shielding something from injury. Prevention is anticipating an event and thereby being in a position of avoiding it. Our antique doors and mantels can take a terrible beating from just ordinary use. Mantels can get candle spills, perhaps hot casserole and cigarette burns. Doors are often the recipient of kicks, claws, and condensation. In what is to follow we will learn how to shield things from injury.

As to prevention we can certainly anticipate and avoid some of the destruction that stalks our rooms. Staircase rails are subjected to years of hand grasping, climbing, and sliding. Protective finishes and suitable repair can assist in preventing their weakening. Keeping down dust and sand prevents the wear of floor finish, proper window coverage prevents direct sunlight from injuring sills and window seats, and double or, better, triple glazing helps prevent condensation on window sashes.

THE ENEMIES OF WOOD

Years ago a cartoon character named Pogo said, "We have met the enemy, and he is us!" I'll always remember that. Much later Chicago's famous mayor blamed the 1968 Democratic Convention riots on "outsiders." You know something—both Pogo and Mayor Daly were right. With regard to those factors that hurt trim and woodwork it is both we who live in our houses and the environmental (outside) forces that do the damage.

What are these environmental factors? They are dust, moisture, temperature, humidity, dryness, sunlight, atmospheric pollution, and nature's pests. The "we" factors are poor housekeeping, plants, pets, and people.

Dust

Upon close examination there are several kinds of dust. In the country it is the dust of the fields, the roads, the plains, and the mountains, most of which is loose topsoil. I call it "clean" dust because it is devoid of petrochemicals. There is grit to it, however, giving it a definite abrasive quality.

People living near the sea are subject to a second kind of dust—sea dust. It is a mixture of salt crystals and moist sand and is carried to one's house and into rooms by wind and fog. It is not so abrasive as it is corrosive. Most of you who live by our oceans know how it infiltrates even closed bookcases and can ruin books. Those of us who live on the beaches of the Great Lakes often wake up to find that overnight, cobwebs have appeared between ceiling beams, across corners, and over doorways. I call this "lake dust."

In the city dust is less the result of loose topsoil, the sea, and the lake (although port cities get that, too). There, dust is the combination of steel mill flue dust, utility coal burning, and auto and truck dust. Add to that all the petro chemicals, and the result is a greasy, gritty dust that not only settles but also clings to all surfaces.

Ordinary dust is destructive because the sharp edges of dust particles cut into and scratch fine woodwork surfaces. What can be done about dust? Besides good housekeeping, which will be covered a little later, one can replace open windows in the summer with air conditioning. More esoteric and also more efficient are the electrostatic dust collectors. Where sandstorms are frequent, about the only remedy is to keep doors and windows shut tight, vacuum and dust often, in addition to using air conditioning and dust collectors. Where sea dust is a problem, all items must be washed and kept free of sea dust at all times. The high humidity that usually accompanies living near a large body of water may make washing counterproductive, however, so let's look next at the problem of moisture.

Moisture

In certain parts of the country—along the ocean and Great Lakes shores and in the state of Florida, for example—one must contend with excessive moisture day in and day out. Where winters are cool or cold, condensation forms on windows and collects on sills and sashes. The inside of outside doors and sometimes even door frames also collect much condensation.

High humidity causes outside paint to bubble and to peel. It assists termites, dry rot, wet rot, and mildew. Inside it can cause doors to warp, veneer to lift, drawers to swell and stick, and everything to smell damp and moldy. Condensation on windows can blacken muntins and sills when it penetrates the sealer; carried to the extreme, it can rot wood the same as if it were outside.

Exterior dampness is almost impossible to control; the recommended procedure, then, is to live with it by proper wood treatment. If you live in a wooded area, or if trees have overgrown around your house, cut some down and thin others so the sun can get through and do its thing. If your house is constructed on a foundation with a dirt cellar or crawl space, prevent ground moisture from rising into your living quarters by laying heavy 9 × 12-foot plastic drop cloths on the dirt. If possible, install air conditioning, as it removes moisture from the air. If it's as cool in the summer where you live as where we live, you don't need air conditioning; you need dehumidification only. When we shut down our lake house at Labor Day for weekend use only, we install a dehumidifier to dry out the place until winter heat takes over.

If there is a gray or white fuzzy mold on your woodwork, it is mildew. Wash it off and try to get some sunlight and air on the surface. The smell of dampness can also be removed by washing and airing doors, woodwork, and built-ins. Keep drawers smelling nice by keeping a bar of scented soap in them.

Dryness

Dryness, the opposite of moisture, is also destructive, especially when combined with heat. Paradoxically, natural dry air is a preservative, as noted before. Overheating is the real culprit, because it brings with it a lack of oxygen and moisture. This can cause wood to crack (split or check) or buckle and veneer to lift. Door panels shrink, exposing unfinished edges.

If you detect any of these symptoms, you probably *need* humidity. Humidifiers, the opposite of dehumidifiers, are really necessary in the heated homes during northern winters. All together now, it's *dehumidifiers* in the summer and *humidifiers* in the winter. Good!

Sunlight

Although sunlight is good for dampness and will help destroy and prevent mildew, it has a fading and a drying effect on wood surfaces. We can move our antique furniture pieces away from direct sunlight, but we cannot move our sashes and our sills. The sun's rays that penetrate window glass bleach wood, and the heat dries out the natural oils in wood.

I suggest that you use awnings. Not only can they protect your woodwork, but if properly placed they can also protect your trim. If these don't fit your decorating scheme, then by all means use heavy shades, especially for the south exposures in the winter, and the west in the summer. Even the best paint and polyurethane are no match for the constant exposure your sashes get to direct sunlight.

Atmospheric Pollution

This form of destruction is almost impossible to control. Even we who live in the country are now subjected to it, they tell us. Pollution drifts in huge clouds many miles from its source. An illustration of this is acid rain, now said to be contaminating Wisconsin's lakes and streams hundreds of miles from Milwaukee, Chicago, and Minneapolis. Public utilities, paper mills, and mining operations put particles into the air in the country just as the steel mills do in our cities. Again, keeping windows and doors closed helps, although some authorities say that most homes also have polluted air because of their closed-up condition. What's an old house woodwork lover to do?

That's the inside. What about your exterior? When we hear that the façades of important ancient edifices in Athens and Rome are being destroyed by the atmosphere polluted by cars and factories (the Taj Mahal is the latest victim), it appears like a losing battle. Nonetheless, it is better to go down fighting. Therefore, keep your trim clean by washing it at least once a year, and when it needs another finish coat, lay it on. Inside your home use air conditioning, electrostatic dust collectors, and regular cleaning. Also, join the fight for clean air!

Termites and Other Pests

The destructiveness of termites is infamous. What is even more fascinating than what they can do to an old house is the fact that so many people are not aware of them. So if you see ants with white wings flying about or crawling on the floor, you've got termites, all right. Since they thrive on wood, I recommend you call a termite exterminator.

Though bats and other critters like squirrels do not destroy wood, they can disturb your peace and tranquillity. Old houses are frequently troubled with these, and rats and mice as well. Houses that have been uninhabited for a while often collect all sorts of creepy, crawly things. Again, the answer seems to be an exterminator, the two-legged kind, for everything but mice and rats. The four-legged exterminator I recommend for the latter is a good feline mouser. Some will also help rid you of squirrels. Try mothballs for bats. Bats will become weakened by them and lie on your lawn at dawn. All you have to do is go outside and kill them with a shovel.

Poor Housekeeping

Now we come to the "we" culprits. The first is poor housekeeping. There are very few people I know who consider themselves poor housekeepers, yet I have personally observed a vast range of cleanliness.

Who do you know who washes their woodwork twice a year, or their walls even once a year? Even more weird, who do you know who washes their house trim, or their clapboard siding? Typically, new exterior paint is laid over dirt and pollutants on the trim, and the new woodwork finish goes on over everything under it, including greasy fingerprints. Try this as an experiment if you think the outside air is clean. Leave a window open and place a well-finished table under it overnight. Check the surface in the morning. Now multiply that film by 365 to get your annual windowsill deposit. Now who's fussy?

Even though your house is not a landmark, protect your investment, preserve your future, provide heirlooms for your children, and prevent the destruction of your heritage. Good housekeeping will certainly help you achieve these objectives.

Plants

A book could be written on what plants have done to old house woodwork, exterior trim, and antique furniture. Plant pots leak, dent, and scratch. They leave white rings, black rings; they lift veneer and, carried to excess, cause splits and warping. Their leaves drip, drop, and mark; their petals get pushed under their pots and stick. They ooze and attract bugs. In short, plants are a menace!

Now, your restored mantels, window seats, and stair treads, if refinished according to my suggestions made earlier, *will* resist more than past finishes, to be sure. But plant pots will get them, too, eventually. There are two things you can do. One is don't leave your plants on refinished woodwork or trim in the care of a plant sitter while you go to the country for the summer. Take your plants along with you. If you can't do that, put them in one place where the lighting is good and set them on a protective cover, like heavy-duty plastic.

Second, use a waterproof, scratchproof pot and *always* set it on a protective pad when its base is the built-in sideboard or some other refinished woodwork piece. Granted this is a lot of trouble, but it's a lot easier than a second restoration. Remember all the fun you had stripping all the paint off the front steps? Memories.

A no-no if you want to protect your woodwork. Plants should never be set directly on windowsills as these in the kitchen of James J. Glessner House. Use protective mats or coasters. Photo by Edwin Johnson

Pets

Though pets can be very nice, they have teeth and claws, two things woodwork can do without. I have personally restored doors of rooms in which dogs had evidently been locked for some time. The claw marks were so deep that I literally sanded away a quarter inch of the frames and panels to remove them. Some dogs can be trained to stop this practice, but cats are another matter. If your home has some fine antiques, and now restored woodwork, have the animal declawed, at least her front paws.

A short while back a distraught man called me to ask how one could remove dog urine from a newly sanded and unsealed floor. It seems he locked his pet in the room too long and the pup had an accident. I answered him that there was nothing that could be done—that spot had to be resanded. Moral: keep pets off unfinished floors!

People

By now you're thinking, this guy doesn't like plants and pets—I wonder what he's going to say about people. Well, I think that people are just great! But we all need a little help, don't we?

Perhaps a few house rules are in order:

1. Doors should be opened and closed only with our hands, and then only on the knobs.
2. Staircase handrails are also for hands only, not bottoms.
3. As only birds perch, stay off the windowsills.
4. Fireplace mantels are the exclusive turf of trophies, old photographs, and other such mementos. Keep your butts off, including cigarettes.
5. Do not write or draw on the wainscot. Use paper, it's a lot neater.
6. Ceiling beams are only for looks and not for hooks; library shelves are only for books and not for schnooks.

Well, I guess that about says it all. And now that we better understand the enemies, let's see how we can handle them.

This heavy maple log (firewood) box skims over floors on heavy-duty mover's casters. Photo by Edwin Johnson

No-no's for good door care! Photos by Edwin Johnson

You can protect your good hardwood floors with heavy plastic furniture glides like these.
Photo by Edwin Johnson

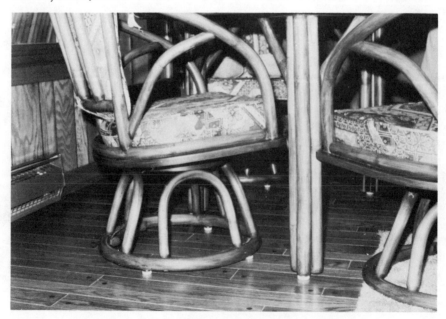

WOODWORK AND TRIM CARE

The care in use of old house woodwork pieces and trim items has been discussed and I think the message is pretty clear. Everyone in the family has to learn to live with old stuff. Old inside louvered shutters were rather delicate when they were originally fabricated. Time has not changed anything, except that today, ninety years later, the wood is more brittle, and the stripping operation probably didn't help any. Sash cords on old windows are dry and stiff; sudden raising and lowering may indeed snap the cord, necessitating repair. And the newel at the bottom of the staircase already rocking a little doesn't need any assistance.

These native cedar beams are rough-sawed. Therefore, they defy washing, but a good vacuuming will take care of sea dust, cobwebs, spiderwebs, and assorted other intruders. Photo by Edwin Johnson

The premise here is that you realize the antiquity that may surround you, and you *have* been careful. Or at least everyone has tried without making it a *cause célèbre*. But you have a question about dusting or maybe washing your woodwork. How? How often?

At the great risk of being simplistic, I will venture to say first that there are special dustcloths on the market impregnated with a dust settler and collector and made of a very soft material. Using one of these cloths prevents pushing dust from one side of, say, a door surface to the other, thus reducing potential scratching. Sills, like all horizontal surfaces, collect more than their share of dust; hence a vacuum cleaner duster seems a good tool for picking up residue.

As I don't have much faith in spray products designed to aid dusting, I would not recommend them. They appear to be putting another material on the surface that may well hold dust better than protect the finish. And finally, who has to be told that regular dusting is better than irregular? Practically nobody.

Washing

If you were reading carefully a while back, you may have noted I stated that water is one of the enemies of wood. Now I am going to recommend washing. Inconsistent? No, not exactly. You see by water I meant a *lot* of water. When you wash woodwork, you should use as *little* water as possible. In our home woodwork is washed twice a year, whether it needs it or not. And believe me, it needs it.

Woodwork is best washed with a fine soap like Murphy's Oil Soap. Here's what my wife does. She mixes about a tablespoon of the soap in a small pail of warm water. She gets her cloth full of this solution, wrings it out, and covers the entire surface, say, a door. Then she gets another cloth wet in a pail of rinse water, wrings it out, and rinses. Immediately she dries the surface with a third cloth. It not only dries but also polishes.

Washing woodwork as well as wood paneling and doors begins with proper mixing of the soft soap. Here, Murphy's Oil Soap is being hand-mixed in a small pail of warm water. Photo by Edwin Johnson

The soap solution is being applied with a small piece of Turkish towel. Pails are held on TV table for reach and portability. Small ladder is handy. Oak floor is protected with clean drop cloth. Photo by Edwin Johnson

The rinse solution of clean water will now be applied. Turkish towel is being wrung out. Photo by Edwin Johnson

The last step in woodwork washing is to wipe with a well-wrung-out piece of Turkish towel. This also has a polishing effect. Photo by Edwin Johnson

You can tell when doors and sills are clean. They look clean—clean and polished, for Murphy's has an oil in it. And everything feels clean, not its former sticky self.

Outside, such care is not required; however, washing, I think, is. I used to wash all the fasciae on a brick house and the clapboard attached garage with a solution of warm Spic 'n Span or Soilax, whichever was around the house. My neighbors thought I was nuts! But it cut down on the paint jobs and looked a lot better in between them.

Protective Coatings

Protective coatings is a subject nearly as controversial as tung oil. One manufacturer says that lemon oil is the best, but only his brand, because it is not greasy like some other lemon oils. The S. C. Johnson Company pushes Pledge on television. A book on furniture care states that oils should not be used. Instead, it recommends the traditional standard, wax, preferably paste wax. Then, some old refinishing pros swear by beeswax combined with elbow grease. Finally, a producer of furniture refinishing and touch-up products advises that wax should not be used. Instead, they feel that a furniture cream is best, especially their brand. So which will it be, oil, wax, or cream?

Don't be so confused that you use nothing, for wood should be fed. The Johnson household, since you ask, likes furniture creams the best, and Wyman's in particular. Why? Oils and waxes are sticky and serve to hold dirt and dust, we feel. Further, wax tends to build up, particularly in surface areas not subject to normal use, washing, or dusting. This buildup can discolor and mask the natural beauty of the wood grain. The cream, we believe, provides sufficient feeding and protection, and wears and washes off. This is merely my feeling on the subject, okay?

THE ART OF TOUCH-UP AND PATCHING

Despite your best care and housekeeping, accidents will happen. You nick the door woodwork moving furniture from one room to another. After several years of vacuuming the carpeting, wear marks from the machine begin to appear on the baseboard, especially at the outside corners and doorways. The inside of the bathroom door hits the towel bar on the wall in back of it every time it is fully opened and five hundred hittings later a gouge has been dug in the panel. Don't worry about them; they can be patched. Here's how.

Everyman's Touch-Up and Patching

There are some techniques, tools, and materials available for the most common surface woodwork defects that can make the weekend retoucher nearly as good as the pro. They are far from the skills and supplies one needs for antique furniture touch-up, but they work well on woodwork.

The defects we are going to look at are missed areas, scratches, dents, gouges, water marks and rings, white stains, candle wax, cigarette burns, and blushing. As for materials, available at a local supplier, we have interior paint, touch-up solutions, stain, toothpaste, wax sticks, crayons, and putty. As you will see, there is no special mystery in touch-up and patching.

MISSED AREAS. In the refinishing process there are apt to be areas that you missed staining or places where the stain did not take well. These will be lighter than adjacent woodwork surfaces and are typically in corners or on edges. Missing a spot can be corrected, providing the surface has not been sealed, by brushing on some more stain. Light spots caused by the stain not penetrating are caused by insufficient stripping, sanding, or both. Shame on you!

Such light spots can be corrected in several ways. One, if you notice the spot while you're staining, sand it with number 180 production sandpaper, wipe, and stain again. But for corners like those in door panels, complete your staining, seal, and then touch up, which I will discuss shortly.

HARD-TO-REACH PLACES. As mentioned in an earlier chapter, but which I will repeat here just in case you forgot or missed it, out-of-the-way, hard-to-reach finishing spots have to be handled by cheating. Yes, cheating!

Take the ceiling beam decorative trim problem previously mentioned. White paint could not be stripped out of deep decorative grooves, so it was left there and painted over with semigloss paint that color-matched the stain when sealed.

Still another hard-to-reach place is the groove between bead board. This tongue-and-groove wood is frequently found in the backs of built-ins, in wainscot, and even in some ceilings. Getting paint out of the groove is not only time-consuming but impossible to accomplish 100 percent. So I stain, seal, and brush matching semigloss paint in the deep grooves, wipe, let dry, and brush on the finish coat. This is cheating that works.

TOUCH-UP. Touch-up covers scratches and nicks. The material readily available to you for limited touch-up may come in different brands, but is to be purchased in your local hardware store.

Here in the Midwest we have Scratch Magic made by Magic American Chemical Corporation of Cleveland, Ohio. It comes in a number of shades in a small thirty-milliliter bottle with a brush in the cap.

It is too thick for my taste, so I thin it with lacquer thinner. And the brush supplied by the producer is too stubby, so I use a pointed sable brush. Clean yours in lacquer thinner when you're through with it. You can mix several colors to get what you want. To use it, just brush the length of the scratch or the nick and carefully wipe off the excess to avoid a "patched" look.

Another common touch-up material is paint mixed to match your woodwork color. For limited patching it works; but for extensive work it will show. Finally, stain can be used for touch-up. Once I was asked to do a cheap and quick touch-up and staining job in an old apartment building near De Paul University. The scene was a dimly lit staircase. I stained the floor near the balusters so they matched. Then I brushed stain on the string going from the first-floor landing to the third floor. It beautifully covered thousands of nicks, some going back forty years. Later the string was sealed and varnished all over the original, old, badly worn and nicked surface. Admittedly this was sloppy, but in that light and in that building it looked magnificent. So try stain that matches, too!

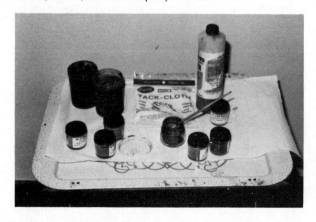

Filling and retouching materials. In front are jars of professional furniture retouching colored powders. The author has over sixty different colors which, when mixed with the solvent (back row right), produce a fast-drying color touch-up which covers lacquer, varnish, polyurethane, and shellac. A tack cloth is shown, center, and colored putty is at left.

The correct color has been found and is being poured into an empty mixing jar.

DENTS, GOUGES, AND NAIL HOLES. Scratches are two-dimensional and can usually be nicely touched up; dents, gouges, and nail holes are three-dimensional and are corrected by filling. The filling materials available to everyman are the wax stick (e.g., the Weldwood Blended Stick), color-matching crayons, and colored putty. The so-called wax stick comes in a variety of shades and can be purchased at your neighborhood hardware store. To use it, take a small piece of it with a small screwdriver, rigid blade knife, or narrow putty knife and force it into the gouge or hole. One can also heat a knife with an alcohol burner and melt some of it into the spot to be filled. The wax stick, while easy to use, will come out of shallow gouges in time through normal wear and tear. So with very shallow gouges, filling may not work so well as touching up.

Deep nail holes are successfully filled with colored putty. This product, like the others mentioned so far, also comes in a variety of colors. It is much superior to wood filler, as filler can rarely be made to match the wood color. To apply putty, use your finger and wipe the excess with a rag. As this material is slow-drying and quite soft, it will not stay in gouges too well. If you are using putty, crayon, or wax stick in the refinishing process, fill *after* sealing but *before* the finish coat. In this manner you will usually get a better color match, and the finish coat will protect the filler.

Minor dents can be steamed out of wood, particularly softwoods. So before you try to sand them out, fill them, or touch them up (they are frequently discolored), try steaming them out. Here's how to do it.

After the old finish has been stripped off, and before you begin the refinishing process, try to remove the dent by placing a wet rag over it and then put a hot clothes iron over the rag. Allow your iron, turned to low, to sit on the rag from a few minutes to a few hours, checking progress every once in a while. It may just work for you. And if it doesn't, perhaps you should leave it be and consider it a beauty mark.

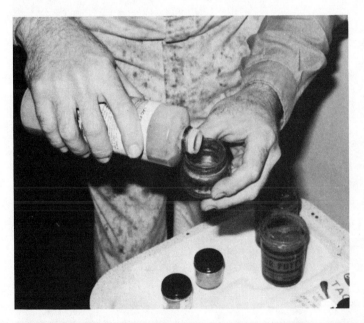

Author mixing a color for touch-up. These colors are available only to professional furniture touch-up people. Here, the solvent is being poured over the color powder.

Author checking touch-up color with door color. He subsequently covered the bad spots shown. Neither stripping nor sanding removed them, so they had to be touched up after sealing. A fine camel's-hair brush did the job. Photos by Jim Kuba

1. Filling nail holes. Whether the nail has already been set . . .

2. or is flush with the surface and must be set . . .

4. Wipe excess putty, keeping filling level with the woodwork surface.

5. A filled nail hole in an 1889 solid oak door in the south bedroom, Frank Lloyd Wright Home and Studio, Oak Park, IL. Photos by Jim Kuba

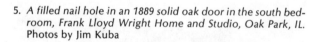

3. fill it with colored putty after the sealing step and before the finish coat has been brushed on. Match the putty color with the woodwork color. Push putty in hole with your finger.

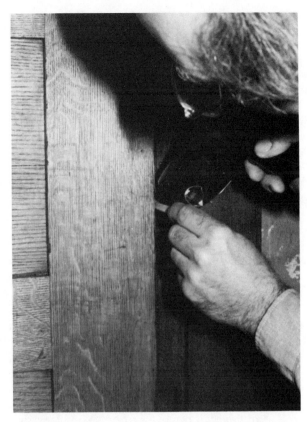

Here is a problem common with oak, a splinter. Now, you could pull it off, but bare wood and a gouge would show. So . . .

you glue it back so it won't snag fingers or dustcloths. Here, the author is using his hot glue gun, putting glue between the splinter and the door rail.

Finger pressure is enough to hold the splinter to the door rail until it sets—a few minutes via hot glue.

The splinter is back where it belongs and will never catch another unwary finger! Photos by Jim Kuba

WATER MARKS AND RINGS. From talking to people and reading the literature one would think that there are many cures and home remedies for marks and rings. The cures range from rubbing paste wax on grade 0000 steel wool to applying a few drops of salad oil on the blemish and on a rottenstone and working with the wood grain.

White rings are the easiest to remove. All you do is mix baking soda and toothpaste, put it on a damp cloth, and rub the troubled spot with the grain into a strong light so you can periodically check your progress. After this rubdown, wash the area with oil soap like Flax or Murphy's. If the ring is still there, repeat the process. Then dry and apply furniture cream.

Not so easy to remove are black rings. These are caused by water that penetrated the old finish and has entered the wood surface. The three possible correctives are sanding, bleaching, and touching up. Though I am pretty much sold on touching up, let me discuss the other two possibilities.

Sanding will remove not only the black ring but also color and material. If you remove color, you are going to have to touch up; if you sand after stripping, less color will be removed, but a spot lighter than the adjacent area will have been created. So one must sand beyond the trouble spot. Sanding also removes material, creating a dished area. Such a dish shows prominently on large areas like door panels. So if you choose to sand, be discrete. Sand following the black ring, and if it appears that too much wood is being removed, stop. Creating a very light area can be corrected by staining it darker and feathering it later.

Now that I have developed some skill in touching up defects, I prefer this method. I just touch up the darkness over the sealer. Touching up successfully first depends on exact color match of the touch-up solution with the color of the piece. In the case of covering a dark brown stain, the touch-up must be quite light to do the job. Second, one should brush carefully and accurately so as to make the touch-up literally disappear into the woodwork. Finally, a finish coat must be put over the touch-up to protect it from being subsequently worn off.

CANDLE WAX. Often the end of a perfect evening is candle wax on your fireplace mantel. Don't fret. Allow it to harden overnight. Then in the cool gray dawn use your fingers to remove as much wax as possible, scrape gently with a plastic cooking utensil followed with a brisk rub of the area with a dry cloth and a generous application of furniture cream over the whole mantel top.

CIGARETTE BURNS. Your fireplace mantel, built-in sideboard countertop, or even staircase tread can be the scene of a nasty cigarette burn. Instead of silently cursing the guest who did the deed, perhaps one should be happy the place wasn't burned down! In any event the burn is a big problem because it not only discolors the wood but causes a dent and softens the wood below that dent. A triple threat, indeed. This makes sanding of little avail, as both the darkness and the softness go pretty deep. That leaves touching up or filling in.

Edges of pieces, like mantels, are pretty difficult to fill successfully, especially with the relatively soft wax stick. If the burn causes a gouge away from the edge, you may try filling. Otherwise, touch it up.

BLUSHING. You may have noticed that one of your old paneled doors has a sort of white haze on part of it. That was caused by moisture that has entered the finish, generally via condensation. So *before* stripping it try to remove the haze by rubbing the grain back and forth with a piece of super-fine steel wool that has been dipped in linseed oil. If this removes the blushing, wash off the oil with oil soap and dry the door. And if the finish is satisfactory, you have just saved yourself a restoration job.

Professional Patching

The professionals in this business use materials, tools, and techniques different from those I outlined earlier. We use alcohol stains (I have over fifty colors) and three different solvents for touching up defects. And filling is often accomplished with a burn-in knife and solid lacquer. I say this not to put you down, but to make you aware that there are more satisfactory methods around. Most of us have taken special training to use these techniques and materials, and the firms that supply them do not wish to deal with the public at large. What I have told you, however, should enable you to deal with most of the problems you will encounter in a most satisfactory manner.

CONCLUSION

Well, you now possess much of what ten years of experience in antique furniture and old house woodwork restoration has taught me. In those years I have not only practiced but I have discoursed, lectured, consulted, and observed. And what I have been able to put into words and pictures I have done to help make your project a success.

And I am continuing to learn. Perhaps this is because I experiment and because once in a while, anyway, I listen to what others have to say. It embarrasses me to write this, but I do not know all of the answers; I do not hold all the solutions to all the woodwork restoration problems.

I sincerely hope that this will not only assist you but will spur you on to starting your project—*and* completing it before you're an old lady or an old man!

Bibliography

A. J. Bicknell and William T. Comstock. *Victorian Architecture*. Watkins Glen, N.Y.: American Life Foundation, 1976.

H. Allen Brooks. *Prairie School Architecture*. Toronto: University of Toronto Press, 1975.

Joseph Byron. *Photographs of New York Interiors at the Turn of the Century*. Text by Clay Lancaster. New York: Dover Publications, Inc., 1976.

Harold Donaldson Eberlien and Cortlandt Van Dyke Hubbard. *American Georgian Architecture*. Bloomington, Ind.: Indiana University Press, 1952.

Charles Rahn Fry, ed. *Art Deco Interiors*. New York: Dover Publications, Inc., 1977.

Talbot Hamlin. *Greek Revival Architecture in America*. New York: Oxford University Press, 1944.

Henry Hudson Holly. *Holly's Country Seats*. New York: D. Appleton and Company, 1863.

John Mead Howells. *Lost Examples of Colonial Architecture*. New York: Dover Publications, Inc., 1963.

Late Victorian Architectural Details (Combined Book of Sash, Doors, Blinds and Mouldings). Chicago: Rand, McNally and Company, 1898.

Clem Labine, ed. *The Old-House Journal Compendium*. Woodstock, N.Y.: The Overlook Press, 1980.

Hugh Morrison. *Early American Architecture*. New York: Oxford University Press, 1952.

George Nash. *Old Houses: A Builder's Manual*. Englewood Cliffs, N.J.: Prentice-Hall, Inc., 1980.

Anne Randall and Robert P. Folly. *Newport—A Tour Guide*. Newport, R.I.: Catboat Press, 1976.

Helen Shropshire and Winston Elstob. *Where California Began*. Monterey, Calif.: Herald Printers, 1978.

Paul E. Sprague. *Guide to Frank Lloyd Wright and Prairie School Architecture in Oak Park*. Oak Park Landmarks Commission, Village of Oak Park, Ill., 1976.

George Stephen. *Remodeling Old Houses*. New York: Alfred A. Knopf, 1977.

Bruce J. Talbert. *Victorian Decorative Arts*. Originally published in 1867 and 1876. Watkins Glen, N.Y.: American Life Foundation, 1978.

William A. Vollmer, ed. *A Book of Distinctive Interiors*. New York: McBride, Nast and Company, 1912.

Index

NOW . . . Announcing these other fine books from Prentice-Hall—

THE BEGINNERS' HANDBOOK OF WOODWORKING, by Tom Pettit, revised by Jack J. Colletti. This illustrated guide—designed for the beginner yet sufficiently detailed to satisfy the serious woodworker's needs—covers specific tools and techniques employed by professionals and presents easy-to-follow directions on how to fashion, join, and finish wood safely and effectively.

$9.95 paperback $18.95 hardcover

OLD HOUSES: A REBUILDER'S MANUAL, by George Nash. Covering everything from floors, walls, and windows to basic heating and electrical systems, this do-it-yourself guide shows how to recover and preserve the spirit of an old house while making structural and cosmetic repairs to suit personal tastes. Includes valuable tips on how to make essential repairs, when to do the job, the types of materials available, how to finance it, and much more.

$12.95

To order these books, just complete the convenient order form below and mail to **Prentice-Hall, Inc., General Publishing Division, Attn. Addison Tredd, Englewood Cliffs, N.J. 07632**

Title	Author	Price*
_____	_____	_____
_____	_____	_____
_____	_____	_____

Subtotal _____

Sales Tax (where applicable) _____

Postage & Handling (75¢/book) _____

Total $ _____

Please send me the books listed above. Enclosed is my check ☐ Money order ☐ or, charge my VISA ☐ MasterCard ☐ Account # _____

Credit card expiration date _____

Name _____

Address _____

City _____ State _____ Zip _____

Prices subject to change without notice. Please allow 4 weeks for delivery.